LORD DUNSANY

**Recent Titles in
Contributions to the Study of
Science Fiction and Fantasy**

LORD DUNSANY

Master of the Anglo-Irish Imagination

S. T. JOSHI

Contributions to the Study of Science Fiction
and Fantasy, Number 64
C. W. SULLIVAN III, Series Adviser

GREENWOOD PRESS
Westport, Connecticut • London

Library of Congress Cataloging-in-Publication Data

Joshi, S. T.
    Lord Dunsany : master of the Anglo-Irish imagination / S. T. Joshi.
      p. cm.—(Contributions to the study of science fiction and
fantasy, ISSN 0193–6875 ; no. 64)
    Includes bibliographical references and index.
    ISBN 0–313–29403–8 (alk. paper)
    1. Dunsany, Edward John Moreton Drax Plunkett, Baron, 1878–1957—
Criticism and interpretation. 2. Fantastic fiction, English—Irish
authors—History and criticism. 3. Ireland—In literature.
I. Title. II. Series.
PR6007.U6Z726 1995
828′.91209—dc20   94–24571

British Library Cataloguing in Publication Data is available.

Library of Congress Catalog Card Number: 94–24571
ISBN: 0–313–29403–8
ISSN: 0193–6875

First published in 1995

Greenwood Press, 88 Post Road West, Westport, CT 06881
An imprint of Greenwood Publishing Group, Inc.

Printed in the United States of America

The paper used in this book complies with the
Permanent Paper Standard issued by the National
Information Standards Organization (Z39.48–1984).

10 9 8 7 6 5 4 3 2 1

Copyright Acknowledgment

Extracts from assorted works by Lord Dunsany are reproduced with permission
of Curtis Brown Group Ltd., London on behalf of the Trustees of the Estate
of Lord Dunsany. Copyright the Lord Dunsany Will Trust.

To the memory of my father

T. M. JOSHI

1910–1994

Contents

Contents

Abbreviations

JH	*Jorkens Has a Large Whiskey*
JRA	*Jorkens Remembers Africa*
KED	*The King of Elfland's Daughter*
L	Hazel Littlefield, *Lord Dunsany: King of Dreams*
LBW	*The Last Book of Wonder*
LR	*The Last Revolution*
LT	*The Little Tales of Smethers and Other Stories*
MAP	*The Man Who Ate the Phoenix*
MF	*Mr. Faithful*
MI	*My Ireland*
MT	*My Talks with Dean Spanley*
OF	*The Old Folk of the Centuries*
OH	*The Odes of Horace*
PEA	*Plays for Earth and Air*
PGM	*Plays of Gods and Men*
PNF	*Plays of Near and Far*
PS	*Patches of Sunlight*
RB	*Rory and Bran*
SiW	*The Sirens Wake*
SJ	*The Strange Journeys of Colonel Polders*
SMC	*Seven Modern Comedies*
SMS	*The Story of Mona Sheehy*
SW	*The Sword of Welleran and Other Stories*
TAP	*To Awaken Pegasus*
TG	*Time and the Gods*
TT	*The Travel Tales of Mr. Joseph Jorkens*
TTH	*Tales of Three Hemispheres*
TW	*Tales of War*
UFT	*Unhappy Far-Off Things*
UH	*Up in the Hills*
WP	*War Poems*
WS	*Wandering Songs*
WSS	*While the Sirens Slept*
Y	*The Year*

Preface

The ignorance—amounting, it seems to me, to a deliberate avoidance—of the work of Lord Dunsany (1878–1957) by the critical establishment and, in particular, the Irish critical community is at once understandable and mystifying. It is mystifying because the distinctiveness, originality, and consistently high quality of Dunsany's work would seem to mark it for praise and analysis; and it is understandable if one looks not to Dunsany's actual work but to the subsequent course of Irish literature and history and to certain trends in literary criticism. Three significant factors have militated against Dunsany's recognition: first, the fact that, as an unwavering Unionist, he was, as it were, on the "wrong" side of Irish politics in the early decades of the century—wrong in the sense that the position he supported did not ultimately prevail and was not the one backed by most of those associated with the Irish Renaissance; second, the fact that his work did not bear a distinctively Irish cast until the 1930s and later, so that he remained—even to friends like Yeats, Stephens, AE, and Gogarty—an outsider in the Irish literary revival; and third, the fact that the bulk of his work falls into what is now termed fantasy or horror fiction (what I prefer to call weird fiction), a branch of literature that has always failed to receive its due from mainstream critics. Dunsany continually maintained that he was one of the least-read Irish writers in Ireland, and also that many held it against him that he was a nobleman living in relative comfort; as he remarks with a certain cheerless humor, ". . . the greatest barrier over which my dreams have had to climb appears to have been the belief that titled dilettantes trying to write, in order to take the bread out of the mouths of honest men, should be discouraged by every man of independent spirit" (PS 117). It is at this point in time difficult to assess the merits of this assertion, but the many instances of this reverse snobbery cited by Dunsany in his letters and autobiographies may lend some credence to it. In any event, the situation remains that Dunsany is virtually a cipher in Anglo-Irish literature. *The Field Day Anthology of Irish Writing* (1991) includes nothing of his work—not a story, play, poem, essay, or novel excerpt—and scarcely mentions him save in connection with his discovery and support of Francis Ledwidge.

Dunsany lives, if at all, as a respected but ill-understood figure in the modern fantasy movement, an acknowledged influence on such later figures as H. P. Lovecraft, J.R.R. Tolkien, Ursula K. Le Guin, and others. From the 1920s onward, however, all the genres—weird fiction, science fiction, detective fiction, the western—suffered what can only be called a "ghettoization," a product, I believe, of the dominance of cheap pulp magazines during this period, especially in America. As a result, there developed a rather ignorant and small-minded unwillingness on the part of mainstream critics to consider any material of this type as falling within the realm of genuine literature; the smallest fantastic element was enough to damn a literary work in such critics' eyes. Dunsany naturally suffered from this prejudice, even though he had never appeared in the pulp magazines. Accordingly, the preservation and interpretation of weird and fantasy fiction fell to the not always capable hands of critics and enthusiasts within the field. And yet, the fantasy community itself must share some of the blame for Dunsany's obscurity: the mass and complexity of his work have evidently deterred many full-scale analyses, and he is relegated to the status of an honored precursor. *Probitas laudatur et alget.*

I have written this book largely from the perspective of weird fiction, since that has been the focus of my previous studies. Although I have attempted to give some hints as to Dunsany's relation to Irish literature, they are no more than hints and I must leave to others the task of placing Dunsany's work more concretely in the realm of Irish history, literature, and culture. Space limitations have also prevented me from discussing in detail Dunsany's poetry or several of his purely mainstream works.

The difficulties in writing about Dunsany are many. In the first place, the sheer bulk of his work—thirteen novels, hundreds of tales and poems, more than forty plays, dozens of essays, five autobiographical volumes, along with reviews and letters—makes the task of writing an integrated study a daunting one, even though I believe that Dunsany's work returns obsessively but with great variation to a few basic themes. In the second place, the relative obscurity of this material—indeed, the near-total obscurity of the work he wrote subsequent to, say, 1935—requires a greater amount of plot synopsis than I would ordinarily be inclined to give, and reduces the amount of space I might otherwise have for analysis. This study cannot, therefore, be assumed to be anything but preliminary: it displays the array of Dunsany's work, arranging it by theme or trope along a generally chronological framework, but leaves more detailed analysis of individual works or bodies of work to later hands. If I have not cited other critics as frequently as is the custom in academic work, it is frankly because I have not found much of their work very enlightening. Critical study of Dunsany is at an extremely primitive stage, and has been hindered largely by an ignorance of the overall scope and direction of his work.

I trust that my methods of citation of works by Dunsany are not confusing. I have assigned abbreviations to nearly all of Dunsany's books, citing them by abbreviation and page number in the text; editions used are indicated by an asterisk (*) in the bibliography. I have rarely cited specific page numbers for uncollected works, since they are on the whole brief; full information on them is supplied in the bibliography.

I do not wish to sound like an uncritical admirer of Dunsany's work, a proselytizer attempting to convert the heathen; but I should be dishonest to myself if I were to deny that I have derived a great deal of pleasure from reading Dunsany. Much of my career as a critic has been an attempt to unearth unjustly forgotten works and to show both the pleasure and the edification that may be derived from them. Lord Dunsany's work has, I think, been unjustly forgotten, and my sole interest is in exhibiting it to the world and hoping that it may affect others as it has affected me.

S.T.J.

LORD DUNSANY

Introduction

Edward John Moreton Drax Plunkett, who in 1899 became the 18th Baron Dunsany, was born on July 24, 1878, at 15 Park Square near Regent's Park, London. This may be the most important biographical fact about him; for, although there have been Dunsanys in Ireland since the twelfth century, and although Dunsany spent much time in Dunsany Castle in County Meath, his birth in England and his frequent and lengthy habitation at Dunstall Priory, his home in Kent, mark him emphatically as an Anglo-Irish writer, with perhaps a slightly greater emphasis on the former element of that compound. Dunsany may have been the friend of Yeats, AE, Stephens, Gogarty, and Lady Gregory, but he attended the Cheam School in Kent, then Eton and Sandhurst; he may have had his early plays staged, with considerable success, at the Abbey Theatre, but they achieved greatest renown at the Haymarket in London and on Broadway, where in 1916 Dunsany became the only playwright in history to have five plays running simultaneously. To this schizophrenic life as an Anglo-Irishman he engrafted an equally schizophrenic career as an aristocrat-writer: he was a huntsman, traveler, and soldier, but also a poet, novelist, and lecturer. He unsuccessfully ran for Parliament; he was one of the greatest chess players of his day (he played Capablanca to a draw in 1929); he travelled all across Europe, Africa (especially the Sahara), and India; he served in the Boer War, was injured in the Dublin riots of 1916, joined a division of the War Office during World War I, and during World War II was part of the Home Guard reporting on incoming German aircraft. In 1904 he married Beatrice Villiers, daughter of the earl of Jersey; they had one son, Randal. He died on October 25, 1957.

Dunsany wrote five autobiographical volumes, although two of these—*Unhappy Far-Off Things* (1919), a series of sketches on the devastation of France after the war, and *My Ireland* (1937)—are not very illuminating in regard to Dunsany's life and attitudes. When, at the age of sixty—and at his publisher's request, as he is careful to note (PS 1)—he came to write a formal autobiography, he was already a grand old man of English and Irish literature. *Patches of Sunlight* (1938) is one of the most delightful autobiographies in English, and one need know nothing about Dunsany to derive pleasure from its wry but unaffected account of his early years. It ends, however, at the end of World War I. Some years later Dunsany took up the account, producing *While the Sirens Slept* (1944) and *The Sirens Wake* (1945) in quick succession. These autobiographies are not nearly as interesting, becoming tedious in their undigested annals of Dunsany's travels (mostly in Africa, and mostly for the purpose of hunting big game) and being remarkably unrevelatory as regards his motives and beliefs. Nevertheless, all three formal autobiographies contain useful information on the sources, composition, and purpose of his writing.

There were few indications in Dunsany's early upbringing, as the scion of a privileged aristocratic family, of his future career as a writer of fantastic fiction. It is true that he read Grimm and Andersen at an early age (PS 22) and, a little later, Poe ("the haunted desolation and weird gloom of the misty mid-region of Weir remained for many years something that seemed to me more eerie than anything earth had" [PS 32]); but he did not take to writing early in life, and no examples of any juvenile work are known to me. His first published work was a poem, "Rhymes from a Suburb," written in 1896 and published in *Pall Mall Magazine* in September 1897. Undistinguished as it is, it already underscores what may be the single overriding theme that unites nearly the whole of Dunsany's work: the need for reunification with the natural world by a repudiation of industrial civilization. The "smoke" and "dust" that clog the "downs of Kent" are dispelled by the flight of geese, who

> . . . brought us glimpses as they flew
>   Of that which lived beyond the town
> Where rushes by the water grew
>   And all the hills went sloping down
> To meet the moor, where ever blew
>   The wind that turns the woodlands brown. (PS 67–68)

One thinks of a comment Dunsany made on AE—"He had a prophetic feeling that cities were somehow wrong" ("Four Poets" [1958]; GHL 157)—a comment that more emphatically applies to himself. But why choose fantasy to express the idea? Dunsany, who does not seem to have been especially well-read in the literature of fantasy—and whose work is, accordingly, so unlike that of his predecessors in this field that analogues, sources, or influences are almost impossible to identify save in insignificant details—seems to have had a natural sense of the symbolic function of fantasy; and his work, both early and late, is a systematic demonstration of how fantasy can be used for philosophical purposes.

It is the distinguishing feature of fantastic fiction that it can wholly or partly dispense with the "real" world and replace it with a world of the author's imagination, a world whose creation—however much it may draw upon myth, legend, or history—is strictly governed by the author's world-view. Insofar, however, as there is a very obvious if tacit understanding between writer and reader that this world *is* purely a product of the imagination, the fantastic universe becomes an aesthetic creation whose entire raison d'être resides in its embodiment, almost as a sort of utopia, of what the author wishes the "real" world to be. All fantasy is, in the most literal sense of the term, wish fulfillment—or, perhaps more precisely, the concretization of wish fulfillment. Dunsany's uniqueness lies in his creating such a world out of whole cloth and in making it serve as an exhaustive criticism of the world as he saw it.

I have already stated that the overriding inspiration for all Dunsany's work is a plea for a return to Nature and the simplicity and immediacy of life associated with it. Such a formulation takes on many different aspects, among them the diminution of the human (because it is so clearly tied to the rise of cities and industrialism), the glorification of the past, the preference for dreams (and art, the distillation of dreams) over mundane reality, and a sympathy for the animal world, frequently at the expense of the human.

Two critical passages in *Patches of Sunlight* make very clear that Dunsany's fantasy lands have as their principal symbolic function the evocation of the natural world. In the first, Dunsany recounts how at an early age he saw a hare in the garden of Sir Joseph Prestwich:

If ever I have written of Pan, out in the evening, as though I had really seen him, it is mostly a memory of that hare. If I thought that I was a gifted individual whose inspirations came sheer from outside earth and transcended common things, I should not write this book; but I believe that the wildest flights of the fancies of any of us have their homes with Mother Earth . . . (PS 9)

The second passage is more general:

The source of all imagination is here in our fields, and Creation is beautiful enough for the furthest flights of the poets. What is called realism only falls far behind these flights because it is too meticulously concerned with the detail of material; mere inventories of rocks are not poetry; but all the memories of crags and hills and meadows and woods and sky that lie in a sensitive spirit are materials for poetry, only waiting to be taken out, and to be laid before the eyes of such as care to perceive them. (PS 20–21)

Here again it becomes clear that, for Dunsany, the creations of a fantastic world serve as symbols for the natural world, a natural world whose "realistic" portrayal does not interest him because it is too concerned with petty details and not with imaginative overtones.

Perhaps it is just as well that Dunsany did little writing before his maturity; for when he did begin to write, in 1904, the result was an outpouring of inspired writing unparalleled in the history of fantasy fiction. Dunsany had to pay for the publication of *The Gods of Pegāna*, which appeared in 1905; but its critical success led to the publication, over the next fourteen years, of some of the most influential works in the field: *Time and the Gods* (1906), *The Sword of Welleran* (1908), *A Dreamer's Tales* (1910), *The Book of Wonder* (1912), *Fifty-one Tales* (1915), *The Last Book of Wonder* (1916), and *Tales of Three Hemispheres* (1919). These early volumes—with their introduction of an exotic world of pure imagination complete with its own cosmogony and theology, their simple yet musical prose, and their seamless mixture of naïveté and sophistication, sly humor and brooding horror, chilling remoteness and quiet pathos—attracted a wide, devoted, even idolatrous following, although some readers and reviewers were left baffled and even hostile, unused to the rhetoric of fantasy and striving feebly to find analogues for this anomalous work in the plays of Maeterlinck or the fairy tales of Oscar Wilde.

By 1916 Dunsany had become one of the most critically acclaimed writers in both Great Britain and—thanks in part to the reprints of his work by the Boston firm of John W. Luce and the publication of his tales in H. L. Mencken's *Smart Set* and other fashionable periodicals—the United States. A token of this celebrity is the appearance of Dunsany's moving poem "A Dirge of Victory" in the London *Times* on Armistice Day 1918. It was the only poem published in the issue.

Dunsany's early fame was augmented—indeed, really established—by his plays. The story of how Dunsany began writing plays—Yeats, who wished to "get him into 'the movement' "[1] (that is, the Irish Renaissance), asked him rather offhandedly to write a play for the Abbey Theatre—is sufficiently well known, and Dunsany himself tells it wittily in *Patches of Sunlight* (149–50). When Yeats made his offer, Dunsany said that he had an interesting idea for a play but didn't think he could write it; Yeats replied that he would have to get someone else to do it, and this stung Dunsany enough to write the play in an afternoon. This was, of course, *The Glittering Gate*, performed at the Abbey in April 1909. It was nearly two years before his next play, *King Argimēnēs and the Unknown Warrior*, was performed, in January 1911, and it was really the spectacular success of that play and of *The Gods of the Mountain*, performed in London in June 1911, that established Dunsany as a playwright of note. His best early plays were collected in *Five Plays* (1914) and *Plays of Gods and Men* (1917); his remaining early plays appeared in *Plays of Near and Far* (1922), and the longer ones were issued separately: *If* (1921), *Alexander* (1925), *The Old Folk of the Centuries* (1930). Nearly all his plays, early and late, were published at one time or another in separate acting editions.

Many of the plays continue to dwell in an imaginary realm, but gradually they yield to the real world, although still retaining elements of fantasy and the supernatural. The tales of the later teens undergo this same development, and eventually seem to become parodies of themselves. What exactly is happening? Was Dunsany becoming tired of fantasy? Did the course of world events—whether the onset of the war in August 1914 or the Easter rebellion in April 1916, in which Dunsany, attempting to aid the government, was seriously injured by the rebels—jolt him from his languid dreams? Douglas A. Anderson ponders the matter:

[T]he year 1916 may be seen as a turning point—for Dunsany's mother died, and he sued his brother over the estate, thereby alienating him for the rest of his life. . . . In the same year Dunsany was shot in the face during the Easter rebellion in Dublin, and imprisoned by both sides. Then he was sent off to the carnage of the Somme in World War I, where he fully expected to die. . . . It is entirely understandable that his output after such a year would be entirely different.[2]

There is much to this, but Anderson himself ignores other vital pieces of evidence. Doubtless the war and the Dublin riots jolted Dunsany, but the transformation of his work was already underway long before 1916. "Why the Milkman Shudders When He Perceives the Dawn" (LBW), an exquisite parody of his own early manner, was published in the *Saturday Review* of December 26, 1914, hence probably written either just before or just after the start of the war. Some of the stories in *The Book of Wonder* were written as early as 1910, and they too are full of arch satire, irony, and self-parody.

In effect, the *Gods of Pegāna* style had already run dry by around the time of *A Dreamer's Tales*; Dunsany had said all he had to say in that vein.

Another factor to be taken into consideration in this gradual abandonment of imaginary-world fantasy is the effect of Dunsany's wide travels upon his writing. He notes (PS 74) that the celebrated line in *The Gods of the Mountain*, "Rock should not walk in the evening," was inspired by a trip to the Alps taken around the turn of the century; other works were analogously inspired by his stay in Gibraltar and South Africa during the Boer War. But Dunsany did not become a world traveler until around 1912, when he canvassed the Middle East, Africa, and elsewhere in search of big game. I think his witnessing the wondrous sights of the real world had much to do with his inability or unwillingness to create worlds of pure imagination. On one of these trips he admits, "I wrote nothing in these days, for I had no need to" (PS 234). Some lines in *A Journey* (1944) perfectly encapsulate this development:

> I told a Turkish lady I had dreamed
>   Long of the East, but mosques now visited,
> Domes, spires, gates, gardens, songs and legends, seemed
>   More lovely than I ever dreamed. (J 34)

In any event, the fantasy quotient begins to decline in a more or less systematic way during the last thirty-five years of Dunsany's literary career. Early in *Patches of Sunlight* he makes the telling admission that, "disappointed at the reception of my short stories, I turned to writing novels" (PS 10). In the first three of these novels—*The Chronicles of Rodriguez* (1922), *The King of Elfland's Daughter* (1924), and *The Charwoman's Shadow* (1926)—the fantastic element is certainly present, but in a significantly altered way: the first and third of these are set in a nebulously defined Spain of the "Golden Age," while the second—which stylistically marks a stunning return to that bejewelled, prose-poetic manner typical of his early work—contrasts Elfland and the real world, but not always to the disadvantage of the latter. With *The Blessing of Pan* (1927), fantasy—embodied in the figure of Pan and his seductive music—serves almost wholly as a transparent symbol for the wonders and mysteries of the natural world.

The course of Dunsany's later playwriting career is even more startling in its wholesale abandonment of fantasy. *The Lost Silk Hat* (1913) may be an anomaly in being a light comedy of manners at a time when Dunsany was still summoning the presence of gods and kings in his plays; but then comes *Cheezo* (1917), another play wholly devoid of fantasy, and some years later, in *Seven Modern Comedies* (1928), fantasy, when it is present at all, is used almost wholly as a satiric prop. The same is true of most of the *Plays for Earth and Air* (1937).

Perhaps an important anticipation of this renunciation of fantasy is the series of tales Dunsany wrote about the clubman Joseph Jorkens. The first of these, "The Tale of the Abu Laheeb," was written in 1925; when it appeared in the *Atlantic Monthly* the next year, it constituted the first short story Dunsany had published in six years. The break from his earlier work could not be more emphatic: stylistically it is written in that flat, deadpan, and ironic manner that would serve him for the bulk of his remaining career; in substance it deals, to be sure, with a fantastic creature, but one whose existence we can never quite accept because we can never be quite convinced that Jorkens is not pulling our legs. The Jorkens tales were tremendously popular—more than his early tales ever were—and were printed in the best-paying middlebrow magazines in America (*Atlantic Monthly, Cosmopolitan, Saturday Evening Post, Harper's Bazaar, Harper's Magazine*) and England (*Graphic, Britannia and Eve, Pall Mall Magazine, Spectator*). They were collected in five volumes over twenty years: *The Travel Tales of Mr. Joseph Jorkens* (1931), *Jorkens Remembers Africa* (1934), *Jorkens Has a Large Whiskey* (1940), *The Fourth Book of Jorkens* (1947), and *Jorkens Borrows Another Whiskey* (1954).

Dunsany, of course, continued to write non-Jorkens stories of all types from the 1920s to the 1940s, including a large number for *Punch* in the 1940s. Many of these are admittedly slight, although I think it is simply false to say (as Douglas A. Anderson does) that they "became merely bags of tricks." Several—"The Policeman's Prophecy" (1930), "The Finding of Mr. Jupkens" (1932), "Helping the Fairies" (1947), "The Speech" (1950), "The Romance of His Life" (1952)—are of great power even though they have largely abandoned the imaginary world or fantasy altogether. Even the Jorkens tales, lighthearted as they are, address a number of serious concerns. Some of the non-Jorkens stories were collected in two late collections, *The Man Who Ate the Phoenix* (1949) and *The Little Tales of Smethers and Other Stories* (1952), the latter of which contains "The Two Bottles of Relish" (1932), one of the most frequently reprinted stories in modern literature. A great many tales, however, remain uncollected.

After a six-year hiatus in novel writing, Dunsany published *The Curse of the Wise Woman* in 1933. This was his first "Irish" novel, and really his first work to utilize Irish themes in a significant way. It won the Harmsworth Literary Award from Yeats' Irish Academy of Letters. From this point on Dunsany incorporated Irish elements in his work with increasing frequency, whether in such a reminiscent volume as *My Ireland* (1937) or in novels such as *Up in the Hills* (1935), *Rory and Bran* (1936), and *The Story of Mona Sheehy* (1939). Many of his *Punch* stories feature Irish characters, although not always in a favorable light. It may seem peculiar that Dunsany took to writing about Ireland so relatively late in his career; but for a variety of reasons he remained apart from the Irish Renaissance in his early years, and he would not alter the manner or substance of his work merely in accordance with others' wishes that he join "the movement." *The Curse of the Wise Woman* is regarded by many as his finest novel, but not necessarily because it is about Ireland.

By the 1940s Dunsany's creative energies appeared to be waning. It is not that he was writing less—right to the end of his life he remained a prolific short-story writer and poet—but that his work was becoming increasingly thin and insubstantial. At the outbreak of World War II he joined the Local Defence Volunteers (the Home Guard), watching for incoming German airplanes from Dunstall Priory. Then, at the age of sixty-two, he was asked to serve as the Byron Professor of English Literature at Athens University. He made the laborious trip to Greece in late 1940, but early the next year was forced by the German invasion to evacuate; he returned home by an extraordinarily circuitous route, travelling through Egypt, down to South Africa, and then back to Ireland by ship. This entire adventure served as the inspiration for several works, among them the long poem *A Journey* (1944) and the war novel *Guerrilla* (1944).

Given the disruptions in his life, he found poetry more manageable, and in addition to *A Journey* he wrote *War Poems* (1941), *Wandering Songs* (1943), and *The Year* (1946) in quick succession. He also translated *The Odes of Horace* (1947) in two months. Autobiographical writing also came to him easily, and he wrote his final two autobiographies during the concluding stages of the war. He delivered a fine series of Donnellan Lectures in 1943 at Trinity College, Dublin. Dunsany managed to summon up the energy to write *The Strange Journeys of Colonel Polders* (1950), one of the best of his later novels, but his final two, *The Last Revolution* (1951) and *His Fellow Men* (1952), are undistinguished.

If Dunsany's career petered out toward the end—if, as with so many other writers, he lived too long and wrote too much—his effortless command of very diverse literary forms (short story, novel, play, poem, essay) and the remarkably large output of consistently meritorious work are sufficient to establish him as a writer of significance. Even among his supporters, however, there is a tendency to ignore, even to scorn, his later work, as if the last thirty-five years of his career represent some uniform excursion into futility. This tendency—evinced even by H. P. Lovecraft, his most ardent disciple and one of the acutest of his commentators—is in some sense understandable, given the utter uniqueness and brilliance of his early tales, from *The Gods of Pegāna* to *Tales of Three Hemispheres*; but we will see, firstly, that these tales are by no means monolithic either in substance or in quality, and, secondly, that his later writing has distinctive features of its own. In any event, this later work has received such little attention that even the most cursory analysis might help to redress the balance.

I do not wish to devote much attention to Dunsany the man. It is not that I think his biographer, Mark Amory, has done an especially good job at delineating the course of his life and opinions; indeed, a more wooden, lifeless, and unenthusiastic biography would be difficult to find. It is rather that the essence of Dunsany's life can be found in his work—and not in the obvious sense that most writers do nothing but write (a patently false assertion as regards Dunsany in any case), but rather in the sense that the true complexity of Dunsany's thought is much more evident in his creative work than in his essays or autobiographical writing. Many of his essays harp rather obsessively, repetitively, and not very interestingly on the same subjects—laments on the decline of the purity of English, condemnations of the laxity of modern poetry, and protests against the cruel practice of cutting off dogs' and horses' tails. Even his autobiographies are remarkably cagey, full of engaging details on certain aspects of his life and writings but very circumspect regarding his beliefs, sensations, and even some personal details. (One would never know, for example, from reading his autobiographies that Dunsany even had a brother, much less that he was not on good terms with him.)

One point on which Dunsany was never reluctant to speak was the high calling of the genuine artist. The popularity of his work is the more puzzling because it was so manifestly unlike the fashionable literature of his day—whether the arch sophistication of Edgar Saltus or the mawkish sentimentality of Robert W. Chambers, to say nothing of the avant-garde work of Eliot, Joyce, or Gertrude Stein—and remained aggressively so right to the end. Dunsany never wrote to please anyone but himself: "no man more narrows his work by unnecessary limitations than the man who, having been told, or thinking he knows, what the public wants, carefully writes for this supposed need. It is hard enough to give one's own message aright. It is a million times harder to give a million other men's" ("Good Plays and Bad—Why?" [1928]). This stance leads directly to a hostility toward didacticism in art. Didacticism is not so much giving what you think people want, as telling people how you think they should behave, and as such it can be stated more effectively through simple exhortation.

But while Dunsany's adjuration not to "hunt for allegories"[3] in his work is well taken, it is nevertheless evident that many of his tales are transparent and consciously crafted parables. Perhaps there is no contradiction in all this; as he states elsewhere: "If an allegory is not so clear that all beholders can see it, it fails at its little job" (PS 114).

Dunsany early evolved a coherent theory of drama, and he addresses it in a number of important essays: "Romance and the Modern Stage" (1911), "Artist and Tradesman" (1918; GHL), "The Carving of the Ivory" (1928; GHL), and the third section of *The Donnellan Lectures* (1945). He was aware that the "material of the dramatist is events" (DL 48), not principally language or character as such; the latter must be subordinate to, and an outgrowth of, the former if the play is to be genuinely dramatic. It may sound odd for a writer so given to prose-poetry to state that "poetry can greatly ornament a play, but it cannot construct one" (DL 49); but nearly all his plays conform to this dictum. Dunsany was fond of making the analogy that dialogue is to drama as bricks are to a house; if one praises a play solely for its dialogue, it is as if one were to attend a dinner party and say that a house was built of very good bricks; and "you would know that there must have been something very wrong with the dinner-party" (DL 47). Dunsany repeatedly scorned the idea of learning the "rules" of dramatic technique; but, just as his early tales reveal a remarkable intuitive grasp of story construction, his plays are almost unfailingly dramatic in their scenarios and their denouements, and he was able to adjust his style to this different medium with great skill. This is demonstrated vividly in three late plays—*The Use of Man*, *The Bureau de Change*, and *Golden Dragon City*—that are adapted from short stories and which are on the whole considerably superior to their originals.

Dunsany's plays, both early and late, display some highly piquant, elaborate, and carefully etched psychological portrayals. It is entirely false to assume, as Mark Amory does, that the general absence of such portrayals in the early tales is an indication of Dunsany's "complete lack of interest in any connection with the real world or in human character" (Am 46): in fact Dunsany observed human beings, individually and collectively, with a shrewd eye, and his later stories reveal an increasing interest in psychological motivation, an interest evident in all the plays.

"Nowadays" (1912), the finest of his early essays, is a moving paean to artists (he speaks of poets, but his remarks are more general than that) as the interpreters, and perhaps the saviors, of the age. Amid the clangor of cities, amid the deceitful advertising (one of Dunsany's bêtes noires), the poet alone can "come at the meaning of life and the scheme of man" (GHL 131). What is it to be a poet?

It is to see at a glance the glory of the world, to see beauty in all its forms and manifestations, to feel ugliness like a pain, to resent the wrongs of others as bitterly as one's own, to know mankind as others know single men, to know Nature as botanists know a flower, to be thought a fool, to hear at moments the clear voice of God. (GHL 138)

However naive or fin-de-siècle this may sound, it was a view to which Dunsany remained faithful to the end of his career.

Some other features of his life and thought may, however, be obstacles toward the appreciation of his work, and these need to be addressed. Dunsany himself felt that his membership in the titled nobility presented such an obstacle, but I cannot imagine that this is much of an issue anymore. A more important consideration is his penchant for hunting, something that fills many of us with loathing. Dunsany was aware of the criticism he might receive on this issue, but he was not apologetic:

I was taught to shoot by the gamekeeper, Joseph Reid, who had also taught my father; though shooting did not become the favourite occupation of my life until a few years later. When it did it took me out into the woods and over the countryside, once again to destroy, as when I collected butterflies, but learning something of the ways of the world where they are untainted by cities; which fishermen, sportsmen, soldiers and many another will agree is a knowledge that seems only to be able to be acquired with the help of killing. (PS 28–29)

I do not know how many will accept that final argument, but that Dunsany developed a greater intimacy with Nature as a result of his far-flung hunting expeditions seems undeniable. It is not a paradox—or, at least, Dunsany did not see it as such—that he could rail so vehemently against cutting off dogs' tails while shooting thousands of animals over the course of his life; for the former was merely a barbarous and irrational practice that served no useful purpose (surely, Dunsany argued, Nature had bestowed dogs with tails for a reason), whereas a good deal of his shooting was done either for the purpose of sustenance—he would frequently shoot his dinner for an entire season when at Dunsany Castle—or (in the case of foxes) for the protection of livestock or poultry. In the end, however, Dunsany made no excuses for his pastime: he shot because he was good at it and because he enjoyed it. And it really did make him "feel that one is part of the country" (WSS 86).

In other ways Dunsany was considerably in advance of his time. It seems undeniable that his lifelong opposition to the docking of animals assisted in some small way toward the abandonment of the custom.[4] He was rather less successful in his attacks on advertising, which has now reached levels Dunsany could not have conceived, but he would have been grateful for the movement toward purity in food which he anticipated by half a century. *Cheezo* (1917), at once a broadside against advertising and against harmful chemical additives in food, is one of his most vicious satires.

Dunsany's protests against the decay of English—carelessness in punctuation, misuse of nouns as adjectives, the fossilization of dead metaphors, and a general imprecision and ignorance in the use of language—again have a tendency to sound reactionary and pedantic, but they come from one whose own use of language was a model of clarity, precision, and simplicity. I think a case could be made that Dunsany's prose is, qua prose, one of the finest in English, and his words on style and language are always perspicacious and insightful.[5] Late in life he became particularly exercised at the seeming irrationality and formless-ness of modern poetry, wondering "how on earth this land that knew Shakespeare, Milton, Shelley, and Keats, and has never been without a poet between Spenser and de la Mare" ("The Fall of the Muses" [1952]) could have been "taken in" by the poetry of T. S. Eliot and its analogues. Such remarks too seem very reactionary, but if we pause to wonder why modern poetry has become so utterly irrelevant to the intellectual lives of most cultivated people, then we may perhaps conclude with Dunsany that poets have indeed "failed in their duty" to express their age in a way that others can enjoy and understand.[6]

It was clear to Dunsany that these seemingly diverse issues—bad English, bad poetry, bad food, advertising—were all the evil products of industrial civilization, itself a product of the dominance of the machine. Dunsany was of a generation that still retained its ties to the rural country-side, and he saw the machine as a loathsome aberration:

[I]t seems to me, as I watch the glare of our factories, or hear the roar of our towns and the sound going up from Progress upon her ravenous path, it seems to me that man has sailed out of his course and is steering by bad stars. And the terrible evil of it is this: that the further he goes, the harder it becomes for him to hear any voice that calls him back. ("Nowadays" [GHL 133])

If we smile at this sort of thing, it is because we know the battle to be lost. Dunsany himself lived long enough to suspect that the cause was hopeless, but he went down fighting.

Nearly the whole of Dunsany's work—even those early tales that, of anything of his, are valued, to say nothing of his later tales (including all the Jorkens volumes), most of his novels, all his plays and poetry, and his autobiographies—is out of print, and his uncollected stories, essays, and poems remain buried in the anthologies and magazines in which they were first published. It is hardly surprising, therefore, that critical study of Dunsany has not progressed very far. In his own day he was the subject of countless articles and one full-length book, Edward Hale Bierstadt's quite mediocre *Dunsany the Dramatist* (1917; revised 1919). His work, early and late, was reviewed in leading journals by Elizabeth Bowen, Evelyn Waugh, J. B. Priestley, Seán O'Faoláin, Edwin Muir, L. P. Hartley, Padraic Colum, Joseph Wood Krutch, Graham Greene, Austin Clarke, Carlos Baker, Diana Trilling, William Rose Benét, Desmond MacCarthy, V. S. Pritchett, Alexander Woollcott, and many others. And yet, as he continued to live and write, he drifted insensibly but inexorably into obscurity. Many who had been entranced by *The Gods of Pegāna* or *The Queen's Enemies* in the early decades of the century probably thought he had died long before he actually did in 1957.

Writers and critics of fantastic fiction have also been curiously slow in acknowledging Dunsany, perhaps because, as with the Irish Renaissance, he never allied himself with their movement. Lovecraft discovered Dunsany in 1919 and saw him lecture in Boston in October of that year; he subsequently wrote "Lord Dunsany and His Work" (1922), but it was merely a lecture given to a small circle of amateur journalists and not published until 1944. He devoted significant space to Dunsany in *Supernatural Horror in Literature* (1927; revised 1933–35), but that essay was published only in small-press magazines. In the 1940s and 1950s, when fantasy fandom burgeoned, Dunsany's work was championed in brief articles and reviews by Anthony Boucher, Arthur C. Clarke, and Fletcher Pratt. August Derleth struck a coup for his fledgling publishing firm of Arkham House by issuing the American edition of *The Fourth Book of Jorkens* in 1948. The volume did not sell especially well, but the presence of Dunsany—as well as such other eminent British authors of weird fiction as L. P. Hartley, Algernon Blackwood, and Cynthia Asquith—helped to lend prestige to his small press, which had initially been founded solely to publish the work of Lovecraft. Dunsany's tales continued to be reprinted in anthologies of fantasy, horror, science fiction, and detective fiction, and also—although with decreasing frequency—in general anthologies of stories, poems, and plays. But critical work was almost nonexistent.

In the 1970s things began to change slowly. Lin Carter compiled three collections of Dunsany's tales and plays for his Adult Fantasy series from Ballantine; they attracted some attention, but quickly went out of print.

More successful was E. F. Bleiler's *Gods, Men and Ghosts: The Best Supernatural Fiction of Lord Dunsany* (1972), a volume that remained in print for nearly twenty years, although I have no figures on how many copies were sold. His work began to be seen as an anticipation of, and perhaps an influence on, the now popular work of J.R.R. Tolkien; Ursula K. Le Guin, L. Sprague de Camp, and others in the fantasy community extolled his achievement. The first full-length critical study of Dunsany's entire work came out of this community—Darrell Schweitzer's *Pathways to Elfland: The Writings of Lord Dunsany* (1989), a summation of many articles he had published over the previous fifteen years. In 1993 Schweitzer and I published a bibliography of Dunsany's work.

In 1972 Collins published Amory's biography and reissued *My Talks with Dean Spanley* (1936) and *The Curse of the Wise Woman*. All three received fairly polite reviews. Seamus Heaney remarked of the latter novel, "The emotional division in the heart of a Unionist landlord, living in the heart of a Unionist Ireland, is emblematically realised in the setting . . . there is a seam of memorable beauty running through the whole story."[7] Theses, dissertations, and articles in scholarly journals and books are slowly appearing, but Dunsany has far to go to achieve general recognition.

A word should be said about foreign interest in Dunsany. Some of his work was translated as early as the 1920s and perhaps earlier: Dunsany himself saw a Czech version of *The Laughter of the Gods* performed in Prague in 1920 (WSS 34). The first book publication I have traced is a Lithuanian edition of three of his plays in 1923; translations of stories into French, Spanish, and German appeared the next year. Dunsany's work has subsequently appeared in Dutch, Japanese, Polish, Italian, and Norwegian. Perhaps the most notable item is a volume of his tales and plays edited by Jorge Luis Borges, which has appeared in Italian (1981), German (1983), and Spanish (1986). His plays have appeared in the Spanish *Nosotros*, the French *Revue Européenne*, and the Italian *Il Dramma*.

Criticism of Dunsany's work abroad has not been extensive but in some ways surpasses Anglo-American work. Louis Paul-Dubois wrote a penetrating article on Dunsany in *Revue des Deux Mondes* in 1933, and other scattered criticism has appeared in French, German, and Italian. The pinnacle was reached with Max Duperray's enormous and comprehensive dissertation in 1979 from the Université de Lyon, portions of which have appeared as separate articles. This dissertation is substantially superior to the several American and English dissertations that have been devoted to Dunsany over the last four decades. Dunsany is perhaps less obscure in Europe than in Great Britain and the United States, but only slightly so.

I do not know what place Lord Dunsany will eventually occupy in Irish literature, general literature, or fantasy literature. He is reasonably secure in that last group, although his work is more praised than read. The Jorkens tales, if nothing else, establish him as an ingenious storyteller and dry wit; his early plays ought to be reprinted if for no other reason than their distinctive exoticism and their historical importance; a judicious selection of his best poetry may be worthwhile. But I am still unable to understand the stony silence regarding Dunsany from the Irish critical community: Is it truly because he did not support the rebellion? That he did not join the Irish Renaissance? That he achieved spectacular popular success when other, perhaps worthier, Irish writers did not? That he wrote about Ireland only late in life, and then not always flatteringly? Dunsany did not wish to be restricted within the confines of "Irish literature"—but neither, I imagine, did Joyce, Beckett, or even Yeats, and this has not prevented Irish critics and readers from embracing them. Dunsany, of course, is not to be compared with these figures; he is not a great writer (save specifically within the realm of fantasy literature), but a good, entertaining, and diverse writer whose work is not nearly as out-of-date or old-fashioned as one might think. It is exactly because, in most of his work, he repudiated narrow realism and spoke of the "big" issues of life, death, time, and the cosmos that he has at least the potential of remaining perennially relevant.

NOTES

1. W. B. Yeats, letter to Lady Gregory, 23 May 1909; in *The Letters of W. B. Yeats*, ed. Allan Wade (London: Rupert Hart-Davis, 1954), 530.

2. Review of *The Weird Tale* by S. T. Joshi, *Lovecraft Studies* Nos. 22/23 (Fall 1990): 65.

3. Letter to Emma Garrett Boyd (n.d.); cited in Edward Hale Bierstadt, *Dunsany the Dramatist* (Boston: Little, Brown, 1917; rev. ed., 1919), 160–61. See also Linda Pashka, " 'Hunting for Allegories' in the Prose Fantasy of Lord Dunsany," *Studies in Weird Fiction* No. 12 (Spring 1993): 19–24.

4. See such essays as "A Barbarous Rite" (1950) and "Arming Our Ignorance with a Knife" (1953). He also wrote many letters to the *Times* (London) on the subject. See also the delightful essays "Tales about Dogs" (1951) and "A Moment in the Life of a Dog" (1953; GHL).

5. Among his essays on language are "England Language Conditions!" (1928), *Building a Sentence* (1934), "Among the Ruins" (1944), and "The Charwoman and the Hyphen" (1950).

6. Among Dunsany's many essays on modern poetry are "What Have We Here?" (1934), "A Dissenting Opinion on Modern Poetry" (1950), "The Fall of the Muses" (1952), and "The Poets Fail in Their Duty" (1957).

7. Seamus Heaney, "The Labourer and the Lord," *Listener* (28 September 1972): 409.

1

Pegāna and Its Analogues

PEGĀNA

Our first order of business, when considering *The Gods of Pegāna* (1905) and *Time and the Gods* (1906), is to probe the exact significance of the otherworldly realms created in these two collections of tales. It would seem that the creation of a "new" theogony, with entirely new gods, heroes, prophets, and creation myths, would at the very least suggest some dissatisfaction with the standard theogonics of humankind, specifically the one—Christianity—in which Dunsany was raised. I shall examine the anticlericalism of Dunsany's mythos, as well as his possible atheism, at a later stage; here it is significant to specify the precise nature of the mythology and its philosophical, theological, and aesthetic ramifications.

The superficial "purpose" of *The Gods of Pegāna* is the delineation of the "Pegāna Mythos" (a term of my own invention, not one ever used by Dunsany); as his preface declares: "There be islands in the Central Sea, whose waters are bounded by no shore and where no ships come—this is the faith of their people" (GP [v]). Where is the Central Sea, and who are the people who dwell in it? These are not questions we can answer at the moment, and matters are not helped much when it is declared in the very first sentence of *The Gods of Pegāna* proper: "Before there stood gods upon Olympus, or ever Allah was Allah, had wrought and rested Mānā-Yood-Sushāī" (GP 1). The mentions of Olympus and Allah are the only references in the entirety of *The Gods of Pegāna* and *Time and the Gods* to entities in the "real" world, and the statement clearly denotes a temporal precedence of the gods of Pegāna to those of other religions known to humanity. Does this mean that the gods of Pegāna are the "true" gods? By prefacing his book with the remark "this is the faith of their people," is Dunsany acting merely as a reporter and disavowing intellectual or even aesthetic belief in the theogony he is writing? I am not sure that I know the answers to these questions, or that there are meaningful answers to them. Let us merely investigate who the gods of Pegāna are and what they stand for.

Mānā-Yood-Sushāī is the Jupiter or Yahweh of the Pegāna Mythos, but his connection with the rest of creation is highly tenuous and indirect: he "made the gods" (the lesser ones, such as Mung, Sish, and Kib) and then, tired from this exertion, fell asleep. He remains asleep because of the constant drumming of Skarl the Drummer. "Some say that the World and the Suns are but the echoes of the drumming of Skarl, and others say that they be dreams that arise in the mind of Mānā because of the drumming of Skarl . . ." (GP 3). All this is not very reassuring, nor is the final outcome: "But at the last will Mānā-Yood-Sushāī forget to rest, and will make again new gods and other worlds, and will destroy the gods whom he hath made" (GP 1–2). The ephemerality and fragility of all creation can have no more resounding expression than this.

The lesser gods of Pegāna are all embodiments, symbolizations, or representations of the vast forces that govern the cosmos and the smaller but still mighty forces animating the natural realm of this planet. Kib appears to be the god of Life, for it is by his doing that "Earth became covered with beasts" (GP 8). "Time is the hound of Sish" (GP 13), so that one imagines that Sish is a symbol for Time. "The soul of Slid is in the Sea" (GP 17), although there are separate, and evidently lesser, gods— Eimes, Zanes, and Segastrion (GP 36)—who are river gods, hence presumably subordinate to Slid. Mung is the "Lord of all Deaths between Pegāna and the Rim" (GP 20). Dorozhand is the god of Destiny (GP 41). Many other gods are introduced in *The Gods of Pegāna*, their powers varying in accordance with their functions as cosmic or terrestrial forces.

What is the purpose of this prodigal invention of gods? Dunsany is aware, as he says in "The Relenting of Sardinac," that gods are "of the childhood of the world" (TG 182): they are the product of primitive man's responses to a world whose manifestations he does not have the scientific knowledge to comprehend in natural terms. Unlike the materialist Lovecraft, however, Dunsany is not interested in the supersession of primitive myth with the cold rationalism of modern science; for the value that Dunsany sees in animism—the primitive deification of the forces of Nature—is exactly in the sense of unification it creates between human beings and the natural world. Animism of the purest and most exquisite sort is expressed in "The Coming of the Sea," which discusses the battle of Slid (the sea) and the land, protected by the gods:

But Slid advanced and led his armies up the valley, and inch by inch and mile by mile he conquered the lands of the gods. Then from Their Hills the gods sent down a great array of cliffs of hard, red rocks, and bade them march against Slid. And the cliffs marched down till they came and stood before Slid and leaned their heads forward and frowned and stood staunch to guard the lands of the gods against the might of the sea, shutting Slid off from the world. Then Slid sent some of his smaller waves to search out what stood against him, and the cliffs shattered them. But Slid went back and gathered together a hoard of his greatest waves and hurled them against the cliffs, and the cliffs shattered them. (TG 91)

And yet, it would be naive to imagine that Dunsany presents this animism with the expectation of intellectual belief on the part of his readers; he is not a primitive, and he knows his readers are not primitives, and so the real significance of his animism is an attempt to restore the magic and poetry of the natural world. In "The Relenting of Sardinac" a character speaks of the abandonment of earth and its people by the gods, a scarcely veiled metaphor for the loss of wonder and closeness to Nature by industrial civilization:

But I, . . . when already three [of the gods] had passed me, leaving earth, cried out before the fourth:
"Gods of my childhood, guardians of little homes, whither are ye going, leaving the round earth to swim alone and unforgotten in so great a waste of sky?"
And one answered:
"Heresy apace shoots her fierce glare over the world and men's faith grows dim and the gods go. Men shall make iron gods and gods of steel when the wind and the ivy meet within the shrines of the temples of the gods of old." (TG 181)

The gods of Pegāna have no more business on the earth, now that they have been replaced by gods of iron and steel: the natural world slips away under the onslaughts of technology.

The archaistic tone that is the most immediately noticeable feature of Dunsany's early work as a whole, and of *The Gods of Pegāna* in particular, plays an important function in this revival of aesthetic animism. There can hardly be a doubt that the multiplicity of gods in Pegāna is meant to recall the paganism of Greco-Roman antiquity in contrast to the lonely god of Judaism, Christianity, or Islam; Dunsany makes this very clear when remarking on his inability to master Greek in his youth, which "left me with a curious longing for the mighty lore of the Greeks, of which I had had glimpses like a child seeing wonderful flowers through the shut gates of a garden; and it may have been the retirement of the Greek gods from my vision after I left Eton that eventually drove me to satisfy some such longing by making gods unto myself, as I did in my first two books" (PS 30). It is also hardly to be wondered at that Dunsany, imbued from childhood with the sonorous rhythms of the King James Bible, would employ biblical prose for his theogony. Random scraps of Dunsany's classical and biblical readings appear sporadically throughout his early work. When, in "In The Land of Time," an army cries, "Alatta! Alatta!" (TG 177), referring to an imaginary realm, we are clearly meant to see this as a recollection, and perhaps a parody, of the cry of the Ten Thousand, "Thalatta! Thalatta!," in Xenophon's *Anabasis*. In "The Vengeance of Men" it is stated: "All feared the Pestilence, and those that he smote beheld him; but none saw the great shapes of the gods by starlight as They urged their Pestilence on" (TG 108), a transparent echo of the celebrated passage in Vergil's *Aeneid* where Venus shows Aeneas that the gods, though invisible to mortals, are assisting the Greeks in their destruction of Troy (*Aen.* 2.594–623). Several early tales—"The Revolt of the Home Gods" (GP), "The King That Was Not" (TG)—are textbook cases of hubris.

This echo of classical antiquity has, however, the broader function of suggesting the superiority of the past over the present. If the gods of Pegāna are remote and capricious, if they know nothing of wealth and love (GP 77), they at least allow human beings to retain that intimate bond to Nature which Dunsany sees as the distinguishing condition of the childhood of the world. His later work will express this longing for the unmechanized past in many different ways, but Dunsany's first two books have lain the groundwork by erasing modern history altogether and replacing it with a theogony and cosmogony that place the vast forces of the natural world onstage as the ultimate originators of all life, human or otherwise.

The Gods of Pegāna and, to a lesser degree, *Time and the Gods* are remarkable in their complex intermingling of a childlike aesthetic animism and a highly sophisticated expression of very advanced philosophical views. It is as if they were an anomalous collaboration between biblical prophets and Sir James George Frazer. But this is all in accordance with Dunsany's own philosophical perspective: the deification of Nature as an aesthetic act, and the awareness of the inconsequence, minuteness, transience, and godlessness of the earth and all its inhabitants as revealed by modern science. We know little of Dunsany's readings in modern philosophy or literature, although Amory remarks that he read Nietzsche around 1904 (Am 40). He hardly need have remarked on it, for the influence of Nietzsche and other thinkers on Dunsany's early work is pronounced.

The gods of Pegāna "sat in the middle of Time, for there was as much Time before them as behind them, which having no end had neither a beginning" (GP 5). Here is a strange theology indeed, denying to the gods the origination of time. Similarly, "Pegāna was The Middle of All, for there was below Pegāna what there was above it, and there lay before it that which lay beyond" (GP 5). Before Einstein's notion of curved space, the idea of the infinity of space, although clearly traceable to the pre-Socratic philosophers, was the predominant belief of the leading physicists and philosophers of the later nineteenth century. Mung, the god of Death, tells the man who has unwittingly walked the road of death, "Had it been possible for thee to go by any other way then had the Scheme of Things been otherwise and the gods had been other gods" (GP 21). This is nothing more than the philosophy of determinism, a tenet that is also Greek—as Dunsany acknowledges in creating Dorozhand, the god of Destiny (GP 41), and even more pronouncedly by having Fate and Chance as coeval with Mānā-Yood-Sushāī (GP [vii])—but which many physicists of the later nineteenth century were adopting. And what of the fact that when "Fate and Chance had played their game and ended, and all was over," Fate then said to Chance, "Let us play our old game again," with the result that "under the same bank in the same land a sudden glare of sunlight on the same spring day shall bring the same daffodil to bloom once more and the same child shall pick it, and not regretted shall be the billion years that fall between" (TG 189–90)? Is this not Nietzsche's eternal recurrence?

In "Pegāna" Imbaun the prophet wants to know "where shall the life of a man abide when Mung hath made against this body the sign of Mung?" (GP 80); in other words, what of life after death? The god Yoharneth-Lahai rejoins with a paradox: "Thy life is long, Eternity is short" (GP 81). How can this be?

So short that, should thou die and Eternity should pass, and after the passing of Eternity thou shouldst live again, thou wouldst say: "I closed mine eyes but for an instant."

There is an Eternity behind thee as well as one before. Hast thou bewailed the aeons that passed without thee, who are so much afraid of the aeons that shall pass? (GP 81)

The idea is vaguely Epicurean—recall Lucretius' berating the man who fears death, as if his consciousness will be around to fear it (*De Rerum Natura* 3.894–911)—but it is in fact a virtually exact echo of a remark attributed by Boswell to David Hume: "I told him [Johnson] that David Hume said to me, he was no more uneasy to think he should *not be* after this life, than that he *had not been* before he began to exist."[1]

As if it were not enough that Dunsany is covertly introducing secularists like Nietzsche and Hume into the divine fabric of his theogony, we find Darwin making anomalous appearances. Kib, the creator of all earth life, first populated the planet with beasts, then he "made Men: out of beasts he made them" (GP 9). Still more explicitly, "When the Gods Slept" relates how Ya, Ha, and Snyrg, "the lords of evil, madness, and of spite" (TG 112), cross the world to find men who will worship them, but in vain; at last they come upon some baboons, who agree to worship them when Snyrg says that "he would make them men" (TG 118). And what does the future hold? A prophet in "The Journey of the King" tells King Ebalon, who wishes to live forever:

Lastly, O King, thou shalt perceive men changing in a way thou shalt not comprehend, knowing what thou canst not know, till thou shalt discover that these are men no more and a new race holds dominion over the earth whose forefathers were men. . . . Then . . . the hills shall fling up earth's long stored heat back to the heavens again, when earth shall be old and cold, with nothing alive upon it but one King. (TG 217)

All this is spoken in the most resonant of prose-poetry, but the conceptions behind it—the further evolution of mankind into a different species, the eventual cooling of the sun and extinction of all life upon the earth—are those of modern biology and astrophysics.

This latter idea is expressed in one of Dunsany's most affecting early tales, "A Legend of the Dawn." This story is nothing more than a parable about the rising and setting of the sun. Inzana, "the child of all the gods" (TG 97), plays with her golden ball, tossing it far into the sky; but on successive days various evil figures—Umborodom, "whose hound was the thunder" (TG 98); the North Wind; the Fog, "behind [whom] slunk the Night" (TG 103)—contrive to hide the ball, and darkness overwhelms the earth. Each night the ball has to be rescued and returned to Inzana, so that she will stop crying for her golden ball.

But some day the Night shall seize the golden ball and carry it right away and drag it down to its lair, and Slid shall dive from the Threshold into the sea to see if it be there, and coming up when the fishermen draw their nets shall find it not, nor yet discover it among the sails. . . . And men, no longer having light of the golden ball, shall pray to the gods no more, who, having no worship, shall be no more the gods. (TG 104–5)

In another way Dunsany seems very modern in spite of the jewelled archaism of his language; and this is in his many traces of atheism or, at the very least, anticlericalism. Amory states bluntly that Dunsany was an atheist (Am 33), but cites no evidence for the claim; I am not entirely sure of the matter, but we have already seen in "Pegāna" the implication of the non-endurance of the soul after death, so that actual atheism on Dunsany's part is likely enough.

The first hint of anticlericalism comes remarkably early in *The Gods of Pegāna*. After the introduction of the important gods, we find a chapter entitled "The Chaunt of the Priests," specifically the priests of Mung, god of Death: it is useless, they tell us, to pray to Mung, for he comes heedless of our prayers or desires;

> Rather bring gifts to the Priests, gifts to the Priests of Mung.
> So shall they cry louder unto Mung than ever was their wont.
> And it may be that Mung shall hear. (GP 23)

Whom are these priests trying to fool? Indeed, priests and prophets do not fare especially well in *The Gods of Pegāna*: in a series of stories about various prophets, we find that Yonath, "burdened with the wisdom of great years, and worn with seeking, know[s] only that man knoweth not" (GP 54); Yug claimed that "I know all things" (GP 56), but Mung got him; Alhireth-Hotep made a similar claim, and "men brought gifts to him" (GP 57), but Mung got him as well; Kabok, "fattened upon the gifts that men had brought him" (GP 58), also finds Mung awaiting him one day.

Imbaun the prophet endures a little longer, but some of his remarks are highly curious for a religious man. He is denied "the secret of the gods" (GP 80); concerned that he will no longer be thought a prophet and "another would take the people's gifts instead of me" (GP 81), he weaves a story that "the people when they die shall come to Pegāna, and there live with the gods, and there have pleasure without toil" (GP 81). His subsequent description of Pegāna is uncannily like conventional descriptions of Heaven. But it is all a myth, and Imbaun is fully aware of it. Later he declares explicitly that it is the prophet's function to "speak the hopes of the people, and tell the people that their hopes be true" (GP 86). All this is somewhat Nietzschean, although without Nietzsche's violent hostility toward priests as manipulators of religious doctrine for the purpose of maintaining power over their followers.

Time and the Gods becomes much more explicit on the matter of actual atheism. I am not at the moment concerned with the apparently increased fragility of the gods—who now fear time ("Time and the Gods"), the sea

("The Coming of the Sea"), and their possible end ("The Vengeance of Men"), and who now lament that they are old and that there is nothing new in the world (TG 111–12)—for I believe the significance of these things lies elsewhere. What is remarkable in this volume is a succession of tales that are clearly atheistic in their implications.

The first, and most exhaustive, of these is "The Sorrow of Search." This is a transparent parable suggesting that all established religions are false. King Khanazar seeks knowledge of the gods; his "master prophet" (TG 131) tells him instead a story:

> Far and white and straight lieth the road to Knowing, and down it in the heat and dust go all wise people of the earth, but in the fields before they come to it the very wise lie down or pluck the flowers. By the side of the road to Knowing—O King, it is hard and hot—stand many temples, and the doorway of every temple stand many priests, and they cry to the travellers that weary of the road, crying to them:
> "This is the End." (TG 131)

But, of course, it is not the end. Some continue along the path, stopping at each temple but failing to find satisfaction there. The road itself offers no hope, for the travelers can see nothing because of the dust, some of which "is stirred up by the feet of all that travel upon it, and more arises from the temple doors" (TG 131–32). But one traveler did indeed come to the "utter End" (TG 133):

> [A]nd there was a mighty gulf, and in the darkness at the bottom of the gulf one small god crept, no bigger than a hare, whose voice came crying in the cold:
> "I know not."
> And beyond the gulf was nought, only the small god crying. (TG 133)

All religions think they, and they alone, have the answer, but both they and the seekers after knowledge only disseminate obfuscation (dust); the "End" is merely the absence of knowledge. Perhaps it were better to follow the lead of the wise men and pluck the flowers along the side of the road.

"The Men of Yarnith" has a slightly different message. Yarni Zai is the god worshipped in Yarnith. The myths of the land tell how he created all animals, birds, and human beings, and it is also by his sufferance that the god of spring and the god of winter continually chase each other year after year. There then come drought and famine to Yarnith, first attacking animals and then the people. There can be no recourse but to offer prayers to Yarni Zai, whose temple is situated in a remote valley; but all are afraid to go. Finally Hothrun Dath agrees to undertake the arduous journey; but when he traverses the valley of Yodeth to find the colossal figure of the god, he discovers that it is no more than a statue carved by human beings. Initially he suffers crippling disillusion: "There are no gods, and all the world is lost" (TG 144). But not long afterward the men of Yarnith gain a new resolve: "And they said: 'If no help cometh from Yarni Zai then is there no help but from our own strength and might, and we be Yarnith's gods with the saving of Yarnith burning within us or its doom according to our desire'" (TG 145). And by their own initiative they end the famine. Paradoxically, however, a thousand years later the descendants of the people of Yarnith still pray to Yarni Zai—one might as well not take a chance!

"For the Honour of the Gods" tells of the ancient time when "listless peace" (TG 147) hung heavy over the lands of the Three Islands; the people "played like children about the feet of Chance and had no gods and went not forth to war" (TG 147). But this state of affairs does not last for long: sailors come to the islands and urge these "happy people which had no gods" (TG 147) how much happier they would be if they would worship gods and fight in their honor. The people of the islands are gradually converted, setting sail for other lands to conquer and pillage in the name of the gods. Soon all the people on the three islands are fighting each other:

> And from one of the isles all the folk came forth in ships to battle for gods that strode through the isle like kings. And from another they came to fight for gods that walked like humble men upon the earth in beggar's rags; and the people of the other isle fought for the honour of gods that were clothed in hair like beasts; and had many gleaming eyes and claws upon their foreheads. But of how these people fought till the isles grew desolate but very glorious, and all for the fame of the gods, are many histories writ. (TG 150–51)

It may be a glorious thing to fight for the gods, but the end result is death, destruction, and desolation.

And let us remember "The Relenting of Sardinac." All the gods are forsaking the earth, but a lame dwarf, Sardinac, who sees them marching in a row into the sky, follows them. The people, thinking that Sardinac himself is a god, plead with him not to leave the earth entirely godless; he relents and is made a god. Can there be any clearer message as to the haphazard way in which unworthy and (spiritually) deformed entities are made into gods? The criticism of theism in the tales in *Time and the Gods* goes far beyond mere anticlericalism, beyond merely a display of the duplicity and avariciousness of the priesthood: there is a fundamental questioning of the very foundations of religion and of the very dubious rewards it bestows upon a duped and easily swayed populace. Once again it is important to note that this criticism is in no way confounded by Dunsany's own bountiful creation of gods; for these latter are purely aesthetic inventions that are meant to herald our closeness with Nature.

Related to atheism and Nature worship is what can only be called, in the most literal sense of the term, Dunsany's antihumanism. I have suggested that this is a dominant motif in the whole of his work, but it does not take the form of Ambrose Bierce's cheerful misanthropy or H. P. Lovecraft's bland indifference toward human concerns; rather, it strives to reintegrate human beings into the natural world. In *The Gods of Pegāna* antihumanism is expressed by means of a frigid cosmicism—a depiction of the spectacular vastness of time and space and the resultant inconsequence of human beings within the boundless universe. It is this quality—exhibited in *The Gods of Pegāna* far more potently than in any of his later work—that led Lovecraft to claim hyperbolically that "[h]is point of view is the most truly cosmic of any held in the literature of any period."[2]

The known universe—the worlds and the lesser gods—is only the product of the dreams of Mānā-Yood-Sushāī; one day he will awake and it will all be forgotten. We have already seen that human beings are a sort of second-order creation: we were created by Kib, who was created by Mānā-Yood-Sushāī. Time and space are infinite, and there is no afterlife for us: our tenure on this planet is of the most fleeting and insignificant sort.

The game motif that pervades *The Gods of Pegāna* is central to Dunsany's devaluation of human importance. In the prefatory note to the volume, we learn that Fate and Chance "cast lots to decide whose the Game should be" (GP [vii]); but no one knows who won the cast. The very creation of the universe is seen as the result of a moment of frivolity, and one day Fate and Chance will clear the board and play the game all over again (TG 189–90). Once the lesser gods are made, they declare, "Let Us make worlds to amuse Ourselves while Mānā rests" (GP 5). The gods play with the worlds, but after a million years "Kib grew weary of the first game of the gods" (GP 8); he created beasts and "played" (GP 8) with them. A million more years passed, and "Kib grew weary of the second game" (GP 9) and created human beings. Zodrak the prophet declares:

The gods have many moods. Thousands of years ago They were in mirthful mood. They said: "Let Us call up a man before Us that We may laugh in Pegāna."
They took me from my sheep upon the hill that slopes towards the sea. They carried me above the thunder. They stood me, that was only a shepherd, before

Them on Pegāna, and the gods laughed. They laughed not as men laugh, but with solemn eyes. (GP 76)

And yet the gods are themselves potentially transient and ephemeral, for they all fear the waking of Māna-Yood-Sushāī. The god Hoodrazai learns why the gods were made; "and . . . he was the god of mirth and of abundant joy, but became from the moment of his knowing a mirthless god" (GP 47). This idea is expressed more elaborately in *Time and the Gods*, where it becomes clear that the gods themselves are subject to many of the ills that afflict human beings. In this volume, more than in its predecessor, the great figure of Time becomes the titan foe of the gods. Time is the gods' "swarthy servant" (TG 87), "yet he cast furtive glances at his masters, and the gods distrusted Time because he had known the worlds or ever the gods became" (TG 87). The gods are powerless to defend their peerless city Sardathrion against the onslaughts of time, and all they can do is mourn its loss. In "When the Gods Slept" the gods themselves become weary of the monotonous passing of time: " 'Will no new thing be? Must those four march for ever round the world till our eyes are wearied with the treading of the feet of the Seasons that will not cease, while Night and Day and Life and Death drearily rise and fall?' " (TG 111). The gods have no recourse but to sleep and to hope: "It may be that the worlds shall pass and we would fain forget them" (TG 112).

But if Time is a terrible foe to gods, how much more terrible is it to human beings! Two of the most poignant tales in *Time and the Gods* tell of quixotic quests by human beings to overcome Time and its ravages. In "The Cave of Kai" King Khanazar yearns for his lost yesterdays. Syrahn the prophet tells the king that they now lie in a cave, "and over the cave stands sentinel one Kai, and this cave Kai hath guarded from the gods and men since ever the Beginning was made" (TG 125). Undaunted, the king makes an expedition to the cave, but Kai refuses him entrance. Returning forlorn from his journey, the king encounters a harpist, who tells him, "I have a golden harp; and to its strings have clung like dust some seconds out of the forgotten hours and little happenings of the days that were" (TG 127). This exquisite fable of the power of art to preserve some fragments of our past will be elaborated upon in many of Dunsany's later tales and poems.

Still more affecting is "In the Land of Time," in which King Karnith Zo, seeing the evidences of Time's handiwork—temples of old gods falling to ruin, gardens overrun with weeds, a woman with her face furrowed with wrinkles—resolves to battle this monstrous foe. He and his weary army march across the plains, going from city to city; on each occasion they find not Time, but only his withering effects. Finally they find the castle of Time atop a hill and seek to ascend it:

But as the feet of the foremost touched the edge of the hill Time hurled five years against them, and the years passed over their heads and the army still came on, an army of older men. But the slope seemed steeper to the King and to every man in his army, and they breathed more heavily. And Time summoned up more years, and one by one he hurled them at Karnith Zo and at all his men. And the knees of the army stiffened, and the beards grew and turned grey . . . (TG 176)

This remarkable scenario will be reused in a somewhat less fantastic but no less poignant manner in *The King of Elfland's Daughter* (1924), when Alveric gathers a motley band of companions to search in vain for Lirazel, the daughter of the king of Elfland.

Dunsany was aware that *Time and the Gods* was only a partial sequel to *The Gods of Pegāna*; as he charmingly puts it, "The early part of that book was of a world ruled over by the Gods of Pegāna, but as the book progressed I became heterodox to my own heterodoxy and wrote tales of peoples that worshipped other gods" (PS 121). With Dunsany's second volume the "Pegāna Mythos" comes to a close, and the gods, lands, and peoples of that cosmos make no appearance in his later work, aside from a fleeting mention in "The Avenger of Perdóndaris" (1912; TTH). But the themes that were broached in these two books—fantasy as Nature, the glories of the unmechanized past, antihumanism, the awesomeness of Time and the power of art and dreams to combat it—would receive many distinctive variations and elaborations in his subsequent story collections, plays, novels, and poems. And yet, in some ways Dunsany never excelled *The Gods of Pegāna* and *Time and the Gods*: their assured tone and aesthetic richness are as far as can be imagined from the apprentice work of a beginning writer; and their unique style and subject matter have made them landmarks in the literature of fantasy.

FANTASY AFTER PEGĀNA

The Sword of Welleran (1908) and *A Dreamer's Tales* (1910) solidly established Dunsany as a vigorous new voice in English and Irish literature, although there was still very little that was distinctively Irish in his writing. Whereas only a single tale in *Time and the Gods* had been published in a magazine prior to book publication (the title story appeared as "The Lament of the Gods for Sardathrion" in the *Shanachie*), a good many of the tales in the next two collections received periodical appearances, most in the English *Saturday Review* and a few in E. Nesbit's rare periodical, the *Neolith*. Dunsany even acknowledges, in the preface to *A Dreamer's Tales*, the editor of the *Saturday Review* "for the opportunity afforded me by his review of reaching a wider public than my books have attained to yet" (DT [vi]). The *Saturday Review* also published a good many of the prose-poems in *Fifty-one Tales* (1915), which shall be studied here because of their general similarity in tone to *The Sword of Welleran* and *A Dreamer's Tales* and because most of them were published between 1909 and 1912.

One of the first things that strikes us when we read *The Sword of Welleran* is that the "real" world has not been wholly banished, as it was in Dunsany's first two books. The title story is set in a dream city, Merimna, although—as I shall note presently—this does not immediately imply any ontological subordination to the "real" world. But in "The Fall of Babbulkund" we encounter mentions of pharaohs and Araby (SW 127), and it shortly becomes clear that Babbulkund is actually in or near Arabia: ". . . when we came to the land of which Babbulkund is the abiding glory, we hired a caravan of camels and Arab guides, and passed southwards in the afternoon on the three days' journey through the desert that should bring us to the white walls of Babbulkund" (SW 128). Later the Baltic, Ceylon, Ind, and Cathay are cited (SW 131). There were once Europeans in Bethmoora (DT 54). In "The Idle City" the unnamed city of the title requires those who wish to enter it to tell an idle tale as a sort of toll, and one man tells a tale of Rome (DT 111). Several other tales are set in the empirically real world of England, although populated by elves and other inhabitants of fairyland.

All this bespeaks a significantly different relation between fantasy and reality from that obtaining in *The Gods of Pegāna* and *Time and the Gods*. The "real" world is no longer replaced with a fantasy realm; instead, that fantasy realm and its denizens are, as it were, now being inserted into the "real" world. What this means is that the land of fantasy is much more accessible than Pegāna and its analogues, and there is now always the possibility that any of us could fall into a fantasy realm at any moment.

Critical to this shift of perspective is the function of dreams. Dunsany's early tales have, with careless inclusiveness, frequently been termed dream narratives, but only a few can be so classified. It is not the case that Dunsany wishes to contrast the "real" world with a dreamworld: in his first two books his fantasy world *is* the "real" world, and there is no other; in his later work the fantasy world occupies some tantalizingly ill-defined position within the "real" world, sometimes in the past and sometimes simply off the beaten track, usually in "the East." Dunsany himself once ruminated, in a lengthy passage in *Patches of Sunlight* (PS 83–85), on why his early work was set so uniformly in lands that suggested Arabia, Greece, North Africa, and India, when he at that time had little firsthand experience of them. He himself was not clear on the matter, but gave a five-part answer: first, his reading of the Bible, later combined with his study of Greco-Roman antiquity; second, a very brief glimpse of Tangier around the turn of the century; third, his father's tales of Egypt; fourth, his early reading of Kipling; and fifth, his sight of South Africa during the Boer War. All this may or may not be a satisfactory answer; and we must keep in mind that Dunsany's imagination was fueled as much by anticipations of future voyages as by actual voyages: he notes that "The Fall of Babbulkund" and "The Fortress Unvanquishable, Save for Sacnoth" were inspired by the sight of Gibraltar (PS 80), but that "Idle Days on the Yann" was written while looking forward to a trip down the Nile (PS 143–45).

"Idle Days on the Yann," indeed, is the story that may provide a key toward the solution of the relation among dream, fantasy, and reality. Let us recall, however, a fleeting utterance in *The Gods of Pegāna* in reference to Yoharneth-Lahai, "the God of Little Dreams and Fancies" (GP 28), that may be of relevance: "Whether the dreams and the fancies of Yoharneth-Lahai be false and the Things that are done in the Day be real, or the Things that are done in the Day be false and the dreams and fancies of Yoharneth-Lahai be true, none knoweth saving only Mānā-Yood-Sushāī, *who hath not spoken*" (GP 28–29). Is it possible that dreams are not merely the products of imagination, but that they instead provide access to some other, perhaps more favored, realm? This may well be the implication of "The Sword of Welleran," which opens: "I have never seen a city in the world so beautiful as Merimna seemed to me when first I dreamed of it" (SW 111). This statement is, however, remarkably ambiguous: does "in the world" mean "in the real world," so that the dream city of Merimna is superior to all terrestrial cities? Is Merimna merely the product of the narrator's dreaming? The tale proceeds as if Merimna is a truly existing city: no reference to lands in the "real" world is made, and the narrator never returns to wake up from his dream.

In "Idle Days on the Yann" the narrator "came down through the wood to the bank of Yann and found, as had been prophesied, the ship *Bird of the River* about to loose her cable" (DT 59). He announces to the captain of the ship that he comes "from Ireland, which is of Europe" (DT 60); the narrator evidently feels that this laborious circumlocution is necessary on the chance that the crew have not heard of such a place, but it is of no use: "the captain and all the sailors laughed, for they said, 'There are no such places in all the land of dreams'" (DT 60). It gradually becomes evident that there is both a common dreamland and a dreamland specific to individuals; for the narrator admits to the crew that "my fancy mostly dwelt in the desert of Cuppar-Nombo, about a beautiful blue city called Golthoth the Damned" (DT 60), at which the crew "complimented me upon the abode of my fancy, saying that, though they had never seen these cities, such places might well be imagined" (DT 60–61). As the narrator is departing after his long journey, he goes back

> to find my way by strange means back to those hazy fields that all poets know, wherein stand small mysterious cottages through whose windows, looking westwards, you may see the fields of men, and looking eastwards see glittering elfin mountains, tipped with snow, going range on range into the region of Myth, and beyond it into the kingdom of Fantasy, which pertain to the Lands of Dream. (DT 91)

There now seem to be three different realms: the "real" world; an intermediate world ("those hazy fields that all poets know") full of natural beauty; and the Lands of Dream.

The significance of all this is clarified by two later stories, "The Shop in Go-by Street" and "The Avenger of Perdóndaris," both published in 1912 but not collected until *Tales of Three Hemispheres* (1919). Both are deliberate sequels to "Idle Days on the Yann." In the former tale the narrator yearns to see the Lands of Dream again and to meet the captain of the *Bird of the River* and his crew; but he has evidently lost the ability to attain this realm by dreaming, as he had done in "Idle Days on the Yann." He learns that a shop in Go-by Street, London ("not far from the Embankment" [TTH 105]), affords entry to the Lands of Dream through its back door. Passing through this door, he finds that the *Bird of the River* now lies in decayed ruins: evidently dream time and real time function very differently.

"The Avenger of Perdóndaris" is still more interesting. Passing once again through the back door of the shop in Go-by Street, the narrator has a revealing conversation with an old witch who occupies that intermediate realm that poets know:

> "I have come from London," I said. "And I want to see Singanee. I want to go to his ivory palace over the elfin mountains where the amethyst precipice is."
> "Nothing like changing your illusions," she said, "or you grow tired. London's a fine place but one wants to see the elfin mountains sometimes."
> "Then you know London?" I said.
> "Of course I do," she said. "I can dream as well as you. You are not the only person that can imagine London." (TTH 128)

This really brings us back to that statement regarding Loharneth-Lahai in *The Gods of Pegāna*. If London and the Lands of Dream are both "illusions," it argues for a sort of relativism whereby fantasy becomes purely a matter of perspective. The "real" world is just as capable, in principle, of producing a fantastic scenario as the world of dreams; and the key to that scenario, as many tales in *The Sword of Welleran* and *A Dreamer's Tales* attest, is imagination.

What imagination does is to vivify and—more importantly for Dunsany, whose aesthetic very likely derives from that fin-de-siècle credo encapsulated by Wilde's imperishable dictum, "The artist is the creator of beautiful things"[3]—*beautify* everything with which it comes into contact, even the most seemingly prosaic. The narrator of "The Sword of Welleran" "dreamed" of the city of Merimna: now that we have done away with any ontological distinction between dream and "reality"—or, at least, any derogation of the ontological status of the former in relation to the latter—we can say that the narrator's imagination has either conjured up, or granted him access, to this glorious city whose streets are "given over wholly to the Beautiful" (SW 111). This tale, the highest of high fantasy, is a magnificent epilogue to some of the tales of fantastic battle in *Time and the Gods*, especially "The Cave of Kai" and "In the Land of Time"; the "real" world has been abolished wholly and utterly.

We have already noted the difference of "The Fall of Babbulkund" in this regard, but in its aesthetic of beauty it continues the pattern that we will find persisting throughout the whole of Dunsany's early work. The narrator and his friends wish to journey to Babbulkund "that our minds may be beautified" (SW 127); Babbulkund, indeed, is, as a traveler asserts, " 'the most beautiful city in the world' " (SW 136). What, then, are we to make of several stories in this collection and *A Dreamer's Tales* that are clearly set in the real world? "The Fortress Unvanquishable, Save for Sacnoth" (SW) is another tale of high fantasy without any admixture of the real; but it is followed directly by "The Lord of Cities," which takes place in England. A river and a road debate as to who is the lord of cities. The road argues that it is Man, but the river counters:

Beauty and song are higher than Man. I carry the news seaward of the first song of the thrush after the furious retreat of winter northward, and the first timid anemone learns from me that she is safe and that spring has truly come. Oh but the song of all the birds in spring is more beautiful than Man, and the first coming of the hyacinth more delectable than his face! (SW 202)

The spider, however, argues that it is the lord of cities, not Man: "'What is Man? He only prepares my cities for me, and mellows them. All his works are ugly, his richest tapestries are coarse and clumsy. He is a noisy idler. He only protects me from mine enemy the wind; and the beautiful work in my cities, the curving outlines and the delicate weavings, is all mine'" (SW 205).

This tale may perhaps be among the earliest to enunciate what I wish to call Dunsany's "Prayer of the Flowers" motif. "The Prayer of the Flowers," one of the most affecting prose-poems in *Fifty-one Tales*, tells of the sorrow of the flowers under the spread of "cancrous cities" (FOT 36) filled with noise and smoke; but Pan comes to comfort them, saying, "'Be patient a little, these things are not for long'" (FOT 37). This notion that the natural world awaits with eagerness the ultimate destruction of the human race so that it may resume its sway upon the earth—a neat conjoining of Dunsany's dominant themes of the glorification of Nature, the loathing of industrialism, and the denigration of human striving—will be found in tales, plays, and poems throughout his career, and emphasizes what appears to be a rigid and unbridgeable gulf between the human realm and the realm of Nature. An early essay, "Two Hundred Times in a Blue Moon" (1910), starts out as a review of Maeterlinck's *The Blue Bird* but wanders off on this theme: "I wonder if [in the far future] . . . the Dog grown wild and banded together in packs, and the Cat prowling more solitary still, and Bread waving his bearded head in the natural, savage state shall outlive the doom of Man, and if Sugar shall luxuriate undisturbed with no dark men to gnaw it as they go by the banks of the Nile." And, of course, Dunsany adds his usual explanation for the downfall of the human race: "We are taking too much to cities." "The Hurricane" is another very early exposition of this idea, as those two great forces of Nature, the hurricane and the earthquake, look forward to destroying cities so that "all the lovely forests may come back and the furry creeping things" (SW 178).

Fifty-one Tales is a virtual litany of this theme. In "The Death of Pan," "travellers from London" find Pan lying apparently dead in Arcady; but at the sound of an "idle song" Pan "leaped up and the gravel flew from his hooves" (FOT 14–15), a transparent symbol for Nature's rejection of cities. "Time and the Tradesman" tells of Time's hair being gray "with the dust of the ruin of cities" (FOT 38): is it that cities, because of their alienation from the natural world, are unusually susceptible to the ravages of Time? Fog, in "Wind and Fog" (FOT), tallies up all the ships he has destroyed over the centuries: how easily can Nature overwhelm the puny works of

Man! In "Nature and Time" the former asks the latter, "'When will the fields come back and the grass for my children?'" and the latter replies, "'Soon, soon'" (FOT 122). And yet, there is perhaps hope for human beings, for Nature refers to "'My child Man'" (FOT 121): can it be that, once cities are gone, human beings will once again turn to Nature? "The Workman" presents less of a contrast between human beings and Nature, but it is nonetheless enormously powerful for its gleeful anticipation of the end of urbanized life: the ghost of a workman who has fallen from the scaffolding of a building notes with contempt, "'Why, yer bloomin' life 'ull go by like a wind . . . and yer 'ole silly civilization 'ull be tidied up in a few centuries'" (FOT 27). This staggering use of colloquialism—far indeed from the perfumed prose-poetry of most of the other tales in this collection and in Dunsany's early work generally—and the notion that civilization is some sort of vile stain that requires "tidying up" make this prose-poem one of the most poignant in his entire corpus.

But not all cities are "wrong" in Dunsany's eyes: Merimna may be "only" a dream city, but it has more than its share of quintessential beauty; Babbulkund, the most beautiful city in the world, must be somewhere in Arabia. In "Poltarnees, Beholder of Ocean," all the cities of the Inner Lands have a "broad, green way" (DT 2): they are at one with Nature. These cities may be very dissimilar to those cities of the modern industrial world we know, but what then do we make of "Blagdaross"? In this exquisite tale an old cork, an unstruck match, a broken kettle, an old cord, and an old rocking horse tell of their origins and their heyday. The match declares boldly: "'I am a child of the sun . . . and an enemy of cities; there is more in my heart than you know of. I am a brother of Etna and Stromboli'" (DT 26); but the kettle counters: "'I am the friend of cities. I sit among the slaves upon the hearth, the little flames that have been fed with coal'" (DT 26). And Blagdaross, the cast-off rocking horse, exults when a young boy takes him up from the garbage heap on which he has been thrown and imagines himself to be Coeur de Lion: "'I am Blagdaross again!'" (DT 31). Can it be that even the detritus of urban life has its poetry? Yes, but only if it is enlivened by the imagination.

The word "romance" was, for Dunsany, a code word for imagination, specifically the fantastic imagination. We will find it in his essay "Romance and the Modern Stage" (1911), and we find it in an uncollected prose-poem called "Romance" (1909). Romance "has a way of touching quite common things," like a spider's web: "When Romance came I guessed the history of the dust that lay in the spider's web. It came on an old east wind from Babylon. He has despoiled Assyria to pave his court. Where are the colours faded from old tapestry?"

Two further essays or prose-poems from this period, "Gondolas" (1908), and "Pens" (1909), continue on this theme of finding "romance" in distinctive objects of the real world. These essays are paeans, respectively, to gondolas and quill pens, and in both cases their "romance" is tied precisely to their symbolization of the world of Nature. Gondolas are "the descendants of the old sea-horses"; "theirs is the grace of princely bygone times"; they scorn to be "distrusted by the snorts of a modern ship made out of machinery without a soul": "And they have carried me into their favourite haunts, to and fro through little darkening ways where strange faces peer from little windows and songs begin to arise, when the sunset unseen from the waterways is turning the palaces into haunts of faery in which dwelt the princes of Once-upon-a-time and the people of Over-the-hills-and-far-away." This single essay encapsulates the essence of Dunsany's vision: the creative imagination that transforms objects of the real world into things that suggest the beauty of Nature and (what is metaphorically the same thing) the realm of faery; the disdain of the soulless machine; the yearning for the past when our ties to Nature were so much stronger and clearer. "Pens" tells a similar story, ruminating on the imaginative associations of quills taken from a wild goose's wing.

"The Beggars" is a fictional instantiation of these ideas. The narrator concludes that the streets of London "were all so unromantic, dreary" (DT 138); but then a flock of beggars comes into town. One of them addresses a street lamp: "'O lamp-post, our brother of the dark, are there many wrecks by thee in the tides of night? Sleep not, brother, sleep not. There were many wrecks an it were not for thee'" (DT 139–40). The beggars even find romance in the "ugly smoke" (DT 141) that billows up from factories: "'Behold the smoke. The old coal-forests that have lain so long in the dark, and so long still, are dancing now and going back to the sun'" (DT 141). It is true that one of the beggars enunciates the "Prayer of the Flowers" theme: "'Art thou weary, street? Yet a little longer they shall go up and down, and keep thee clad with tar and wooden bricks. Be patient, street. In a while the earthquake cometh'" (DT 140); but the fundamental message that wonder can be found even in the clangor of a very real metropolis, if one has the proper vision, is manifest.

There are, indeed, different types of cities, as "The Madness of Andelsprutz" makes clear: "There are cities full of happiness and cities full of pleasure, and cities full of gloom. There are cities with their faces to heaven, and some with their faces to earth; some have a way of looking at the past and others look at the future; some notice you if you come along them, others glance at you, others let you go by" (DT 32–33). Andelsprutz lacks that subtle charm that cities can have—it "had no way with her and no air about her" (DT 34)—and so the narrator knows that it is mad and dead. And what of London? "The Field" offers a harsh contrast to "The Beggars." In the summertime the call of the country is imperious: "No volume of traffic can drown the sound of it, no lure of London can weaken it" (DT 175). There are parts of London where "ugliness reaches the height of its luxuriousness, in the dense misery of the place, where one imagines the builder saying, 'Here I culminate. Let us give thanks to Satan'" (DT 177). Ugliness is a sin in Dunsany's aesthetic, and London has its share of it.

But let us consider what happens when we turn to "The Avenger of Perdóndaris." The narrator, yearning for the Lands of Dream, comes upon the palace of Singanee and there encounters Saranoora, "a lady . . . of marvellous beauty" (TTH 131), with whom he dances. Then it comes time for the narrator to return to London, although he is reluctant to do so and fears he will never again see Saranoora. Instead of returning the same way he entered, however, he attempts to go through a different alley; but he has forgotten that dream time and real time are not in congruence, and just as he found the *Bird of the River* in decay after only two years in the "real" world, he now returns to a London thousands of years after his own time. The city has returned to a state of primitivism, with rude huts having thatch roofs and shepherds leading flocks of sheep along streets overgrown with grass. Surely, to someone who so yearns for the simplicity of a nonindustrial age and who hates cities as all Dunsany's sympathetic characters do, this must be a blessing; but instead the narrator finds that he feels "the call of the fields we know" (TTH 139). He becomes keenly nostalgic when he hears a man speaking a variant of Cockney: "I know that that very language that was carried to distant lands by the old, triumphant cockney was spoken still in his birthplace" (TTH 143).[4] He appeals to the old witch and her cat, hoping that they can lead him back to his own time; he even says, " 'I'm tired of the Lands of Dream' " (TTH 146). The witch tells him to go back through the same alley by which he came, and when he does so he finds to his relief the London of his own day.

"I'm tired of the Lands of Dream"? Who is speaking here, the narrator or Dunsany? As early as 1910, in the prose-poem "Roses," Dunsany had written, "I hope that when London is clean passed away and the defeated fields come back again, like an exiled people returning after a war, they may find some beautiful thing to remind them of it all; because we have loved a little that swart old city" (FOT 53–54). This theme will be developed fascinatingly in Dunsany's later work.

The conclusion of "The Avenger of Perdóndaris" leads us naturally to a discussion of the role of Time in the tales of this period. Time is still a mighty power, but there are glimpses that certain forces—even human forces, such as art—can combat its worst effects. "Carcassonne" tells heartrendingly of the quest of Camorak to overcome Fate, which has decreed that he shall never see the glorious city of Carcassonne. Fate may here be no more than a substitute for Time, for—as with Karnith Zo in "In the Land of Time"—Camorak dares to take Fate on and gathers an army in order to find the sought-after city. But decades pass, the army grows old, and finally Arleon, the king's poet and prophet who has been their guide, is forced to admit: " 'My King, I know no longer the way to Carcassonne' " (DT 166). The king, in turn, learns the lesson stated at the outset of the quest: "We must wrestle with Time for some seven decades, and he is a weak and puny antagonist in the first three bouts" (DT 148). We are reminded of a grim simile in "Romance": "And there in the corner stands the tall old clock, swinging his long pendulum to and fro, even as a headsman that has grown old at his trade swings up and down his axe—and not in idleness but to strike the deadlier blow."

Time, in the tales of this period, is to be dreaded most when it impinges upon human beings. The narrator of "The Avenger of Perdóndaris," finding that he has lost the London of his time, remarks with poignant simplicity: "I began to feel that I had missed the world" (TTH 141). One of the most powerful tales of Dunsany's entire early period, and perhaps his first true horror tale, is "Where the Tides Ebb and Flow." Here a man has committed some nameless sin, so that even upon his death his spirit cannot rest; a band of men continually unearths his body. Centuries elapse; London "was passing away" (DT 47); "the cause of Nature had triumphed" (DT 48). The entire human race becomes extinct, and the birds, looking down at the poor unburied corpse, remark, " 'He only sinned against Man . . . it is not our quarrel' " (DT 48), and the man's soul climbs up to heaven on the notes of bird song.

But there is reason to hope. The people of Astahahn, as the narrator of "Idle Days on the Yann" learns, "have fettered and manacled Time, who would otherwise slay the gods" (DT 69): everything continues to be done in the old way. This conception is so piquant that Dunsany can be excused for failing to provide even the remotest explanation of how Astahahn has accomplished this great feat. The sphinx at Giza has actually conquered Time: "Time hath loved nothing but this worthless painted face" (FOT 16).

But it is art that has the greatest capability to blunt the ravages of Time. "The Raft-Builders" is one of the most exquisite prose-poems in all Dunsany's work, and is a transparent parable of writing as a bulwark against Time: "All we who write put me in mind of sailors hastily making rafts upon doomed ships" (FOT 24). It is true that most of our rafts are merely fodder for Time, which, "like a whale, feeds on the littlest things" (FOT 25); but every now and then some transcendent creation of human art persists: "Our ships were all unseaworthy from the first. There goes the raft that Homer made for Helen" (FOT 25).

"The Giant Poppy" is a slight variant on this idea. The poppy, emblem of forgetfulness, destroys much; but the poet thinks that his clan can turn the tide in some slight way: " 'We think we have saved Agamemnon' " (FOT 52). The worm, in "The Worm and the Angel," can destroy the physical tokens of civilization, but not great art (a line of Homer is quoted; FOT 43). " 'The world is not for ever,' " says a swan in "The Return of Song"; " 'only song is immortal' " (FOT 80).

An essay or prose-poem contemporaneous with these tales, "Jetsam" (1910), perfectly embodies this conception. Dunsany sees the jetsam that washes upon the shores of a deserted beach as emblematic of the fate of human beings. Bringing the earlier essays, "Gondolas" and "Pens," as well as the story "Blagdaross" to mind, he remarks on the scattered little objects that may survive our civilization: "old kettles whose songs are sung, forgotten toys of children grown up and gone afield, and I know not what else besides." But the things that combat the "sea of time" most are "the slender things . . . small songs and delicate rhyme."

One prose-poem in *Fifty-one Tales* provides a transition from art to religion, the latter a dominant motif in the tales of this period. "A Moral Little Tale" is a vicious story in which the Devil praises a Puritan for doing his work by prohibiting dance. The Puritan vehemently objects, but to no avail: the Devil takes him away to hell, where "it was that Puritan's punishment to know that those that he cared for on Earth, would do evil as he had done" (FOT 78). The violently hostile tone of this story may lend support to the belief in Dunsany's atheism, even if he is here only attacking what he perceives to be a social evil caused by religion. There are, however, a string of tales in *The Sword of Welleran* and *A Dreamer's Tales* that present a strong critique of religion and the religious from many different perspectives.

Babbulkund, the most beautiful city in the world, was destroyed by a rival religion. King Nehemoth of Babbulkund worships the god Annolith, and the people pray to the dog Voth, "for the law of the land is that none but a Nehemoth may worship the god Annolith" (SW 134). But a traveler whom the narrator and his companions meet on the way to Babbulkund remarks portentously: " 'I could love Babbulkund with a great love, yet am I the servant of the Lord the God of my people, and the King hath sinned unto the abomination Annolith, and the people lust exceedingly for Voth' " (SW 137). The traveler moves on, and when the narrator reaches the site where Babbulkund once stood, he finds that "in the empty desert on the sand the man in rags was seated, with his face hidden in his hands, weeping bitterly" (SW 141). He has appeased his religion by destroying Babbulkund, but derives no happiness therefrom.

"The Kith of the Elf-Folk" is a still more obvious atheistic parable. I shall study this tale in greater detail when I discuss *The Story of Mona Sheehy* (1939), for this story is a virtual mirror image of that novel; but here we can remark that the Wild Thing, in the course of desiring a soul and wishing to worship God, begins to lose touch with Nature: "Then something akin to discontent troubled the Wild Thing for the first time since the making of the marshes; and the soft grey ooze and the chill of the deep water seemed to be not enough, nor the first arrival northwards of the tumultuous geese, nor the wild rejoicing of the wings of the wildfowl when every feather sings" (SW 144). But the Wild Thing persists, and is eventually granted a soul by a dean. She is sent to work in a factory in the city, and when she finds that life highly dissatisfying, she is made into an opera star because of the purity of her singing voice. Even this does not please her, and eventually she gives up her soul and returns to her native marshes. This entire story urges us to sympathize with the Wild Thing's plight and, as it were, to root for the nonhuman and the soulless.

"The Highwayman" is very much along the same lines. Three compatriots of a highwayman, Tom o' the Roads, who has been hanged seek to free Tom's soul and let it ascend to heaven by burying his body in consecrated ground. All four, we learn, "had incurred the sorrow of God" (SW 161)—but the owlish gravity with which this utterance is made assures us that parody or satire is intended. The three take the body to the churchyard where an archbishop has just been buried; they exhume that corpse, place the body of their friend in the grave, and place the archbishop's body in a grave just outside consecrated ground. The three friends "knew not that in their sinful lives they had sinned one sin at which the Angels smiled" (SW 164). Is it the case that the highwayman is more deserving of holy burial than an archbishop, or is it that the Angels are merely acknowledging the strong ties of friendship that have led the highwayman's associates to this superficially immoral act?

As if it were not clear enough from all this where Dunsany's sympathies lie, "The Sword and the Idol" in *A Dreamer's Tales* puts a seal on the matter. This tale is not set in some remote fantasy world but in the prehistoric past, "late in the Stone Age" (DT 93). Loz discovers the use of iron by accident, and fashions a sword that makes him the ruler of his tribe; but Ith, "who was of no account" (DT 99), retaliates by inventing an idol—transparently labelled, not God, but Ged—to whom he attributes vast powers: " 'Ged sends the crops and the rain; and the sun and the moon are Ged's' " (DT 100). Ith wins over the credulous people and forces Lod, the successor of Loz, to yield the sword as a sacrifice to Ged.

It can readily be seen that many of Dunsany's antireligious tales are sharply satiric in import. Satire as such was not a significant component of *The Gods of Pegāna* or *Time and the Gods* (save perhaps in "The Relenting of Sardinac"), but it comes to the fore in many tales of this period, especially in *Fifty-one Tales*. "The Day of the Poll" (DT) may be one of Dunsany's earliest political satires, contrasting rather obviously the transience and triviality of politics with the beauty and eternity of Nature. A poet urges a voter to forget about the election and turn to Nature; but the voter "cried for his polling-booth like a child" (DT), at which the poet reflects: " 'See . . . these ancient beautiful things, the downs and the old-time houses and the morning, and the grey sea in the sunlight going mumbling round the world. And this is the place they have chosen to go mad in!' " (DT 184–85). There is nothing supernatural in this tale at all. The antidemocratic bias in this story is echoed in "The Demagogue and the Demi-Monde," which amusingly relates how the two figures of the title fare when they come to the gate of Paradise. The demi-monde, even though she lived her life purely for the sake of money, is grudgingly admitted, but the demagogue, who states that he " 'stood unflinchingly on the plank of popular representation,' " is refused admittance because of heaven's " 'unfortunate lack of interest in those Questions that you have gone so far to inculcate' " (FOT 49–50).

The best tale of this type, however, is "The True History of the Hare and the Tortoise." This story is rather reminiscent of a tale entitled "The Hare and the Tortoise" in Ambrose Bierce's *Fantastic Fables* (1899), although it is not likely that Dunsany knew of it or was directly inspired by it. A vicious satire on political campaigning, it tells of how the tortoise, by his ponderous regularity, defeated the frivolous hare in the race, thereby earning the title of the swiftest animal of all. So far there is nothing to distinguish this tale from Aesop's original; but when a forest fire threatens the beasts and they require someone who can speedily warn all the animals to flee, the inevitable results: "They sent the Tortoise" (FOT 70). What this tale is really satirizing is the frequency with which, in a democracy given to cheap sloganeering, the unqualified are put into positions of power and authority. This message seems more relevant to our time than to Dunsany's.

Dunsany's attack on democracy emerges in another way in *Fifty-one Tales*, in the frequent contrast between art and the stolid populace. People who are interested in "the progress of modern commerce" have no time for song ("The Songless Country" [FOT 46]). In "The City" poets and artists know when a city is doomed, but "[n]othing may warn the people" who are "glad with commerce" (FOT 95). "A Moral Little Tale" is also in part devoted to this idea. From a slightly different perspective, "The Assignation" speaks of the fickleness of Fame in a manner that bears comparison with *Fame and the Poet*. Both "The Food of Death" and "The Reward" are satires on adulterated food, but again the play *Cheezo* is a more dynamic working out of this idea.

When Dunsany remarked in *Patches of Sunlight* that many of his early tales were written "as though I were an inhabitant of an entirely different planet," he added that "then one night I suddenly wrote a story in which all the characters were human" (PS 135). The reference is to "The Highwayman"; and the importance of that tale lies not merely in its being the first that is entirely about human characters, but in that it is the first tale set concretely in the real world—namely, East Anglia (SW 150). It is, accordingly, one of the first of Dunsany's works that can genuinely be classified as a horror story. Horror, especially supernatural horror, can occur only in the "real" world, for it requires the intrusion of the unreal into an objectively verifiable milieu; if the unreal is manifested in a fantasy realm, its effect is not that of *horror* because there is not the sensation, as Lovecraft ably put it, "of that most terrible conception of the human brain—a malign and particular suspension or defeat of those fixed laws of Nature which are our only safeguard against the assaults of chaos and the daemons of unplumbed space,"[5] since the "laws" of a fantasy realm are not "fixed" as in the real world but invented by the author. "The Highwayman" does not, indeed, involve any suspension of the laws of Nature, but its atmosphere of horror—especially the incantatory repetition of the phrase "And the wind blew and blew" throughout the entire story—is potent.

"The Ghosts" is much closer to supernatural horror. This tale too is entirely about human characters, specifically the narrator and his brother, who have an argument about the existence of ghosts. The brother is convinced there are such things; the narrator is much more skeptical. That evening ghosts appear to the brother, but, in an ingenious twist, this manifestation does not turn out to be the source of horror, for they are merely the ethereal presences of stock legendry. Instead, loathsomeness is present in the "sins" of these ghosts: "Over there a lady tries to smile as she strokes the loathsome furry head of another's sin, but one of her own is jealous and intrudes itself under her hand. Here sits an old nobleman with his grandson on his knee, and one of the great black sins of the grandfather is licking the child's face and has made the child its own" (SW 173). Still more disturbingly, the ghosts' sins sense the nearness of the living narrator and, by their mere presence, imbue him with loathsome thoughts, such as the murder of his brother. (I shall not speculate on any autobiographical significance in all this.) But the narrator appeals to logic—he recites an axiom from Euclid—and the sins dissipate. This tale is already written in that flat, relatively unadorned prose that is the hallmark of Dunsany's later work; and its wholesale abandonment of anything approaching fantasy in setting and incident or prose-poetry in style makes it a startlingly early herald of his eventual renunciation of fantasy.

Other tales are keenly horrific but remain within the parameters of Dunsany's early prose-poetic style. I have already noted the magnificent sense of doom and pathos that hangs over "Where the Tides Ebb and Flow," one of his great early tales of horror. "Bethmoora" too is a masterwork of atmosphere, telling in hypnotic prose of the desertion of the lovely town of Bethmoora at the hands of the emperor Thuba Mleen. I do not know that this tale has any particular point aside from the creation of an atmosphere of dread, unless we are to infer that this is one more of Dunsany's Nature-conquers-humanity tales; for some believe that it was the desert that overwhelmed Bethmoora: "For he hates the sound and the sight of men in his old evil heart, and he would have Bethmoora silent and undisturbed, save for the weird love he whispers at her gates" (DT 57).

"Poor Old Bill" is another powerfully atmospheric story. A character tells of a ship that approaches a dubious land:

There was a nasty look about the isles. They were small and flat as though they had come up only recently from the sea, and they had no sand or rocks like honest isles, but green grass down to the water. And there were little cottages there whose looks we did not like. Their thatches came almost down to the ground, and were strangely turned up at the corners, and under the low eaves were queer dark windows whose little leaded panes were too thick to see through. (DT 128–29)

The captain goes ashore and secures something from this dubious place, and gains supernatural powers as a result: when the crew mutinies and leaves the captain on a deserted island with a year's supply of provisions, he nevertheless casts a spell over the ship so that it can never land as long as the captain is alive; and he manages to survive well over a year. This tale, told entirely by one of the crew members as he reminisces in an old tavern, is in its humorous, bantering, but sinister tone another significant precursor of Dunsany's later work, notably the Jorkens tales.

A Dreamer's Tales may well be Dunsany's finest short story collection: in its variety of tone, its mingling of horror, fantasy, pathos, humor, and satire, in its chiselled prose, and in its powerful working out of themes central to his work it represents the pinnacle of his early fiction-writing career. *The Sword of Welleran* is not far behind, and *Fifty-one Tales* presents many powerful vignettes, although perhaps it is not wise to read too many of them at once. After this time, however, there is a significant falling off, as Dunsany seems to have exhausted this vein of writing and had yet to discover a new one. But that falling off is already anticipated in *The Book of Wonder* (1912), one of his most celebrated collections but, to my mind, one that reveals serious problems of conception, motivation, and purpose.

SELF-PARODY

The Book of Wonder consists of fourteen tales, thirteen of which appeared weekly in the *Sketch* in late 1910 and early 1911, with illustrations by S. H. Sime. More exactly, however, Dunsany's tales were written after Sime's illustrations, and were an attempt to infer their import and significance. Dunsany's next collection was *Fifty-one Tales* (1915), but I have remarked that the bulk of those tales were written prior to 1912; the later ones are among the weakest of the volume. There then followed *The Last Book of Wonder* (1916; titled *Tales of Wonder* in England). Six of these stories appeared in the *Sketch* in 1914 with illustrations by Sime, and with the same reverse method of composition; the rest of the tales were written randomly between 1912 and 1915. *Tales of Three Hemispheres* (1919) is easily the weakest of Dunsany's story collections, containing miscellaneous tales written apparently around 1916–19 except for a reprint of "Idle Days on the Yann" and its two sequels, "A Shop in Go-by Street" and "The Avenger of Perdóndaris," both published in 1912.

These three collections, accordingly, represent the latter end of Dunsany's early period (1905–19); they also reveal a significantly different approach to fantasy from that of his early tales. *The Book of Wonder* opens with a magnificent tale of high fantasy, "The Bride of the Man-Horse," in Dunsany's "old" manner; it is the bracing story of Shepperalk the centaur who seeks the "inhuman beauty" (BW 2) of Zretazoola, a city in the realm of Sombelenë. But there follows "The Distressing Tale of Thangobrind the Jeweller," whose first paragraph tells the whole sad story:

When Thangobrind the jeweller heard the ominous cough, he turned at once upon that narrow way. A thief was he, of very high repute, being patronized by the lofty and elect, for he stole nothing smaller than the Moomoo's egg, and in all his life stole only four kinds of stone—the ruby, the diamond, the emerald, and the sapphire; and, as jewellers go, his honesty was great. (BW 7)

What is sad about this is Dunsany's dynamiting of the high seriousness of his early fantastic work for the purposes of self-parody, snickering humor, and cheap satire. Lovecraft, who always remained one of Dunsany's acutest critics, put his finger directly on the problem when he remarked:

As he gained in age and sophistication, he lost in freshness and simplicity. He was ashamed to be uncritically naive, and began to step aside from his tales and visibly smile at them even as they unfolded. Instead of remaining what the true fantaisiste must be—a child in a child's world of dream—he became anxious to shew that he was really an adult good-naturedly pretending to be a child in a child's world. This hardening-up began to shew, I think, in *The Book of Wonder* . . .[6]

I am not always in agreement with Lovecraft's assessments of the later Dunsany, since he—like many of those who have been entranced by the glittering magic of the early work—frequently shows an intolerance toward Dunsany's abandonment of pure fantasy and the revolutionary developments that occurred during the last forty years of his career; but in this instance he has identified the matter faultlessly.

Those who maintain the uniform brilliance of Dunsany's early writing and the uniform mediocrity of his later output have failed to come to grips with the serious tailing off represented by *The Book of Wonder* and its successors. It should already be obvious that this early fiction is by no means a monolithic entity, entirely homogeneous either in focus or in quality. Pure otherworld fantasy; fantasy mixed with reality; supernatural horror; parable; satire: these and other elements we find throughout these stories, and what seems to be happening by the time of *The Book of Wonder* is a certain exhaustion of the vein of writing that gave birth to *The Gods of Pegāna* and *Time and the Gods*. It is not, to be sure, that Dunsany is (as Lovecraft remarks) actually "naive" in his early tales, for we have seen the influence of Nietzsche and other advanced thinkers on that body of work; it is rather that Dunsany, having said all he can in that pseudo-naive manner, now pokes fun at it. The imaginary names in "The Distressing Tale of Thangobrind the Jeweller" are no longer invented for their evocative beauty, but for their comic overtones—Snarp, Ag, Snood (BW 7–8); and the outcome—Thangobrind tries to rob the diamond set in the lap of the spider-idol Hlo-hlo but instead is dispatched by that baleful entity—is deliberately predictable.

The morality of this tale—don't rob from the gods—is so elementary as to be childish: it does not suggest genuine hubris, since Thangobrind does not aspire for anything save the jewel itself, and no broader symbolism of any other sort can be derived from it. Several other tales in *The Book of Wonder* have a very similar import: "The Probable Adventure of the Three Literary Men" tells of three nomads who wish to steal a golden box; "The Injudicious Prayers of Pombo the Idolator" involves a man who seeks out a "disreputable god" (BW 24) to answer a prayer that has been refused by other gods; in "The Hoard of the Gibbelins" Alderic seeks to plunder the Gibbelins' hoard, with predictable consequences; "Now Nuth Would Have Practised His Art upon the Gnoles" is about a burglar who strives to relieve the gnoles of their emeralds; "Chu-Bu and Sheemish" speaks of two rival gods who end up destroying one another. The number of stories about thieves and their comeuppance, and about the pettiness of quaint imaginary gods, betrays a serious poverty of imagination on Dunsany's part; several tales are mere variants of one another.

Things get a little better with the six stories in *The Last Book of Wonder* published in the *Sketch*, although some have that same annoying smart-aleck tone that mars their predecessors. "The Bad Old Woman in Black" is a labored, flippant, and pointless tale of a witch with an evil reputation; Dunsany does not even attempt to write an actual narrative around Sime's drawing, merely maundering coyly about some of the picture's suggestive implications. "The Bird of the Difficult Eye" involves Neepy Thang, the son of Thangobrind, who seeks out emeralds from the Edge of the World. In "The Long Porter's Tale" it is flatly stated at the end that the fantastic narrative uttered by the porter is a lie (LBW 71). The three other tales, however, have some redeeming qualities, and they shall be examined in the course of time.

By the time we get to *Tales of Three Hemispheres*, complete disaster has set in. Now Dunsany's tales of the Edge of the World have become entirely slight, self-parodic, and unmemorable. One wonders whether success was having an adverse effect upon him: it was around this time that he was achieving spectacular fame in America, and many of the tales in this collection appeared in the *Smart Set*, *Vanity Fair*, and other highbrow magazines of the day that were seeking to cash in on Dunsany's name. Accordingly we have things like "The Prayer of Boob Aheera," a silly tale of the rivalry between Boob Aheera and Ali Kareeb Ahash; "A Pretty Quarrel," about a battle between dwarfs and demigods; "How the Gods Avenged Meoul Ki Ning," in which the gods, attempting to avenge the murder of Meoul, end up killing someone else by accident; "The Gifts of the Gods," a simpleminded fairy tale; and on and on. Most of the tales in this volume are so insubstantial that they are forgotten the moment they are read.

It is true that several central themes in Dunsany's work are carried on in the tales of this period; but their flippancy makes them seem like parodies both of themselves and of the very themes they express. The cities-vs.-Nature dichotomy is taken up in a number of the less parodically intended tales. In "The Bride of the Man-Horse" Dunsany expostulates to the reader, "[H]ow shall I tell you, ye that dwell in cities, how shall I tell you what he [the centaur] felt as he galloped?" (BW 3), a sentiment that relates directly to the celebrated brief preface to *The Book of Wonder*: "Come with me, ladies and gentlemen who are in any wise weary of London: come with me: and those that tire at all of the world we know: for we have new worlds here" (BW [vii]). "How Ali Came to the Black Country" is a transparent parable on the evils of industrialization. The Black Country in question is clearly the Midlands, as Dunsany states bluntly (LBW 89). Ali remarks to his companions:

Having heard how evil is the case of England, how a smoke has darkened the country, and in places (as men say) the grass is black, and how even yet your factories multiply, and haste and noise have become such that men have no time for song, I have therefore come at the bidding of my good friend Shooshan, barber of London, and of Shep, a maker of teeth, to make things well with you. (LBW 91–92)

But even Ali has little power in the matter. He urges the "great ones" (the owners of the factories) to give up "the devil Steam" so that "there will come back again the woods and ferns and all the beautiful things that the world hath" (LBW 92–94); but the great ones do not wish to forego their profits. And so the devil Steam begets the still more powerful Petrol, and Ali washes his hands of the matter and leaves England to its fate.

But again, as with the tales of the previous period, all is not lost; and it is again imagination that may be our redeemer. "The Coronation of Mr. Thomas Shap" charmingly tells of an ordinary-seeming salesman who begins to "take little flights with his fancy" (BW 63), imagining a fantastic world for himself. He attempts to justify his daydreaming with a "dangerous theory": " 'After all, the fancy is as real as the body' " (BW 64). He becomes king in the land of Larkar, revelling in the beauty of the region and receiving the obeisances of its people. Gradually, however, the imaginative side of Shap overwhelms his practical side: he misses the train to town one morning, then ceases to go to work altogether. Finally he is put away in a madhouse, and yet, somehow this fate seems oddly more satisfactory than the monotonous grind of his meaningless job.

Somewhat similar is "The Wonderful Window," in which a young man finds wonder in the dingy suburbs of London. Mr. Sladden purchases a strange window from an Arabic-looking man and finds that a magical city set with towers is revealed through the window when it is fit in front of a cupboard in the wall of his flat. As Sladden continues to look through the window, he notes a certain development: a hostile army is approaching the town, and eventually a battle ensues. The city is in grave danger of falling to the invading army, and Sladden frantically attempts to come to its aid; he breaks the window with a poker in order to join the battle, but finds that "[j]ust as the glass broke he saw a banner covered with golden dragons fluttering still, and then as he drew back to hurl the poker there came to him the scent of mysterious spices, and there was nothing there, not even the daylight, for behind the fragments of the wonderful window was nothing but that small cupboard in which he kept his tea-things" (BW 81). The breaking of the window and the destruction of the magical city symbolize the death of wonder in Sladden, who "is older now and knows more of the world, and even has a Business of his own" (BW 81). This poignant tale was transformed into a pungent satire on the unimaginativeness of ordinary people in the late play *Golden Dragon City* (PEA).

From a very different perspective, one that is reminiscent of several tales in *A Dreamer's Tales*, we find such a story as "A Tale of London," in which a hashish eater who has been commanded by a sultan to dream of London remarks:

Its houses are of ebony and cedar which they roof with thin copper plates that the hand of Time turns green. They have golden balconies in which amethysts are where they sit and watch the sunset. Musicians in the gloaming steal softly along the ways; unheard their feet fall on the white sea-sand with which those ways are strewn, and in the darkness suddenly they play on dulcimers and instruments with strings. (LBW 1–2)

What exactly is the significance of this passage, and of the story as a whole? London is here described as magically as any of Dunsany's otherworldly realms; does this mean that fantasy and wonder are merely matters of perspective, that there is a sort of relativism of wonder whereby what is merely unfamiliar to one individual (as London would be to a sultan) becomes a thing of exotic beauty? There is something of this idea in "A Tale of London"; but the overriding message is the power of the imagination to skim off the ugliness of any region, real or imaginary, to distill the essence of its beauty, and to transform it into a land of wonder where the spirit can roam at will. Dreams, says Dunsany in the preface to *The Last Book of Wonder*, written from Ebrington Barracks in August 1916, are "the only things that survive" (LBW [v]).

"A Tale of London" should be compared with "A Tale of the Equator" (LBW), in which a sultan wishes to build a palace on the equator, so that he can (as he fancies) simultaneously experience the pleasures of winter and summer. A poet describes such a palace to him, doing so in such beautiful language that the sultan no longer desires to build the actual palace. It is the triumph of imagination over reality. "The Last Dream of Bwona Khubla" picks up on this theme. Drawing clearly upon Dunsany's hunting expeditions in the Sahara, it tells of a band of travelers who come to the camp where Bwona Khubla—a man from London, although "nothing identified his memory now to distinguish it from the memories of all the other dead but 'Bwona Khubla,' the name the Kikuyus gave him" (TTH 2)—met his death. At night the travelers see a magical vision of London: "Both say they saw it not as they knew it at all, not debased by hundreds of thousands of lying advertisements, but transfigured, all its houses magnificent, its chimneys rising grandly into pinnacles, its vast squares full of the most gorgeous trees, transfigured and yet London" (TTH 6). It is the embodiment of Bwona Khubla's "last dream"—the last thing he wished to recall before he died far from home.

"A City of Wonder" completes the pattern. This clearly autobiographical tale of Dunsany's first visit to New York tells of how the city is "waiting one furtive moment to step from the schemes of man, to slip back to mystery and romance again as cats do when they steal on velvet feet away from familiar hearths in the dark of the moon" (TTH 63). It is, therefore, not only London, but any great city that can trigger the imagination to conceive it without the dross of its advertisements, its factories, and all those other things that for Dunsany sapped wonder from them.

Many tales in the three collections under discussion here add bits of information regarding the relationship—geographical and otherwise—between the "real" world and the realm of fantasy; but it is exactly because so many of these stories are obviously flippant or self-parodic that their evidence on this and other matters becomes problematic. Pombo the Idolater is Burmese but lives in London (BW 22); he has to travel to World's End to find the idol who will grant his prayer, and all we are told is, "It is a long journey from London to World's End" (BW 25). Neepy Thang bought a "purple ticket at Victoria Station" (LBW 57) that takes him to the Edge of the World, and Gerald Jones does the same thing in

"The Long Porter's Tale" (LBW 65)—but how valuable is this testimony, given the fact that the porter is a liar? On the whole, most of the tales in these volumes are set in the emphatically real topography of England, and suggest that the fantastic imagination is entirely capable of carving out realms of wonder within it.

This realism of setting also makes possible a much greater degree of supernatural horror than was possible in the otherworldly tales. "The Bureau d'Echange de Maux," one of Dunsany's most celebrated stories, is unadulterated horror. We are taken to an obscure byway in Paris where an inconspicuous shop, the Bureau Universel d'Echanges de Maux, attracts a certain select clientele of desperate individuals. They wish to exchange an evil they have for another, fancying that nothing could be worse than their own. One man exchanges wisdom for folly; another exchanges life for death; and the narrator himself, about to go on a sea voyage, exchanges a fear of seasickness for a fear of elevators, believing that the latter is infinitely preferable to the former—but is it? "And yet at times it is almost the curse of my life" (LBW 103). The muttered dialogues of the various customers as they bargain with one another about their evils, and the utterly cynical proprietor who continually evades the moral issues raised by his establishment (" 'That was not my affair' " [LBW 102]), makes this a powerful psychological as well as supernatural tale. This story, too, was turned into a play—*The Bureau de Change* (PEA)—and improved in the process.

"The Three Sailors' Gambit" and "The Three Infernal Jokes" (both, LBW) are about dubious bargains with the Devil—in the one case, three sailors obtain a magic crystal that allows them to know what moves to make in chess for victory, in the other a man yields up a virtue of his to acquire three jokes that will make people die of laughter—with interesting if somewhat predictable results. Then there is the extremely peculiar tale "Thirteen at Dinner," in which an ex-master of foxhounds tells of coming upon a remote castle in which he asks to put up for the night because of the lateness of the hour. The butler expresses horror at the idea, but grudgingly lets the man in. He has an extraordinarily odd dinner with the owner of the castle, sitting down at an immense table with what seem to be twelve empty chairs, each of which the owner fancies is occupied by a different woman. The guest at first attempts to humor his host; then, whether from exhaustion or from the effects of the wine, he thinks he actually sees the women sitting in their seats and partaking of the dinner. The host has "wronged" (LBW 25) them in some nameless way, although we never learn how; nor is the issue of whether the tale is genuinely supernatural or one of psychological horror ever resolved.

The atmosphere of weird horror that pervades *The Last Book of Wonder* even manages to bleed over into those tales that are partly or entirely fantastic. "The Bad Old Woman in Black" ponderously but unsuccessfully attempts to infuse the title character with terror. "How Ali Came to the Black Country" is more effective, transforming the dismal smoke-clogged Midlands into a realm of fantastic horror. Finally, "The Loot of Loma" is set virtually in a fantastic terrain, although the sackers of Loma are "Indians" (LBW 72); and yet, their fate as they attempt to descend a narrow mountain path burdened with their loot is not enviable:

Though in the heights the fleecy clouds were idle, yet the wind was stirring mournfully in the abyss and moaning as it stirred, unhappily at first and full of sorrow; but as day turned away from that awful path a very definite menace entered its voice which fast grew louder and louder, and night came on with a long howl. Shadows repeatedly passed over the stars, and then a mist fell swiftly, as though there were something suddenly to be done and utterly to be hidden, as in very truth there was. (LBW 74–75)

Diversity of tone is, indeed, one of the distinguishing features of *The Last Book of Wonder*. From the horror of "The Bureau d'Echange de Maux," the bizarreness of "Thirteen at Table," and the perfumed fantasy of "A Tale of London" and "A Tale of the Equator," we move to the buffoonery of "A Story of Land and Sea" and the poignancy of "The Watch-Tower" and "The Exiles' Club." "A Story of Land and Sea" is nothing more than a shaggy-dog story. Featuring characters from "The Loot of Bombasharna" (BW), it tells of a pirate ship whose captain, in order to escape capture, affixes wheels to his ship and transports it across the Sahara Desert. All sorts of adventures enliven this narrative, but in the end it is nothing more than a lighthearted entertainment. In its deadpan tone it is quite similar to the Jorkens tales.

Very different is "The Watch-Tower." This is perhaps the only story of this entire period to enunciate the "Prayer of the Flowers" theme. The narrator speaks to an old spirit in Provence, who warns him against the Saracens. The narrator bootlessly tries to convince the spirit that the Saracens are no more, that they present no danger: " 'There has not been a Saracen either in France or Spain for over four hundred years' " (LBW 168). But the spirit is not to be persuaded and continues his dire warnings. This brief and affecting tale has perhaps two implications: are we to feel a wistful pity for the spirit who is so misguided and so out of date, or is it the case that the Saracens or their descendants will somehow survive the industrial civilization of Europe? The narrator argues that Europe "had terrible engines of war, both on land and sea" and that "the European railways . . . could move armies night and day faster than horses could gallop"; but the spirit replies in scorn, "In time all these things pass away, and then there will still be the Saracens" (LBW 167–68).

"The Exiles' Club" deals with a dinner party in which exiled kings appear to be the guests, but they turn out merely to be the waiters for some far greater exiles—the gods who are no longer worshipped. This is why the narrator ruminates at the beginning:

When a dynasty has been dethroned in heaven and goes forgotten and outcast even among men, one's eyes no longer dazzled by its power find something very wistful in the faces of fallen gods suppliant to be remembered, something almost tearfully beautiful, like a long warm summer twilight fading gently away after some day memorable in the story of earthly wars. (LBW 190–91)

We have seen several tales in Dunsany's very early work ponder on this theme, and several later tales shall do so as well.

The Last Book of Wonder contains one story, "The City on Mallington Moor" (LBW), that may stand as a summation of many of Dunsany's dominant concerns. A man longs to flee London—"partly because of the ugliness of the things in the shops"—for the countryside. He hears from a shepherd rumors of a beautiful city on Mallington Moor, "all in white marble," and makes an arduous climb over the moor in search of it. One evening he thinks he sees the city—but it is only the mist. Then, on another night, he appears actually to see the city through the mist:

Nothing the shepherd had said was the least untrue or even exaggerated. The poor old man had told the simple truth, there is not a city like it in the world. What he had called thin spires were minarets, but the little domes on the top were clearly pure gold as he said. There were the marble terraces he described and the pure white palaces covered with carving and hundreds of minarets. The city was obviously of the East and yet where there should have been crescents on the domes of the minarets there were golden suns with rays, and wherever one looked one saw things that obscured its origin. (LBW 37–38)

The man walks down into the city; he cannot quite make out the language the people are speaking—"they sounded more like grouse." He reflects: "There was none of that hurry of which foolish cities boast, nothing ugly or sordid so far as I could see. I saw that it was a city of beauty and song." He goes to sleep, and when he wakes he finds that the city is "quite gone."

Did the city on Mallington Moor ever exist? Yes and no. It does not exist in reality, but exists just as truly in the realm of the imagination. It is close to Nature; it is, indeed, a symbol for Nature, and a symbol for all the beauty that the modern world of London has lost or forgotten. The entire story magnificently encapsulates the many polarizations we have seen throughout Dunsany's early tales: the contrast of Nature and civilization, of beauty and ugliness, of past and present, of dream and reality.

The eight collections of tales between *The Gods of Pegāna* (1905) and *Tales of Three Hemispheres* (1919)—excluding *Tales of War* (1918)—form one of the most substantial bodies of work in the history of fantasy fiction. And yet, their remarkable diversity of tone and import make it highly problematical to consider them as a single, unified entity. Even if they return obsessively to the themes that would dominate Dunsany's entire literary output, they do so in such different ways, and from such different perspectives, that they must be regarded as discrete units, each adding its own distinctive treatment of one or more of his central concerns. Those who would seek to detach these early tales from the rest of Dunsany's work would do well to consider how many stories in these volumes anticipate the manner and substance of later ones; and the significant change of attitude toward fantasy exhibited by *The Book of Wonder* and later collections must also be taken into account. Dunsany published no short stories between 1921 and 1926, turning his attention instead to novels and plays. It is clear that the exotic otherworldly fantasy of *The Gods of Pegāna* and *Time and the Gods* was beginning to run dry as early as *A Dreamer's Tales*, and was emphatically over with *The Book of Wonder*. The later tales of this period are for the most part thin and uninspired, and it would take a decade for Dunsany to find a new direction for his short fiction.

In the meantime, however, it will be instructive to backtrack and examine how, and whether, his early plays contribute to the focal themes of this period.

NOTES

1. James Boswell, *Life of Johnson*, ed. R. W. Chapman, rev. J. D. Fleeman (London: Oxford University Press, 1970), 426 (s.d. 26 October 1769).

2. "Supernatural Horror in Literature" (1927), in *Dagon and Other Macabre Tales*, rev. ed. (Sauk City, WI: Arkham House, 1986), 429.

3. Preface to *The Picture of Dorian Gray* (1891).

4. This notion was already expressed in Dunsany's review of Synge's *Deirdre of the Sorrows*: "One wonders if the Cockney dialect when known no longer here will be spoken along the Ganges, as this older and purer English survives in the Arran Isles."

5. "Supernatural Horror in Literature," 368.

6. Lovecraft, letter to Fritz Leiber, 15 November 1936; in *Selected Letters*, ed. August Derleth, Donald Wandrei, and James Turner (Sauk City, WI: Arkham House, 1976), 5: 354.

2

The Fantastic Drama

For a variety of reasons it is worth treating Dunsany's early plays apart from his early tales: firstly, Dunsany evolved a theory of drama that is logically separable from the philosophy or aesthetic governing his prose fiction; secondly, his plays, while covering some of the same ground as his stories, have substantially different emphases and foci; and thirdly, since the plays must function by means of characterization and dialogue—features not notable in the early fiction—and since their effects are, in theory at least, meant to be perceived primarily by performance (and they were in fact very successfully performed), it is to be expected that their impact might differ considerably from that of the tales.

We must first determine the range and chronology of Dunsany's plays, since in several instances—again in contrast to the stories—the dates of production or publication of his forty-seven plays (six of which were not published and may not now survive) do not at all correspond to their dates of writing.[1] Twenty-two of them—in other words, most of those contained in *Five Plays* (1914), *Plays of Gods and Men* (1917), and *Plays of Near and Far* (1922), as well as others published separately—were written between 1909 and 1920; as with so many other branches of his work, Dunsany took to playwriting quickly and produced his best work early. Of particular note, in terms of the discrepancy between composition and publication, are *Alexander* (written 1912, published 1925) and *The Old Folk of the Centuries* (written 1918, published 1930). Accordingly, throughout this study I indicate the date of writing of a play in brackets and the date of publication in parentheses.

I have made note of Dunsany's general theory of drama and of the several essays he wrote on the subject; for our current purposes, however, we are concerned only with "Romance and the Modern Stage" (1911),[2] for this alone provides his rationale for *fantastic* drama. As I have observed before, "romance" in Dunsany is frequently a code word for the fantastic imagination, and this essay seeks to present a raison d'être for its incorporation into modern drama.

As with "Nowadays," "Romance and the Modern Stage" sees in art an antidote to the evils of industrial civilization. The dominance of the machine has disturbed the very fabric of our society:

For our age is full of new problems that we have not as yet found time to understand, that bewilder us and absorb us, the gift of matter enthroned and endowed by man with life; I mean iron vitalised by steam, and rushing from city to city and owning men for its slaves. I know of the boons that machinery has conferred on man, all tyrants have boons to confer, but service to the dynasty of steam and steel is a hard service and gives little leisure to fancy to flit from field to field. (830)

The poet has a unique responsibility to save civilization by restoring to it the sense of wonder at the natural world, a sense of wonder that "romantic" (i.e., fantastic) drama can achieve: "But let the poets give us back romantic drama and all the beautiful things that seemed native once, and the drama of convention in a while will fly from the face of it and will go and hide away with the old fashions" (829). There is a "higher realism" (830) toward which drama must strive: "The kind of drama that we most need to-day seems to me to be the kind that will build new worlds for the fancy, for the spirit as much as the body needs sometimes a change of scene. And though speaking generally contemporary drama is rather conventional than fantastic, yet luckily now and then a few poets make these new worlds for us" (834).

This continual contrast between romantic and "conventional" drama suggests that Dunsany's object of attack is that old whipping boy, the "well-made play" of Arthur Wing Pinero and his followers, or any play that deals narrowly and realistically with contemporary social or political issues. But since Dunsany never names names, it is difficult to be precise on the matter. Indeed, it is for this reason difficult to ascertain what plays might have met Dunsany's approval and therefore might have influenced his own dramatic work: as I will note elsewhere, he clearly admired Synge, and presumably had some respect for Yeats's early poetic dramas, although he never mentions them to my knowledge; and he wrote a very enthusiastic review of Maeterlinck's *The Blue Bird* ("Two Hundred Times in a Blue Moon" [1910]), but I do not in the end find much resemblance between Dunsany's work and Maeterlinck's. Dunsany quotes one critic as saying, "The frequent repetition of words and phrases in the first three plays [of *Five Plays*] reminds one of Maeterlinck,"[3] but this stylistic device is as prevalent in the early stories as in the early plays.

It is scarcely to be denied that "Romance and the Modern Stage" is a sort of justification after the fact of Dunsany's own early dramatic work, for it must have been written after the first six or seven of his plays were written, if not actually performed or published. He in fact makes no secret of this:

Romance is so inseparable from life that all we need, to obtain romantic drama, is for the dramatist to find any age or any country where life is not too thickly veiled and cloaked with puzzles and conventions, in fact to find a people that is not in the agonies of self-consciousness. For myself, I think it simpler to imagine such a people, as it saves the trouble of reading to find a romantic age, or the trouble of making a journey to lands where there is no press. (831)

This revelatory statement allows us to understand why even those plays set in the ancient world—notably *Alexander* and *The Queen's Enemies*— are half-fantastic: Dunsany refrained by design from learning too much about the historical periods in which he was writing, so as not to fetter his imagination with facts.

The early plays are not as varied in range as his early tales—perhaps for the simple reason that there are fewer of them. Very few have as their focus Dunsany's central theme of unification with Nature; indeed, only *The Tents of the Arabs* can be said to be devoted even partly to this theme. The majority of the plays deal with "big" issues: the relations of human beings with the gods, Fate, Chance, and Destiny. Dunsany himself states that the moral of *The Gods of the Mountain* and *A Night at an Inn* is that "there are eternal things that [human beings] cannot cope with" (PS 181); and one of his definitions of drama is "the sudden manifestation of one of Destiny's ways" (DL 46). A play, in Dunsany's view, "should have some air about it as though Destiny had had a hand in its making" (DL 54).

As with the early tales, the question of the exact relationship of the fantasy realms in the plays with the "real" world occurs time and again; and, as with the tales, the question does not seem capable of any simple resolution. In *King Argimēnēs and the Unknown Warrior* there is a random mention of Babylon (FiP 72); in *The Gods of the Mountain* Ethiopia is cited (FiP 13); *The Laughter of the Gods*, perhaps like *The Gods of Pegāna*, is temporally in the "real" world ("About the time of the decadence in Babylon") but topographically in an imaginary world ("The jungle city of Thek" [PGM 3]). Something similar appears to hold for *The Queen's Enemies*: here both the time and place are purportedly real (Egypt in the Sixth Dynasty), but the imaginary names of the leading protagonists—even Nitokris is never mentioned by name—lends an air of unreality to the whole proceeding. Then there is *The Tents of the Arabs*, whose very title seems to suggest some sort of connection with reality, but which is set "[o]utside the gate of the city of Thalanna" in an "uncertain" time (PGM 119). The desert that serves as the setting of the play does indeed appear to be in Arabia, as frequent mentions of Mecca establish; but what are we to make of this exchange?

Chamberlain: There is very much for your Majesty to do. Iktra has revolted.

King: Where is Iktra?

Chamberlain: It is a little country tributary to your Majesty, beyond Zebdarlon, up among the hills. (PGM 128)

It becomes evident that Dunsany's carelessness with regard to the exact relationship, temporally or topographically, between the "real" world and the fantasy world is quite deliberate: this imprecision allows both for the introduction of fantastic elements (e.g., the gods, who make actual appearances in some of the plays) and for a concentration upon the scenario rather than upon any illustory connections to historical events or personages. Even the scattered mentions of places in the "real" world are made with a view toward their evocative qualities, as in *The Gods of the Mountain*: "No traveller has met with cunning like this, not even those that come from Æthiopia" (FiP 13). Nearly all the plays appear to be set in a "primitive" or ancient world; those that are not—notably *A Night at an Inn* and *If*—gain their dramatic tension from a conflict between characters from the prosaic modern Western world and those from the mysterious, ancient East that so frequently serves in Dunsany as a symbol for the fantastic imagination.

Nearly all of Dunsany's early plays tell a relatively simple story; their power lies in their spectacular denouements, their flawless maintenance of a high poeticism in diction, and the pungent satire slyly inserted into the fabric of plays whose surface austerity, nobility, and naïveté are deliberately meant to recall Greek tragedy. Dunsany consciously drew upon what he felt were the strongest features of ancient tragedy:

It was shown by these plays that there were eternal laws: it was preached that there was no escape from them. And over all of these plays there is a grandeur in keeping with the grandeur of creation, and the very dooms in them were grand like thunder. If such plays were written nowadays, showing gods in their wrath, and Fate pursuing men, it would be said that they were fantastic, and yet the men that made those plays must have been very near to nature and must have understood profoundly the spirit of man. (DL 64)

But the introduction of a very modern satire—principally on the efficacy of religious belief and on the veracity of distinctions among gods, kings, and ordinary human beings—rescues these plays from being mere experiments in antiquarianism.

As it is, the dominant surface theme of many of the early plays is the relationship between gods and men; but for Dunsany, the probable atheist, this really resolves into two separate issues: the conflict of human beings with Destiny, and the folly of unthinking religious belief. Both branches of this theme are present in two of his strongest plays, *The Gods of the Mountain* and *The Golden Doom*.

The Gods of the Mountain [1910] tells of Agmar, the leader of a band of beggars, who devises an ingenious plan: seven of their number will pose as the seven green jade gods of the mountain; they will accordingly receive all the food and shelter they want in these days that have otherwise become "bad for beggary" (FiP 11). Agmar orders his underling, Slag, to spread a prophecy "which saith that the gods who are carven from green rock in the mountain shall one day arise in Marma and come here in the guise of men" (FiP 16). The prophecy is believed and the beggars are, at least provisionally, accepted as the gods; but when food is placed before them as a tribute, some suspicions do occur to the citizens: "One who was ignorant, one who did not know, had almost said that they ate like hungry men" (FiP 22). These suspicions persist, and an expedition is sent to the mountain to see whether the gods are really there or have come down to the city. Agmar, learning of this expedition, prepares for the worst; but he is stupefied to learn that the expedition has come back and reported that the gods are indeed absent from the mountain! All the beggars are relieved, since they are now accepted as the true gods, but Agmar is worried: he knows that something is amiss, since he himself saw the gods in their shrines on the mountain two weeks before. Then he hears a disturbing report: a man walks in terrified, pleading with them not to frighten the city by walking about in their true forms at night—"Rock should not walk in the evening" (FiP 34). Agmar attempts to bluff it out ("It is only we that have frightened them and their fears have made them foolish" [FiP 35]), but he knows the jig is up. The gods of the mountain come awkwardly down, turn the seven beggars to stone, and leave. The people come in, find the stone figures, and are now convinced that they were the true gods all along.

The true focus of the play, I think, is the folly of religious belief. The citizens of Marma are taken in extremely easily by the pretenses of Agmar and his crew. Some citizens discuss the false prophecy that Slag has circulated:

Illanaun: Should we not investigate this prophecy?

Oorander: Let us accept it. It is as the small uncertain light of a lantern, carried
 it may be by a drunkard, but along the shore of some haven. Let us be guided.

Akmos: It may be that they are but benevolent gods. . . .

Oorander: Let us make sacrifices to them if they be gods.

Akmos: We humbly worship you, if ye be gods. (FiP 20–21)

This seems to be Dunsany's response to Pascal's wager: the probability of the existence of God is so small that even a provisional acceptance of it is likely to lead one into clownish error. The fact that there are "real" gods in this play is not a contradiction of the fundamentally atheistic message of *The Gods of the Mountain*, for they are symbols for all that is nonhuman and beyond human control. The gods of the mountain are merely the tokens of Destiny.

The character of Agmar, a sort of crude Nietzschean whose cynical manipulation of human folly brings about his doom, is central to the play, and he is masterfully drawn. When one of the beggars, hearing of Agmar's plan, notes tentatively that ". . . it were well not to anger the gods," Agmar replies with sophistry: "Is not all life a beggary to the gods? Do they not see all men always begging of them and asking alms, with incense, and bells, and subtle devices?" (FiP 16). Later, when a citizen of Marma comes to him, thinking him a god, and asks him whether his child, bitten by a death-adder, will live, Agmar asks, "Was it your wont to thwart him in his play, while he was strong and well?" The citizen says no, and Agmar counters that Death is the child of the gods: "Do you that never thwarted your child in his play ask this of the gods?" (FiP 26). Agmar knows that the child will die and that he can do nothing about it, but he must preserve the illusion of his omnipotence as a god. Indeed, it is his bold actions at the outset that convince the citizens that the beggars really are gods: all the beggars except Agmar eat the food placed before them, and he even pours upon the ground the valuable Woldery wine that is offered to him.

Surely a hungry beggar would not do this! He and his crew must be gods. He eats and drinks only when the citizens are away.

Nearly thirty years after its premiere, Dunsany asked of *The Gods of the Mountain*, "Was this not something new to the English stage?" (PS 158). I think he was right to be proud of this play, and it deserved the tremendous popularity it received in its heyday. While creating an aura very reminiscent of Greek tragedy, it enunciates a message that is emphatically modern. And that ingenious double climax—the play does not end with the beggars being turned to stone, but with their being wrongly accepted as the true gods after all—is a masterstroke. The play must have been a highly stirring dramatic spectacle: we can only guess, as it does not seem very likely that it, or any of Dunsany's other plays, will ever be revived.

The Golden Doom [1910], a very short one-act play, is nevertheless an intricate intertwining of many themes—cosmic, religious, and political. A little boy wants a hoop to play with, so he and a little girl approach the King's great door to ask for it. He has with him a lump of gold that he has found in a stream, and on a whim he writes a silly little poem on the wall as dictated by the girl:

> I saw a purple bird
> > Go up against the sky,
> And it went up and up
> > And round about did fly.
> > I saw it die. (FiP 45)

All the while the sentries guarding the King's door "talk awhile and eat bash" (FiP 42), never noticing the children. The inscription is seen and, since it is written with gold, is assumed to have come from the gods. A prophet finds the poem very dire and urges the King to lay down his crown and sceptre by the door as a peace offering to the gods for his hubris. The King does so. The little boy comes back, notices the crown, thinks it is the hoop for which he has asked, and takes it away, playing with it delightedly.

The critical figure in the play is neither the boy nor the King but the Chief Prophet. Just as the prophets in *The Gods of Pegāna* cynically pervert the teachings of the gods for their own benefit, so here the prophet finds in the fortuitous inscription an opportunity to wrest power away from the King. Interpreting the poem as a warning against pride (Who but the King could be the "purple bird"? What else could the phrase "go up against the sky" mean but that the King "has troubled the stars by neglecting their ancient worship" [FiP 51]?), he forces the King to abase himself before the stars and, in consequence, before the prophet himself:

King: What more can a man offer?

Chief Prophet: His pride.

King: What pride?

Chief Prophet: Your pride that went up against the sky and troubled the stars.

King: How shall I sacrifice my pride to the stars?

Chief Prophet: It is upon your pride that the doom will fall, and will take away
     your crown and will take away your kingdom. (FiP 53)

In this formulation it is important to establish that the King is not in fact
guilty of hubris. He himself pleads his own case: "Not for myself I have
a fear of doom, not for myself: but I inherited a rocky land, a windy and
ill-nurtured, and nursed it to prosperity by years of peace and spread its
boundaries by years of war. I have brought harvests up out of barren acres
and given good laws unto naughty towns, and my people are happy, and
lo! the stars are angry" (FiP 51). The prophet indirectly acknowledges the
beneficence of the King's reign when he notes: "It is better to give worship
to the stars than to do good to man. It is better to be humble before the
gods than proud in the face of your enemy though he do evil" (FiP 52).
And that last sentence suggests that the entire play is a sort of Nietzschean
conflict between aristocratic pride and the (false) humility of Christianity.

Dunsany himself said that in *The Golden Doom* "I show a child's desire
for a new toy and the fate of an empire as being of equal importance in the
scheme of things."[4] This is only one of the many strands interweaved in
this short play—the inconsequentality of politics, the role of chance in
human affairs, the cynical manipulation of religion for personal gain.
Perhaps Dunsany is also addressing a very modern concern—the power
of language to govern human action. The little girl remarks airily in regard
to her poem, "Writing frightens nobody" (FiP 43), but we have learned a
very different lesson at the end.

Some of the themes in *The Golden Doom* were anticipated in *King
Argimēnēs and the Unknown Warrior* [1910]; here, however, a satire on
religious belief is united with a social criticism on the perceived differ-
ences between a slave and a king. *The Gods of Pegāna* had already stated
that Yoharneth-Lahai "sendeth little dreams to the poor man and to The
King. He is so busy to send his dreams to all before the night be ended that
oft he forgetteth which be the poor man and which be The King" (GP 28).
Argimēnēs greatly elaborates upon this idea.

King Argimēnēs has been enslaved by King Darniak because "my god
was cast down in the temple and broken into three pieces on the day that
they surprised us and took me sleeping" (FiP 60). He now yearns only for

the most meager scraps of food, as the arresting first sentence indicates: "This is a good bone; there is juice in this bone" (FiP 59). But while digging in Darniak's fields he uncovers an enormous sword, and with it he leads the slaves to a revolt that overthrows Darniak and his god Illuriel. As he states: "Illuriel is fallen and broken asunder. . . . My god was broken into three pieces, but Illuriel is broken into seven. The fortunes of Darniak will prevail over mine no longer" (FiP 76). As the play closes he now reigns in the place of King Darniak.

This play does not have quite the dramatic tensity of the two previous plays studied, and Dunsany was aware that the great promise of the first act was not quite sustained in the second. Nevertheless, the play is rich with meaning. Are the gods so fragile that their mere breakage is sufficient to bring down kingdoms? Or is the real object of scorn the weakness of religious belief? The moment Illuriel is brought down, King Darniak and all his followers are deflated, lamenting, "Illuriel is fallen, is fallen" (FiP 77). Here a prophet who speaks truly about the dangers besetting the king is casually dismissed as "clever" (FiP 74)—a diverting amusement for an idle moment. In contrast to the king of *The Golden Doom*, Darniak is genuinely hubristic, demanding that an entire hill be removed because it is too steep (FiP 72). His queens reveal themselves to be cruel and self-infatuated. Queen Cahafra protests that the work of the slaves in building a garden is too slow: "Then *why* are they not flogged? . . . It is so simple, they *only* have to flog them, but these people are so silly sometimes. I want to walk in the great garden, and then they tell me, 'It is not ready, Majesty. It is not ready, Majesty,' as though there were any reason why it should *not* be ready" (FiP 72–73).

But how seriously are we to take the distinction between kingship and slavery? Zarb, a fellow slave of King Argimēnēs who is now his follower, discusses the matter with him:

King Argimēnēs: When I remember that I have been a king it is very terrible.

Zarb: But you are lucky to have such things in your memory as you have. I have nothing in my memory. Once I went for a year without being flogged, and I remember my cleverness in contriving it. I have nothing else to remember.

King Argimēnēs: It is very terrible to have been a king.

Zarb: But we have nothing who have no good memories in the past. It is not easy for us to hope for the future here. (FiP 59–60)

But that last statement is belied, and the difference between slavishness and nobility shown to be a mere product of mental conditioning, by a critical scene later in the play. As Argimēnēs is leading his revolt, Zarb talks with some other slaves:

Old Slave: Will Argimēnēs give me a sword?

Zarb: He will have swords for six of us if he slays the slave-guard. Yes, he will give you a sword.

Slave: A sword! No, no, I must not; the king would kill me if he found that I had a sword.

Second Slave: (*slowly, as one who develops an idea*) If the king found that I had a sword, why then it would be an evil day for the king. (FiP 69)

There is nothing inherently noble in King Argimēnēs; it is simply that he has the strength of will to resist his fate. There is nothing intrinsically slavish about Zarb and the other slaves; but Zarb and the old slave are rooted in slavish states of mind, while the second slave has not yet had his pride and self-dignity beaten out of him.

   The Tents of the Arabs [1910] has some superficial connections with *King Argimēnēs and the Unknown Warrior*, but fundamentally it reflects the concerns of some of Dunsany's early tales, especially as regards the simultaneous lure and oppressiveness of cities. The King, weighed down with the cares of government, yearns for the freedom of the desert; Bel-Narb and Aoob, two camel drivers, yearn in contrast for the city:

Bel-Narb: Cities are beautiful things.

Aoob: I think they are loveliest a little after dawn when night falls off from the houses. They draw it away from them slowly and let it fall like a cloak and stand quite naked in their beauty to shine in some broad river, and the light comes up and kisses them on the forehead. I think they are loveliest then. The voices of men and women begin to arise in the streets, scarce audible, one by one, till a slow loud murmur arises and all the voices are one. I often think the city speaks to me then: she says in that voice of hers, "Aoob, Aoob, who one of these days shall die, I am not earthly, I have been always, I shall not die." (PGM 120–21)

Neither of them realizes that their views on the respective merits of city and desert life are a product of perspective; they romanticize the city precisely because they are not of it. The King has a very different view:

O Thalanna, Thalanna, how I hate this city with its narrow, narrow ways, and evening after evening drunken men playing skabash in the scandalous gambling house of that old scoundrel Skarmi. O that I might marry the child of some unkingly house, that generation to generation had never known a city, and that we might ride from here down the long track through the desert, always we two alone, till we came to the tents of the Arabs. (PGM 127)

Predictably, both Bel-Narb and the King get their wish. The King declares that he will live in the desert for a year and then return; but when he does return, he meets the camel drivers and allows Bel-Narb to masquerade as himself, while he occupies Bel-Narb's place and goes back to the desert permanently. Here again two messages are interweaved, one political (what does it matter who rules?) and the other aesthetic (is not the desert preferable to the city?). There is also a brief but potent passage in which the King, reflecting on his year in the desert, vows to defeat Time by preserving that year in memory ("He [Memory] shall bring back our year to us that Time cannot destroy. Time cannot slaughter it if Memory says no" [PGM 144]), a theme found in a number of the prose-poems in *Fifty-one Tales*. Still, *The Tents of the Arabs*, although lyrical and poetic, is essentially undramatic, and is among the least interesting of Dunsany's early plays.

The Laughter of the Gods [1911] is another play about gods and human beings, but its import is a little difficult to ascertain. It suffers from a certain diffuseness, especially in the first act, and it might have been better as a one-act rather than a three-act play. King Karnos and his retinue are in the jungle city of Thek, but the wives of the king's courtiers find the jungle tiresome and miss the city; they wheedle their husbands into finding some way to convince the king to leave. All the courtiers can think of is to coerce the prophet, Voice-of-the-Gods, to utter a prophecy that the gods in three days will destroy the city of Thek unless all people desert it. The king is not, however, convinced by the prophet, so it looks as if everyone is obliged to remain in Thek. But after three days the city is indeed destroyed, for, as the prophet stated, "my voice is from the gods and the gods cannot lie" (PGM 31). As he dies, the prophet says with relief, "They have not lied! . . . It is the laughter of the gods that cannot lie, going back to their hills" (PGM 76).

I can only derive from this play a satire, as in *The Golden Doom*, on cynical manipulation of religion; here, however, the manipulative courtiers get their comeuppance. The courtiers are manifestly atheistic:

Ludibras: Who can command a King?

Harpagas: Only the gods.

Ludibras: The gods? There are no gods now. We have been civilised for over three thousand years. The gods that nursed our infancy are dead, or gone to nurse younger nations. (PGM 26)

This itself is an interesting reflection on the growing secularism of civilized societies, and it is partly echoed by King Karnos himself in reply to the prophet's warning:

When the gods prophesy rain in the season of rain, or the death of an old man, we believe them. But when the gods prophesy something incredible and ridiculous, such as happens not nowadays, and hath not been heard of since the fall of Bleth, then our credulity is overtaxed. It is possible that a man should lie, it is not possible that the gods should destroy a city nowadays. (PGM 39)

This sounds reasonable enough, but it suggests that we have reached a stage of civilization where anomalous occurrences can no longer be attributed to the gods (who, in Dunsany, are almost always symbols for Fate or Destiny); the actions of gods must now conform to human notions of probability if they are to be accepted as originating from the gods. The "fall of Bleth," a pendant to this idea, is explained in a later passage. Tharmia, one of the wives who is now frightened at the whole turn of events, chides her husband for flagrantly disbelieving in the gods, remarking: "O do not speak like that. There used to be gods. They overthrew Bleth dreadfully. And if they still live on in the dark of the hills, they might hear your words" (PGM 59). The hand of Destiny perhaps showed itself more clearly in the past, but it is something that must never be discounted.

Religion is the entire focus of Dunsany's first play, *The Glittering Gate* [1909]. This cannot be said to be set in a fantasy land as such (the scene is described merely as a "Lonely Place" [FiP 83]) nor in the past: the time is stated explicitly as being "the present" (FiP 82). This remarkably simple play is, however, full of complications and interpretative difficulties. Bill, a burglar who has just died, finds himself in front of an enormous gate on a rocky ledge, which he assumes to be the gate of Heaven. In front of the gate he finds his old friend Jim, who appears to have been there for some time; he is doing nothing but opening the profusion of beer bottles that lie all around, eternally disappointed to find that they are all empty. Jim has been there so long that he has forgotten virtually everything about the world ("What is Putney?") and lost all sense of time ("What are years?" [FiP 85]); he has also reached a state of utter despair as to the prospect of the gate ever opening. But Bill, who is not quite so unhopeful, feels that, if he is not going to be let into Heaven, he'll break in: he has managed to retain his lock pick, and he begins to play with the enormous lock on the gate. Incredibly, his final act of burglary seems to work, and the gate opens; but all he finds are "Stars. Blooming great stars. There *ain't* no heaven, Jim" (FiP 91).

There are, it seems to me, at least two possible interpretations to this play. First, Bill and Jim have found their own personal Hell; second, there is in fact no Heaven or Hell but merely "blooming great stars." There is something to be said for both views. Bill tries to cheer up Jim, who has lost all hope of ever opening the gate, by saying: "You're thinking of a quotation. 'Abandon hope all ye that enter here'" (FiP 85). This certainly makes one think of Hell, as does the "[f]aint and unpleasant laughter [that] is heard off" and which is "repeated continually throughout the play" (FiP 83). The profusion of beer bottles, all certain to be empty, is a nasty temptation in which Satan would find much pleasure. And what of Jim's concluding remark: "That's like them. That's very like them. Yes, they'd do that" (FiP 91)? Who are "they"? Is this merely a sign of Jim's paranoia, or does he, by virtue of his long stay in this realm, have some special knowledge of the evil forces that take delight in their predicament?

And yet, Bill's statement that "[t]here *ain't* no heaven, Jim" is deemed in a succeeding stage direction as a "revelation" (FiP 91): does this mean that Bill is right? Can there be a Hell if there isn't a Heaven? What is more, Bill doesn't seem like a wholly bad sort. One of the things he most looks forward to in Heaven is seeing his mother again: "She never cared much for the way I earned my livelihood . . . but she was a good mother to me. I don't know if they want a good mother in there who would be kind to the angels and sit and smile at them when they sang, and soothe them if they were cross. If they let all the good ones in she'll be there all right" (FiP 89–90). The first thing Bill says when he opens the gate is: "Hullo, mother. You there? Hullo. You there? It's Bill, mother" (FiP 91). Is this a man who, in spite of his dubious profession, deserves eternal punishment? I think the greatness—and, clearly, the early popularity—of *The Glittering Gate* rests precisely in its interpretability, its refusal to provide simple answers to such questions even if the setting and actions of the play are themselves almost childishly simple.

The Queen's Enemies [1913] and *Alexander* [1912] may perhaps be treated together, although they do not have much in common aside from being founded upon ancient history and being perhaps at the very pinnacle of Dunsany's dramatic work. The former tells the very simple tale—first found in Herodotus (*Histories* 2.100)—of how Queen Nitokris of Egypt killed her enemies by inviting them to a dinner party in an underground temple and inundating them by letting in the Nile. Dunsany heard of the story as he was sailing down the Nile on a ship named *Nitocris* (PS 147), but deliberately avoided reading any more detailed account of it; it is, in fact, quite evident that he did not even read the brief passage in Herodotus from where the account derives, since Dunsany makes no mention of the fact cited in Herodotus that Nitokris's act was in revenge for the death of her brother. Dunsany admitted this studied ignorance—"It is not only easier but more amusing to imagine her character and all the names of her enemies than to be bothered with reading about her"[5]—claiming that too much particularity would have an adverse effect upon his imagination. Indeed, it is not merely that Dunsany has invented all the names of the minor characters in the play; he also fails ever to mention Nitokris by name, referring to her simply as "The Queen." As a result, this play gains a sort of half-fantastic atmosphere not dissimilar to that of *The Gods of the Mountain* and *The Golden Doom*, even though nothing supernatural actually occurs.

The character of the Queen is clearly the focus of the play. In the most literal sense, she "cannot *bear* to have enemies" (PGM 83). Her handmaid, Ackazárpses, notes, "One so delicate, so slender and withal so beautiful should never have a foe" (PGM 83). The critical issue, however, is whether the Queen really is delicate and sensitive or is simply feigning these qualities in order to lure her enemies to death. One of her enemies voices the fear that they might be attacked by her soldiers while dining, to which she replies, "The sight of blood is shocking" (PGM 95). There is no reason to doubt this, and the fact that the Queen has not poisoned the food similarly suggests her sensitive abhorrence of that avenue of death.

Dunsany himself remarks: "What I was concerned about when I wrote the play . . . was the lady's motive; this I invented for myself, as well as the names of all her enemies. . . . I made the queen completely, and rather innocently, selfish, and deeply religious" (PS 147–48). This is a very apt analysis, and is borne out by the text. It is insufficient for the Queen that her enemies merely become her friends, for there can never be certainty on this matter, especially in light of the suspicions her enemies have at being invited to the underground banquet. After the Queen persuades them that they will not be attacked and that the food and wine have not been poisoned, one of her enemies states: "We have eaten your fruits and drunk your wine; and we have asked your pardon. Let us now depart in amity." But the Queen retorts: "No, no! No, no! You must not go! I shall say . . . 'They are my enemies still': and I shall not sleep. I that cannot bear to have enemies" (PGM 104). When she continues, "O feast with me a little longer and make merry and be my enemies no more" (PGM 105), we are to take that final clause in its most literal sense, as the only effective way for the Queen not to have enemies.

This play could be thought of as weirdly feminist, in that it seems to reflect common stereotypes of the weakness of women only to subvert them. The Queen is terrified of men ("They are such huge, terrible men"

[PGM 86]); she dislikes their constant fighting ("Why must men slay one another and make horrible war?" [PGM 84]); she is vain about her appearance ("Set this bow higher upon my head so that it must be seen. . . . The pretty bow" [PGM 87]); one of her enemies remarks, "She is much swayed by whims" (PGM 88); but in the end she kills them. And she does so by being, as Dunsany remarked, "deeply religious." She and her handmaid abruptly rise from the table and prepare to leave; when asked where she is going, she states, "I go to pray to a very secret god" (PGM 111). Her enemies let her go, but all their suspicions, which have been lulled by the apparent security and amity of the banquet, return; they of course fear merely some hidden attack by soldiers. But the Queen prays to the Nile, and the river obliges by overwhelming her enemies. The end of the play can only be quoted:

Queen: O, Ackazárpses, are all my enemies gone?

Ackazárpses: Illustrious Lady, the Nile has taken them all.

Queen: (*with intense devotion*) That holy river.

Ackazárpses: Illustrious Lady, you will sleep tonight?

Queen: Yes. I shall sleep sweetly. (PGM 115)

All that the Queen wanted was a good night's sleep. It's not too much to ask.

The sense of the Queen's innocence, ingenuousness, and weakness is maintained flawlessly to the end. I think we are to believe that she really is innocent and ingenuous: the alarm she expresses at the actual arrival of her enemies toward the beginning—"O, say I am ill, say I am sick of a fever. Quick, quick, say I have some swift fever and cannot see them" (PGM 86)—is entirely sincere, as is her injured affront at being suspected of poisoning the food. At one point she even fears that she will be killed by her enemies: "O Ackazárpses, I am frightened: what if my enemies should slay me and carry me up, and cast my body into the lonely Nile" (PGM 96–97). I do not think this is feigned, for at this moment her enemies really do have the upper hand: they are big, strong men and none of her servitors or soldiers are nearby to defend her. I am not, I confess, certain how that climactic scene—the flooding of the temple by the Nile—would have been handled on stage, but it must have been handled effectively, for *The Queen's Enemies* remained one of Dunsany's most successful plays.

Alexander was originally planned as a collaboration with Padraic Colum, but Dunsany wrote his section (the third and fourth acts) so rapidly that Colum never had a chance to write his segment, and he ultimately

bowed out of the collaboration. The play adheres more closely to the
historical record than *The Queen's Enemies*, and Dunsany states that he
actually read Plutarch's life in preparation for writing it (PS 183). Accordingly, he had somewhat less flexibility in inventing incidents and characters, and was compelled at least to make allusions to the central incidents
of Alexander's life—the destruction of Persepolis, the arduous expedition
to India, Alexander's death by fever—but he still manages to create out of
whole cloth the character of Rhododactilos, the Queen of the Amazons,
who fulfills a critical function at the end.

As with *The Queen's Enemies*, the portrayal of the central character is
at the heart of the first three acts of *Alexander*. It is a masterful portrayal:
at the outset Alexander is depicted as a wise, temperate, god-respecting
king whose accompaniment by Apollo (disguised as an old man) is a
symbol for his prowess in war and his Greek sense of honor, dignity, and
piety, just as the dismissal of Apollo at the urging of Thais portends his
eventual doom from hubris. That doom is spectacularly anticipated at the
very beginning by the simplest of details, when Alexander, speaking to his
friend Clitus, "sits down on some fallen pillar or stone" (A 12). It is
Clitus—who unwisely promised Thais that he would urge Alexander to
send Apollo away—who first voices the hubris that will eventually bring
Alexander down: "It will be said years hence of Alexander: 'He was but
a piece upon the board of one of the games of Apollo which he plays with
Destiny or some other god, as it were a game of chess which the Egyptians
play'" (A 13–14). Alexander still resists, but finally yields, and Clitus
exults: "The thing is done. Thais! The thing is done! I have thwarted
Destiny! I have hindered the gods!" (A 15). This formulation makes us
realize why Dunsany was attracted to the Alexander legend, since it
allowed him to exhibit that conflict of humanity and Destiny, in which the
former is always the loser, which serves as the foundation for so many of
his early fantastic plays, from *The Gods of the Mountain* to *A Night at an
Inn*.

The transformation of Alexander is very gradual. He rues dismissing
Apollo; he has scorn for Sycophantes when the latter proclaims him the
son of Zeus, but then ponders the matter to himself: "No man has done
what I have done. And yet . . . Again Zeus is the father of all, but that is
mere . . . And it were politic to be divine" (A 25). There may be some use
in being thought a god. Over the objections of the Priest, he proves his
divinity by burning Persepolis: "Your ignorance shall be instructed. Learn
then that I am the son of Zeus, as many have said, and not the son of Philip,
or of any mortal man. Learn that I am immortal like my father, whom
Chronos begat in the old time: and in proof of this I will burn Persepolis,

the city of such kings" (A 26). He continues that to burn Persepolis "is a frightful thought, and *I* have thought it. No mortal man durst think it" (A 27), and dismisses Thais's (correct) claim that she was the one who initially thought of it: he is now a god and cannot admit that such a grand conception could have come from a mere mortal, let alone a woman. In effect, he cannot bring himself to admit that he is no longer master of his actions, but is now the dupe of sycophants and mistresses.

And yet, godhead does not have quite the rewards it seemed to promise: "I am no longer what I was," Alexander confesses to Nearchos; "I am greater; but not happier" (A 28). When Clitus, with amusingly jarring modernity of diction, scorns the notion that Alexander is the son of Zeus ("I never heard anything so ridiculous" [A 33]), Alexander kills him in a fit of anger, but then plunges in a fit of suicidal depression at the murder of his dearest friend. Nevertheless, he revives enough to conquer India, but by then he has developed his fatal fever. He admits that he is no longer the son of Zeus ("Philip my father, for how long have I disowned you" [A 81]), but realizes it is too late: "It is not Macedon that I inherit now, but man's sure legacy, the human heirloom—even death. O Philip, my father, by this I know that I am your son and heir" (A 80–81). And yet, he remains defiant to the end: "had I wedded Rhododactilos, that fair and terrible queen, we had reared up such a progeny as had overthrown the gods and taken from them Olympus by force of arms" (A 82).

Alexander's death at the end of the first scene of the fourth act would seem to signal the end of the play; but Dunsany deliberately added the long second scene in order to bring the tragedy of Alexander to its proper culmination. He mentions that his would-be collaborator, Colum, "wanted to end the play on the death of Alexander, while I had thought it tremendously impressive that the world still went on though Alexander was dead, and had said so in my play" (PS 185). That world is a lesser world, where Ptolemy and Perdiccas, two inferior subordinates of Alexander, now find themselves in positions of power and greedily carve up the Mediterranean at their whim, a world in which the seeds of democracy, the advent of the common man, are planted:

1st Archer: It is a hard thing, comrade, that none will bury Alexander.

2nd Archer: What matters it what becomes of Alexander now that we are governed by plain honest men?

1st Archer: Indeed you are right, comrade. And yet he was worthy perhaps of burial.

2nd Archer: Much has come out of late concerning Alexander.

1st Archer: Why yes. Hath it not? They say, do they not, that he was harsh to our
    good leaders?

2nd Archer: Indeed, I have it from Perdiccas himself that this was so. Let us be
    thankful that we are done with him and have plain honest leaders. (A 89–90)

But Rhododactilos, once Alexander's enemy but now his only defender—
and the only one now left to defend the virtues of aristocratic strength in
the face of little men—remains true to his memory, and she alone buries
him.

    Alexander is, aside from *If* and *Mr. Faithful*, Dunsany's only full-length
play, and of these three it may perhaps be the greatest: its carefully etched
portrayal of Alexander and all the other characters in the play, the spectacular anticlimax in which grandeur and nobility are perverted and
scorned by the advocates of the ordinary, and its unfailingly high diction
make it a triumph of conception and style.

    The transformation from pure fantasy (*The Gods of the Mountain*) to
fantastic quasi-history (*The Queen's Enemies, Alexander*) continues in *A
Night at an Inn* [1912] and *If* [1919]. Both plays are initially set in the
present and peopled with modern-day Western characters, but in both there
occurs an insidious incursion of the fantastic that ultimately proves overwhelming. The former was perhaps Dunsany's most popular play, and one
reviewer referred to it as his "perfect melodrama";[6] and yet, there is in it
a trace of that tone of self-parody we have detected in the later tales of
Dunsany's early period, notably *The Book of Wonder*.

    A. E. Scott-Fortescue, nicknamed "The Toff," has, with the assistance
of three lower-class sailors, managed to pilfer the ruby eye of the god
Klesh; the four are currently lodged in an inn (the setting is unspecified,
but the implication is that it is back in England: "it is pleasantly situated,
and . . . it is in a very quiet neighbourhood" [PGM 169]), and are attempting to elude the three priests of Klesh who are on their trail. Things look
pretty bad for them, for the priests have found them and, as the Toff notes,
they are relentless: "These black priests would follow you round the world
in circles. Year after year, till they got their idol's eye. And if we died with
it they'd follow our grandchildren" (PGM 168). What are they to do? The
Toff ingeniously plans a series of booby traps for the three priests and
manages to kill them all; but just as all four criminals are breathing a sigh
of relief, the god Klesh stumbles into the room, gropes for its eye, finds
it, and moves off. It summons the four men one by one, saving the Toff
for last. The awfulness of their fate is left for the spectator to imagine.

    This is all good fun, and Dunsany claims to have a deeper message to
convey, stating that the play "is about a man who is too clever; he deals

triumphantly with every temporary thing as it arises, but, as happened in *The Gods of the Mountain*, there are eternal things that he cannot cope with" (PS 181). And yet the play, with its very elementary theme that crime does not pay, makes one think of such other frivolities as "The Distressing Tale of Thangobrind the Jeweller" and other tales in *The Book of Wonder* where a very simpleminded tit-for-tat justice occurs. It is very hard to bring in any broader philosophical issues into a play of this kind, especially when the actual emergence of the stone idol onstage may have been designed to be consciously self-parodic. Early reviewers compared the Toff with Agmar in *The Gods of the Mountain*, but the resemblance is not very strong: Agmar is a genuinely grand figure in his defiance of the gods, while the Toff is merely a smart aleck who has been caught at his own game. *A Night at an Inn* is a delight to read, but I cannot see that it has much substance to offer.

If is a very different matter. In what may be his most superficially "modern" or actable play, Dunsany presents a searing satire on bourgeois values and a vindication of "romance" and fantasy as the motivating factor of the inner lives of even the most outwardly conventional individuals. John and Mary Beal are a comfortable married couple living in their suburban home. The fatuity of their middle-class life is evident from the beginning:

John: I say, dear. Don't you think we ought to plant an acacia?

Mary: An acacia, what's that, John?

John: O, it's one of those trees that they have.

Mary: But why, John?

John: Well, you see the house is called The Acacias, and it seems rather silly not to have at least one.

Mary: O, I don't think that matters. Lots of places are called lots of things. Everyone does.

John: Yes, but it might help the postman.

Mary: O, no, it wouldn't, dear. He wouldn't know an acacia if he saw it any more than I should.

John: Quite right, Mary, you're always right. What a clever head you've got! (I 13)

Into this scenario bursts the anomalous form of Ali, a man "from the East" (I 19) whom John has apparently aided by the lending of some money. Mary's disapproval of the East—"But the East doesn't seem quite to count, somehow, as the proper sort of place to come from, does it, dear?" (I

19)—is a testimonial to her hardheaded imperviousness to imagination. John, not quite so bludgeoned into bourgeois conventionality, secretly longs for the East—"I've often heard people speak of it, and somehow it seemed so . . ." (I 14)—but lacks the knowledge or experience or imagination even to vocalize his longing. But Ali changes all that: he gives John a crystal that will allow him to go back into his past life, change anything he would like to have changed, and return to his house the next day. It is not certain, however, that he will return to exactly the same circumstances:

> *Ali*: The crystal will bring you back to this house when the hour is accomplished, even to-morrow night. If you be the great banker, you will perhaps come to chastise one of your slaves who will dwell in this house. If you be head of Briggs and Cater you will come to give an edict to one of your firm. Perchance this street will be yours and you will come to show your power unto it. *But you will come.* (I 26)

Artificial as this whole contrivance is, it is nonetheless emblematic of the essential act of fantasy: the creation of an entire ontology and the working out of a scenario based upon it. There is no attempt to provide a plausible rationale for the crystal and its powers: they simply are what they are, and are to be accepted solely for their imaginative ramifications.

Although Mary is violently opposed to it—she does not want the placidity of her bourgeois life disturbed—John finally takes Ali up on the idea, choosing what he fancies to be a relatively harmless episode for replaying: ten years ago he missed a train to the city because of the officious behavior of some railroad clerks. He knows that the train did not crash, and he also knows that the person he was to have met in the city on a job interview never showed up, so he believes that the subsequent course of his life would not change significantly if he caught the train.

Of course, everything does change. On the train he meets Miralda Clement, who bears some superficial similarity to the Queen in *The Queen's Enemies* but who is much more consciously hypocritical and manipulative than Nitokris ever was. She wheedles John into helping her with a fantastic proposal: he is to go to the far side of Persia and take control of a pass that Miralda's uncle has bequeathed to her, where a heavy toll is levied from all who cross it; and he is to exact payment from Ben Hussein, the chief of a tribe in the area, who borrowed a great deal of money from Miralda's uncle and has yet to repay it. Is it Miralda's seductive power or John's weakness of will that compels him to undertake this bizarre errand? Perhaps a little of both. John's brother Archie declares, "We're mostly made what we are by some woman or other" (I 74), and John is indeed the stodgy middle-class husband with Mary but something very different under Miralda's influence.

After six months John has yet to tame Ben Hussein, but he has at least established himself as king of the pass and is reforming the religion of the populace, forcing them to destroy all the gods who require ritual sacrifice. Archie, who comes to visit him, declares, "Well, you haven't changed a bit for your six months here" (I 65), and this much is true enough. But he has at least come to realize that Miralda may not be quite as helpless as she makes herself out to be: he first declares, when Archie asks him what she is like, "somehow she sort of seems like a—like a queen" (I 67), then amends it: "Well, I don't know, only she seemed more like—well, a kind of autocrat" (I 68).

But in the six and a half years that elapse between the second and third acts, there is a fundamental change; he now scorns the comforts of bourgeois life: "Home? Home? . . . What have we in common with home? Rows and rows of little houses; and if they hear a nightingale there they write to the papers. And—and if they saw this they'd think they were drunk. Miralda, don't be absurd" (I 103). Miralda is not quite sure what she has created. He has gotten tougher: "I will have what fancies I please, crazy or sane. Am I not Shereef of Shaldomir? Who dare stop me if I would be mad as Herod?" (I 104). He scorns her pleas to marry her: "Drive me not to anger. If I have you cast into a well and take twenty of the fairest daughters of Al Shaldomir, who can gainsay me?" (I 104). He has had Ben Hussein killed, but other enemies have arisen. His change of character is exemplified by his speech: just as his middle-class diction jarred grotesquely with Ali's flowery style at the outset, so now does his own become grandiose:

And I will exalt myself. I have been Shereef hitherto, but now I will be king. Al Shaldomir is less than I desire. I have ruled too long over a little country. I will be the equal of Persia. I will be king; I proclaim it. The pass is mine; the mountains shall be mine also. And he that rules the mountains has mastery over all the plains beyond. If the men of the plains will not own it let them make ready; for my wrath will fall on them in the hour when they think me afar, on a night when they think I dream. (I 140–41)

But is this genuine strength or mere bluster? When Hafiz el Alcolahn formulates a plot to overthrow him, John is forced to depart ignominiously by a secret passageway to a waiting canoe, and so makes his long, weary, humiliating trip back to England. He is completely shattered—he has lost not only his kingdom but also his will; and the loss is typified by the reversion of his language: "I had been intended for work in the City. And then, then I travelled, and—and I got very much taken with foreign countries, and I thought—but it all went to pieces. I lost everything. Here I am, starving" (I 154). He returns to his house to find Mary married to another man; but—in a rather contrived deus ex machina—the maid destroys the crystal and everything is restored to normal, save that John merely ponders: "I—I thought I'd caught that train" (I 160).

John Beal is the fourth great character in Dunsany's early plays, matching Agmar of *The Gods of the Mountain*, the Queen of *The Queen's Enemies*, and Alexander of *Alexander* in the complexity of his portrayal. It is clear that the very malleability of his character—so dependent upon setting and the influence of others—is a testament to its fundamental weakness and the cause of his spectacular fall. Miralda Clement is also a masterwork of characterization, although her duplicity and low cunning are depicted a little obviously. *If* is Dunsany's most exhaustive meditation on time, and like *The Golden Doom* it stresses the role of chance in human affairs; but in the end it is a character study of the secret, perhaps unconscious longing for imaginative stimulation on the part of those who outwardly seem stolidly bourgeois.

If, written in 1919, is an anomaly in its richness and substance; as with so many other facets of Dunsany's work, his early plays are the strongest and his later ones tend toward flabbiness, superficiality, and self-parody. Only two plays in *Plays of Near and Far* need concern us here, *The Compromise of the King of the Golden Isles* [1919?] and *The Flight of the Queen* [1920]; the other four plays in the volume are only marginally fantastic and are more properly discussed elsewhere. The *Compromise* is set in a fantastic realm, but is wholly human and even mundane in its actual action. The King has angered the Emperor of Eng-Bathai by sheltering a man sought by the latter, and the Emperor's ambassador compels the King to choose one of two goblets of wine to drink; one is a rare and treasured wine and the other is poisoned. The entire scenario resists any sort of symbolization, and Dunsany actually takes pride in the fact, remarking in the preface to the American edition of *Plays of Near and Far*: "it is just the sort of play through which those that hunt for allegories might hunt merrily, unless I mention that there are no allegories in any of my plays" (PNF iv). This may be the case, but in this instance the play fails to broach any broader issues beyond its surface plot.

The Flight of the Queen is beset with similar problems. It becomes very obvious that this play, involving such characters as Prince Meliflor and Queen Zoomzoomarma, is a story about bees: the drones, the workers, and the queen bee. It is verbose, static, and superficial; Dunsany cannot draw any wider message for human life from the life of bees, as Vergil does in the fourth book of the *Georgics*. Dunsany's telltale remark that this is the "most poetical" (WSS 35) of his plays cannot conceal its poverty of substance; the man who rightly wrote that "[m]ere beautiful words alone are hollow" (DL 2) has here failed to take his own advice.

A third minor play, *The Old King's Tale* [1917], is also not worth much attention. The setting is aggressively fantastic—*"Place: A fair country. Scene: Anything in the wide world. Time: Now, or never"* (A 99)—but the action is wholly undramatic. King Hodiathon tells two young lovers of his doleful life as an exile in the desert, far from the land over which he should have ruled. His final exhortation—"Fight them! Fight the gods! They cannot stand against youth" (A 114)—is not, as with *Alexander*, an injunction to battle Destiny, but Time; for it is not Fate but Time that has crippled the King physically and mentally, and he knows that only youth can stave it off, however fleetingly. The atmosphere of gloom that hangs over this play is powerful and effective, but the long speeches by the King render this a play to be read and not acted.

Dunsany's innate sense of drama is evident throughout the course of his early plays: it is not their lofty diction but their remarkably simple dramatic touches—the perpetual background laughter in *The Glittering Gate*; Alexander's sitting on a fallen pedestal; Argimēnēs' killing of the slave-guard as seen hypnotically by the movement of shadows—that make these plays authentic products of the stage and not merely the lyrical emanations of a prose-poet. I wonder, however, whether some scenes involving the actual appearance of gods or idols onstage may not be unintentionally comical: I have already noted that the spectacle of Klesh in *A Night at an Inn* may have been deliberately self-parodic, but nothing of the sort was surely intended in *The Gods of the Mountain*, which nevertheless presents the following scenario: *"Enter in single file a procession of seven green men, even hands and faces are green; they wear green-stone sandals; they walk with knees extremely wide apart, as having sat cross-legged for centuries; their right arms and right forefingers point upwards, right elbows resting on left hands: they stoop grotesquely"* (FiP 36). From another perspective, I wonder about the final transformation in *If*, where the "new" life of Mary and the other characters is abruptly reversed upon the destroying of the crystal: *"The photographs of the four children change slightly. The Colonel gives place to Aunt Martha. The green sofa turns red. John's clothes become neat and tidy. The hammer in Liza's hand turns to a feather duster. Nothing else changes"* (I 158–59). In a film today this could be accomplished with ease, but how is it to be managed on the stage?

And yet, it must have been managed, for *If* had a run of two hundred performances at the Ambassador in London in 1921–22.

If was the last great dramatic triumph for Dunsany, and even it came after years of relative neglect of his dramatic work. In 1916 Dunsany could have been called one of the four or five contemporary masters of English drama; by 1925 his plays were nearly all forgotten. *Alexander*, written in 1912 and published in 1925, was not performed until the Malvern Festival of 1938. And yet, Dunsany doggedly continued the writing of plays; aside from the exquisite comedy *Mr. Faithful*, however, his later plays tend to be brief and insubstantial, although a number of them present many features of interest and thematically complement his tales and novels. Brooks Atkinson, reviewing a 1950 revival of *The Gods of the Mountain*, declared that Dunsany's early plays did not deserve the obscurity into which they had lapsed and were worth resurrecting.[7] Some recent work has been done tracing the possible influence of *The Gods of the Mountain* on Pirandello.[8,9] I am not going to claim that Dunsany somehow anticipated the theater of the absurd or any other avant-garde tendencies in modern drama; such a claim not merely is preposterous but seriously errs as to Dunsany's own aesthetic motivation, which was to address the "big" issues of Time, Destiny, Fate, Chance, and religion in a manner that looked not forward but backward to the Greeks who, for Dunsany, were the first and greatest dramatists of the West. *The Gods of the Mountain*, *The Queen's Enemies*, and *Alexander* do indeed have something of Greek tragedy in them, leavened by a very modern sense of irony, satire, and piquant wit that does not so much undercut as augment the grandeur of the surface action. They and other of Dunsany's early plays are indeed worth revival, although I do not expect that to happen very soon.

NOTES

1. See the appendix to Darrell Schweitzer's *Pathways to Elfland* (Philadelphia: Owlswick Press, 1989), 158–62, for a chronological list of Dunsany's plays, giving dates of composition, production, and publication.

2. "Romance and the Modern Stage," *National Review* No. 341 (July 1911): 827–35. Cited in the text by page number.

3. Letter to E. H. Bierstadt (23 July 1917); cited in Edward Hale Bierstadt, *Dunsany the Dramatist* (Boston: Little, Brown, 1917; rev. ed., 1919), 200.

4. Letter to Stuart Walker, 7 August 1916; cited in Bierstadt, 171.

5. Letter to Stuart Walker, 28 June 1916; cited in Bierstadt, 164.

6. Unsigned, "*A Night at an Inn*—Lord Dunsany's 'Perfect' Melodrama," *Current Opinion* 63, No. 2 (August 1917): 91–94.

7. Brooks Atkinson, "Three One-Acters by Abbe Workshop," *New York Times* No. 33, 724 (25 May 1950): 36.

8. Susan Bassnett, "From Gods to Giants—Theatrical Parallels between Edward Dunsany and Luigi Pirandello," *Yearbook of the British Pirandello Society* No. 6 (1982): 40–49.

9. Alessandro Tinterri, "Pirandello regista e *The Gods of the Mountain* di Lord Dunsany," *Yearbook of the British Pirandello Society* No. 6 (1986): 36–39.

Interchapter: The Great War

It is hardly to be imagined that a conflict so destructive of every phase of European culture as World War I could have failed to leave its mark on Dunsany the man and writer. At the very outset of the war he came to feel that "the world was no longer a place for the spilling of ink" (PS 263), and his response was by no means an isolated one. John Palmer, writing in the *Fortnightly Review* for March 1915, expressed some highly typical sentiments:

At midnight on August 4th, 1914, all that literature hitherto described as "modern" passed quietly away in its sleep. This does not mean that there immediately arose a new generation of authors and readers. Things will superficially go on as before, possibly for years to come. . . . Nevertheless, there is no doubt at all that the ways of literature after the war are to be entirely altered. Already we know that certain literary styles and methods which once were "effective," and admirably adapted to their purpose, have now become detestable. We have no room for insolence as a fine art, for dialectic display, for literary virtuosity. Literary manners are completely to be reformed; and with the manners the matter also will be changed. The return to simplicity, so frequently travestied in the age whose extinction is now decreed, is at last coming in sober truth. . . . We shall shortly be looking back with wonder on the curious rhetorical and logical excesses of the first decade of the twentieth century.[1]

Naive and even philistine as some of this is, it may have expressed the sentiments of a widespread array of middlebrow readers, readers who may have found Dunsany's exotic and ethereal imaginary realms irrelevant to present-day concerns. Perhaps Dunsany did also, although he, like Bertrand Russell and so many others who had already come to maturity in the Edwardian age, did not look back so much with "wonder" as with wrenching nostalgia at what he fancied to be the death of his civilization. Well before the war, however, Dunsany's attention was already shifting to politics and war, and a study of all his war writings up to and just after the Great War will provide us with a key toward understanding the course of his subsequent literary career.

Of "In Zaccarath" (1909), a story in *A Dreamer's Tales*, Dunsany remarks rather oddly that it was inspired in part by "the sense of something impending," namely "the gradually increasing probability of war being brought on by Germany" (PS 150). If this is the case, Dunsany has hidden the source of his inspiration with exceptional skill, for I cannot imagine that any reader, then or now, could have deduced the political undercurrent in the tale—or, rather, its specific object. "In Zaccarath" tells in perfumed prose of a king of that fantastic realm who wishes his prophets to prophesy. One does so, uttering dire warnings: ". . . your fall shall be sore and soon. Already in Heaven the gods shun thy god: they know this doom and what is written of him: he sees oblivion before him like a mist" (DT 170). There does not seem any especially compelling reason why this should be so, except that, in the same prophet's words, "The evilness of thy days shall bring down the Zeedians on thee as the suns of springtide bring the avalanche down" (DT 170). But the king, oblivious, merely remarks, "Is he not splendid?" (DT 171), rather like King Darniak and his court in *King Argimēnēs and the Unknown Warrior.* There is much pomp and ceremony at the court of the King of Zaccarath, with warriors displaying their weaponry prominently; but the tale concludes: "And only the other day I found a stone that had undoubtedly been a part of Zaccarath, it was three inches long and an inch broad; I saw the edge of it uncovered by the sand. I believe that only three other pieces have been found like it" (DT 174). But we are given no explanation of the collapse of the Kingdom of Zaccarath, so that it is entirely unclear how Dunsany intends to liken it to the reign of Kaiser Wilhelm II.

A much more interesting story is the one that directly follows "In Zaccarath" in *A Dreamer's Tales*, "The Field." We have already seen in this tale a prototypical expression of Dunsany's longing to leave the ugliness of London for the fields of the English countryside; but once the narrator reaches one particularly beautiful field, he experiences an unplaceable uneasiness. He queries a man who intimately knows the history of the region, but is told that "nothing of any interest had ever occurred there, nothing at all." The narrator therefore concludes that "it was from the future that the field's trouble came" (DT 179). He takes a poet to the field, and the latter, when asked, "What manner of field is it?" remarks, "It is a battlefield" (DT 181). The horror of this future event is casting a pall backward upon the present. This ingenious premise serves as the basis for a tale that is at once chillingly supernatural and full of wistful pathos. Both "The Field" and "In Zaccarath" were published in the English *Saturday Review* toward the end of 1909, and both point to Dunsany's increasing concern over the potentially explosive turbulence in world affairs.

Once the war actually began, Dunsany's writing turned immediately to the subject, but it initially did so by means of fantasy, not by a repudiation of it. The principal method utilized by Dunsany was parable. "Our Laurels," a tale of scarcely three hundred words, appears to be his first war story; it was published in the *Saturday Review* of November 28, 1914. A poet seeks "laurels" (i.e., fame), but finds that they do not grow until "the shades of the Older Poets came in a time of war, and brought him a cupful of the water of Lethe"; at that point his laurels "put forth their branches over the cities of men and made a verdure for ever in far fields of the world." This exquisite little tale anticipates Dunsany's own burgeoning fame as a poet of World War I.

Also in the manner of a parable is "One More Tale" (1915), which tells of a bedraggled old woman "coming towards the World": "She had the appearance of being outcast for ever from the genteel." The narrator realizes that she is Peace: " 'You can't come here,' I said as soon as I saw what she wanted. 'You can't come here, you know.' The words were on my lips as réveillé woke me." Dunsany plays off the standard, even hackneyed, device of horror fiction whereby a horrific event is dismissed as the product of a dream: here it is the dream of peace that is cast away by the call to battle.

Another tale written early in the war, "La Dernière Mobilisation" (1915), is a perfect blend of fantasy and realism. The narrator sees a strange band of "marching men":

The uniforms of the men—of various sorts, indicating that they are from many commands—are in shreds and spotted with stains of mould and earth; their heads are bound in cloths so that their faces are covered. The single drummer at the side of the column carries slung from his shoulder the shell of a drum. No flag flies from the staff at the column's head, but the staff is held erect.

Gradually the column disappears in the mist, and the narrator realizes that it had come from Belgium: "The dead were leaving their resting places in that lost land." This brief tale has an atmosphere remarkably akin to that

of Ambrose Bierce's grim war story "Chickamauga"; but in that tale—
where a little boy sees the crippled remnants of a battalion leaving one of
the bloodiest battles of the American Civil War—a hideous but natural
event is described in the rhetoric of supernatural horror, whereas in
Dunsany's tale the supernatural is used as a metaphor for the evocation of
a poignant but real event: the deaths of countless soldiers during the
invasion of Belgium.

And yet, Dunsany did not in the end write very much during the four
years of the war. Much of that period, of course, he spent either preparing
to serve in various units or recovering from the injuries he sustained during
the Dublin riots of 1916. Dunsany continued to publish books during the
war years, but the material in them had been written much earlier. Almost
all the contents of *Fifty-one Tales* (1915), *The Last Book of Wonder* (1916),
and *Plays of Gods and Men* (1917) were written prior to 1914; some of
the material in *Tales of Three Hemispheres* (1919) was published during
the war, but it is difficult to tell whether it was composed then or earlier.
Dunsany wrote no plays, as far as I can ascertain, between 1913 and the
spring of 1917, when he wrote three short plays—*The Old King's Tale*,
Fame and the Poet, and *Cheezo*—in quick succession; indeed, he remarks
acidly in the preface to *Plays of Gods and Men* that the plays in that volume
were written between 1910 and 1913, "lest any idle person might think
that I have had time to write plays during the last few years" (PGM [v]).

Dunsany's pen began to flow at last toward the end of the war. Early in
1918 he joined MI7B(i), a division of the War Office devoted essentially
to the dissemination of propaganda for the British side. Dunsany wrote
many short articles and stories which were evidently picked up by newspapers all over the world, although I have myself found only one such
appearance, in the *New York Tribune* of July 2, 1918. He collected his
sketches into two volumes, *Tales of War* (1918) and *Unhappy Far-Off
Things* (1919), which constitute his first entirely non-fantastic writing.
To discuss these works in detail is beyond the scope of this book, but
they by no means deserve the neglect and scorn that they generally elicit
even from Dunsany's supporters; in their own way they continue to probe
his all-pervasive Nature theme with complexity and poignancy.

Both of these volumes have been criticized for being excessively
jingoistic and vindictive against the Germans; but it is difficult to see what
other attitude Dunsany could have adopted, and in fact there are traces of
a relatively balanced view that sympathizes with the suffering undergone
by all peoples involved in the conflict. To be sure, we have random
references to "the hyena-like memory of the Kaiser" (TW 23); and
Dunsany might have been better off not writing things like "An Investiga-

tion into the Causes and Origin of the War" (TW), a heavy-handed satire in which the war is attributed to Kaiser Wilhelm's moustache. "The Punishment" (TW), in which a plantom comes to the kaiser and shows him visions of a Germany that might have been had the war not occurred, is interesting in exemplifying Dunsany's use of the supernatural to point a moral but is too close in conception to *A Christmas Carol* to be effective. And yet, one of the last stories in *Tales of War*, "The Home of Herr Schnitzelhaaser," is a refreshing contrast. Sympathy is here extended to an impoverished German family who have lost four sons to the war and are now forced to receive an officer who is to be billeted with them.

But these two collections gain their greatest interest in the light they shed on Dunsany's own state of mind during the Great War. They, and other documents of this period, provide conclusive evidence that it was the horrors of the war, and not merely personal problems affecting his family, that caused him to rethink his entire approach to writing, especially the writing of fantasy. Let us first consider the very odd and disturbing preface to *The Last Book of Wonder*. "I do not know where I may be when this preface is read," Dunsany writes from Ebrington Barracks in Londonderry on August 16, 1916. He continues:

Just now the civilization of Europe seems almost to have ceased, and nothing seems to grow in her torn fields but death, yet this is only for a while and dreams will come back again and bloom as of old, all the more radiantly for this terrible ploughing, as the flowers will bloom again where the trenches are and the primroses shelter in shell-holes for many seasons, when weeping Liberty has come home to Flanders. (LBW [v–vi])

And yet, the dogged optimism of this paragraph ("dreams will come back again and bloom as of old") seems confounded by the conclusion: "And now I . . . offer you these books of dreams from Europe as one throws things of value, if only to oneself, at the last moment out of a burning house" (LBW [vii]). *The Last Book of Wonder* may be the last dreams Dunsany had prior to the war, and dreams like it may be the last that Europe ever has. This single sentence marks the end of Dunsany's first phase of writing—the imaginary-world phase that had dominated his work up to this time and would never return save fleetingly and in very different ways in things like *The King of Elfland's Daughter*.

The Great War was destroying the civilization Dunsany knew; it was gone and would never come again: "They are gone, those times, gone like the Dinosaur, gone with bows and arrows and the old knightlier days" (UFT 47). Dunsany may have attempted to summon up those "old knightlier days" with *The Chronicles of Rodriguez* and *The Charwoman's Shadow*, but he knew that it was a vain and transient undertaking. The twentieth century is, for all practical purposes, over for those who lived before the war:

> whatever others may write, the twentieth century will not be the age of strategy but will only seem to have been those fourteen lost quiet summers whose fruits lie under the plaster.
>
> That layer of plaster and brick-dust lies on the age that has gone, as final, as fatal, as the layer of flints that covers the top of the chalk and marks the end of an epoch and some unknown geologic catastrophe. (UFT 85–86)

"It is our own time that has ended in blood and broken bricks" (UFT 88), and Dunsany knows that he is only a fossil. Gradually he modified these sentiments and willed himself to continue living in the century of Eliot and Hitler. Gradually, too, he began writing again—novels this time, because his early tales had not been well received, and then the Jorkens tales, which already suggest a significantly different relation to fantasy from that obtaining in his previous work: we are now wholly in the realm of the real, with improbable but not impossible events that strain our credulity to the limit but whose falsity we are never able to demonstrate. What need is there, moreover, of imaginary worlds when the real world—which Dunsany had begun to explore through his far-flung travels—has so much of interest to offer?

> it is worth while to travel to far countries, whoever can, to see one of those books [of Time], and where the edges are turned up a little to catch sight of those strange winged bulls and mysterious kings and lion-headed gods that were not meant for us. And out of the glimpse one catches from odd corners of those volumes of Time, where old centuries hide, one builds up part by guesses, part by fancy, mixed with but little knowledge, a tale or theory of how men and women lived in unknown ages in the faith of forgotten gods. (UFT 81–82)

The Jorkens tales are harbingers of two important trends in Dunsany's later work: the abandonment of the realm of pure imagination for the equally exotic realm of the real, and the initiation of that vein of comic fantasy which would reach its culmination in *The Strange Journeys of Colonel Polders* (1950). Comedy was, to be sure, the last thing on Dunsany's mind as he was writing *Unhappy Far-Off Things*, but the relative calm of the postwar world eventually reconciled him to the destruction of life, property, and a whole civilization that he witnessed firsthand during the war years. Imaginary worlds were gone; it was sufficient to insert the weird into the real. Gradually even this yielded to the complete abandonment of fantasy—or, rather, the insertion of fantasy not into the real world but into the very minds of his characters.

NOTE

1. John Palmer, "Mr. Bernard Shaw: An Epitaph," *Fortnightly Review* 103, No. 3 (March 1915): 443.

3

The Golden Age and Elfland

Dunsany's first four novels, *The Chronicles of Rodriguez* (1922), *The King of Elfland's Daughter* (1924), *The Charwoman's Shadow* (1926), and *The Blessing of Pan* (1927), typify a pattern that can be seen throughout his career, one that Darrell Schweitzer has characterized as follows: "In every phase of his work, he would begin very well and get better, producing his best work of any particular type very early. Then he would remain at a certain level for a while and start to decline."[1] This is a little simpleminded and also not entirely true: Schweitzer himself thinks *The Curse of the Wise Woman* (1933) Dunsany's best novel (although perhaps he believes this is still an "early" work in the novel form), and I for one regard *The Strange Journeys of Colonel Polders* (1950) as a masterwork of its kind. Nevertheless, it is remarkable how quickly Dunsany mastered a form—short story, play, novel—at the very outset. Of the four novels discussed in this chapter, the second and fourth are surely among his very best, and are among the landmarks of modern fantasy literature.

I have noted on several occasions Dunsany's remark that he took to novel writing because he was "disappointed at the reception of my short stories" (PS 10). I have no doubt this was the case (although, given the adulation Dunsany received for his early work in general, one wonders what sort of "reception" would have satisfied him), but one would like to think that Dunsany also wrote novels because he was evolving conceptions that required the spaciousness of the novel form for expression. Aside perhaps from *The Chronicles of Rodriguez*, which may have been a sort of practice novel and which is a picaresque narrative full of incidents that do not cohere especially well, it is possible to maintain that all his novels, early and late, really are novels and not a string of short stories. The cumulative power of *The King of Elfland's Daughter*, *The Blessing of Pan*, *The Curse of the Wise Woman*, and *The Story of Mona Sheehy* testify to the integrity of their construction.

Of these early novels, the first and third and the second and fourth pair themselves naturally together, the former in setting and the latter in import. All four once again underscore the Nature theme that is at the heart of Dunsany's work, but the latter pair do so more intensely and poignantly. All, in various ways, also present striking contrasts between the present and the past, the Christian and the pagan, the city and the country; and Dunsany's preferences invariably tend toward the latter of these dichotomies.

On the surface, the most striking thing about *The Chronicles of Rodriguez* is the incredible buoyancy of its tone. This is just about the last thing one might have expected from a writer who confessed to a profound depression after the war: "I was oppressed at my house in Kent with the thought that I might not do as much work as I felt ought to be done by anyone who had survived the war" (WSS 12). Dunsany did not, of course, begin writing the novel until January 1921 (WSS 38), more than two years after the end of the war, and following his vastly successful American lecture tour of 1919–20. His life seemed to have returned to a state of relative placidity, aside from an anomalous incident in early 1921 in which Dunsany was arrested and fined £25 for keeping weapons (mostly old rifles) at Dunsany Castle "not under effective military control."[2] I shall discuss this episode in greater detail later.

In any event, Dunsany seems to have made a conscious decision to leave the searing effects of the war behind him. *If* was written in eight days in the middle of 1919 (WSS 12), and Rebecca West began her review of it by declaring, "There can be no doubt at all but that Lord Dunsany was sent into the world to aid in the great task of cheering us up."[3] He makes no secret of his mission in *The Chronicles of Rodriguez*: "I have chosen a pleasant tale for you in a happy land, in the fairest time of year, in a golden age" (CR 61). Still more startling, the very quest of Don Rodriguez—a search for "the wars" so that he may distinguish himself in battle and win for himself a castle in Spain—seems an anomaly from the author of *Tales of War* and *Unhappy Far-Off Things*. But if this novel superficially seems a mere venture into innocuous escapism, it does not fail to enunciate several of Dunsany's central concerns.

It does so in several ways, notably by a continual satire at the expense of the modern age. Rodriguez has picked up a Sancho Panza-like comrade, Morano, from an inn, and rewards him by presenting him with a sapphire ring: "Morano's expressions of gratitude were in keeping with that flowery period in Spain, and might appear ridiculous were I to expose them to the eyes of an age in which one in Morano's place on such an occasion would merely have said, 'Damned good of you old nut, not half,' and let the matter drop" (CR 34). This sort of thing recurs time and again; but it is not always so flippant. One of the most stunning tableaux in the entire novel is the arduous climb by Rodriguez and Morano to the nearly inaccessible home of a professor of magic, situated on a lofty cliff. The professor, learning of Rodriguez's quest for the wars, directs him to two magic windows, one of which shows the wars of the past, the other the wars of the future. Morano in particular is regaled by the former, slapping his thigh and urging on the Christians in their battles with the infidel. The latter reveals something much more disturbing. It may be true that Dunsany naively romanticizes the wars of the past—"Through the window to the left was colour, courtesy, splendour; there was Death at least disguising himself, well cloaked, taking mincing steps, bowing, wearing a plume in his hat and a decent mask" (CR 81)—but he is nothing but grimly realistic about the war that would be far in the future for Rodriguez but very close to the present for Dunsany:

But in the other window through that deep, beautiful blue Rodriguez saw Man make a new ally, an ally who was only cruel and strong and had no purpose but killing, who had no pretences or pose, no mask and no manner, but was only the slave of Death and had no care but for his business. He saw it grow bigger and stronger. Heart it had none, but he saw its cold steel core scheming methodical plans and dreaming always destruction. Before it faded men and their fields and their houses. Rodriguez saw the machine. (CR 81–82)

I am a little disturbed at the suggestion that the World War was the self-generated outcome of killing machines, as if this somehow absolves human beings from culpability; but it is evidently something Dunsany on some level believed. The effect on Rodriguez is traumatic: "Rodriguez lifted his eyes and glanced from city to city, to Albert, Bapaume, and Arras, his gaze moved over a plain with its harvest of desolation lying forlorn and ungathered, lit by the flashing clouds and the moon and peering rockets. He turned from the window and wept" (CR 82). Rodriguez himself could have gone on to write *Unhappy Far-Off Things*, but strangely enough he soon recovers and continues his quest for the wars. Finally he finds one—a nice, safe little war between two small forces—and he takes captive a man who claims to own an impressive castle in Spain and who promises to yield it to Rodriguez for his life. But when Rodriguez, Morano, and the captive march back to the man's residence, it turns out to be merely a small farmhouse. Is there some underlying message here about the uselessness of war and its empty rewards? One would like to think so, and perhaps the conclusion of the novel may confirm such a view.

In the course of Rodriguez's wanderings he blunders into a spectral forest named Shadow Valley; here he rescues from hanging a man who proves to be the valley's king. He expresses regret that he cannot stay in this pleasant natural realm; but after his bootless attempt to win a castle, he returns disconsolately to Shadow Valley and meets again the king, who promises to build a castle for him. That castle is built in the very midst of Shadow Valley out of its trees, and one could scarcely ask for a more emphatic symbol of the superiority of Nature over civilization. In speaking of the endurance of the castle even to the present—"the castle weathered the ages and reached our days, worn, battered even, by its journey through the long and sometimes troubled years" (CR 307)—Dunsany echoes the message of so many earlier tales of the ultimate victory of the forces of Nature over the transience of human culture.

The Chronicles of Rodriguez, as a picaresque romance, might be regarded as a sort of catchall for many of the themes, elements, and atmospheric touches that distinguished Dunsany's earlier fiction. And yet, there is at least one new element introduced here, and that is the element of romantic love—the first, so far as I can tell, in all Dunsany's work up to this point. While in Shadow Valley Rodriguez encounters the fetching Serafina, and he yearns to win her hand. Perhaps Dunsany was responding to criticisms (unjustified, I think) that his previous work seemed too remote from human emotions; whatever the cause, this romance is handled rather well, and the novel ends with a lavish rustic wedding in Shadow Valley. Rodriguez becomes the ruler of the valley upon the death of its king, and "[h]e gave his days to the forest and the four seasons" (CR 317).

The very first page of *The Chronicles of Rodriguez* announces that the novel is set "in Spain, in the golden time" (CR 3), whenever that is; the first page of *The Charwoman's Shadow* declares that we are once again in Spain, but with "the Golden Age past its wonderful zenith" (CS 1). Moreover, a minor character is introduced as "the second Duke of Shadow Valley, of whose illustrious father some tale was told in the Chronicles of Rodriguez" (CS 65). This is, really, the only genuine connection between the two novels, for the latter tells the piquant tale of a preternaturally aged crone who unwisely gave up her shadow for a sort of immortality, and is now the charwoman of a wizard in a remote house buried in the woods near the town of Aragona. When a young man, Ramon Alonzo, comes to study with the wizard for the purpose of making gold for his sister's dowry, he becomes fired with a chivalrous desire to rescue the charwoman's shadow and restore it to her, and ultimately does so.

This is certainly a charming fable, but I have difficulty interpreting the exact symbolism of the shadow and its loss. There is a suggestion that the shadow is a metaphor for a person's closeness to Nature, as Anemone, the crone, testifies as she laments its absence:

It lay over the fields once; it used to make the grass such a tender green. It never dimmed the buttercups. It did no harm to anything. Butterflies may have been scared of it, and once a dragon-fly, but it did them never a harm. I've known it protect anemones awhile from the heat of the noonday sun, which had otherwise withered them sooner. In the early morning it would stretch away beyond our garden right out to the wild; poor innocent shadow that loved the grey dew. And in the evening it would grow bold and strong and run right down the slopes of hills, where I walked singing, and would come to the edges of bosky tangled places, till a little more and its head would have been out of sight: I've known the fairies then dance out from their sheltered arbours in the deeps of briar and thorn and play with its curls. (CS 33–34)

But not much is made of this, and the absence of a shadow comes to stand as a symbol for ostracism from conventional human society: " '[T]hey won't let me live with them, speak with them, or pass them by, because forsooth I have been unkind to my shadow' " (CS 37). Ramon, who for a time loses his own shadow and is given an evil counterfeit shadow that is a "mere strip of gloom" (CS 110) which does not grow, comes to feel much the same sentiment. It is true that this counterfeit shadow is *unnatural* in the most literal sense—because it does not grow, it at one point deceives Ramon as to the lateness of the hour (CS 110), a symbol for his increasing alienation from the natural world—but it is later said that "there was growing fast in him the outcast's feeling" (CS 143). The absence of a shadow is also cast in terms of religious intolerance. Some young girls who notice that Ramon's shadow does not grow flee in terror because they realize he has been trafficking with the Black Arts. Later a band of citizens from Aragona chases Ramon away because of his anomaly:

Ramon Alonzo they abjured to stop, calling him by the names of certain famous devils; but he no more heeded them than would these devils have done. Only he noticed that, though they fought or pursued, as their cries indicated, for the Faith, for St. Michael, for St. Joseph, for St. Judas not Iscariot, for all the Saints, for the King, they none of them cried "for a Shadow." And yet that was all that the fuss was about, he reflected irritably. (CS 152).

He comes to learn that "any unusual shape of a shadow was no more tolerated than horns and tail" (CS 220). This religious motif is something we will find very prevalent in *The King of Elfland's Daughter* and especially *The Blessing of Pan*. In those novels, however, the implied contrast between Christianity and paganism shows Dunsany's clear preference for the latter; here the contrast is more explicitly that of Christianity and Satanism, and—although neither Anemone nor Ramon is held blameworthy for a lack of a proper shadow, nor is the wizard more than flippantly condemned for his practicing of the Black Arts— Dunsany tends to favor the former. Father Joseph, Ramon's priest, tells him earnestly that he needs his true shadow to enter heaven: " 'On Earth the shadow is led hither and thither, wherever he will, by the man; but hereafter it is far otherwise, and wherever his shadow goes, alas, he must follow; which is but just, since in all their sojourn here never once doth the shadow lead, never once the man follow' " (CS 225). We are evidently to accept this argument at face value, for Ramon immediately seeks with redoubled vigor to regain his shadow.

   I do not find *The Charwoman's Shadow* a wholly satisfactory novel: it may be, as Darrell Schweitzer has noted, "one of the most delightful treatments of magic in all literature,"[4] but it seems a little frivolous: the loss of a shadow does not serve as the focus of any broader philosophical message, and the quest for its rescue is merely a supernatural adventure without any underlying significance. There are, of course, many delightful touches, especially the scene where Ramon finally comes upon the spell that will open the box in which the wizard has placed his many captive shadows:

Then he opened the lid of the box a little way and took out a shadow in finger and thumb by the heels, as he had seen the magician hold his. This he laid on the floor and put a small jar upon it, which he took down from a shelf, trusting any piece of matter to hold down so delicate a thing as a shadow. Then he took out another and treated it in the same way. Then a third and a fourth. They were shadows of all kinds of folk, men and women, young and old. The red sun peeped in and saw the shadowless man laying out this queer assembly and holding them one by one with little weights. They did not grow as the red sun looked at them, for they were masterless and lost. They lay there grey on the floor, fluttering limply. (CS 256–57)

With passages like this, perhaps the search for a more profound message is needless.

The Chronicles of Rodriguez and *The Charwoman's Shadow* occupy a sort of middle ground in Dunsany's work: stylistically they represent a partial reversion to the archaism that was the hallmark of Dunsany's earliest work, and in setting they continue that carving out of a fantasy realm within the real world which we have seen in some of the later stories of his early period. We are manifestly dealing with the real world of Spain in some form or other; but the temporal setting—a vague, unspecified, and poetical "Golden Age"—and the introduction of a mythical Shadow Valley in the former novel and a forest full of imps and other supernatural entities in the latter provide the escape valve of fantasy that Dunsany at this stage still required. In a remarkably cagey, tongue-in-cheek preface to *The Chronicles of Rodriguez* he enunciates the need for "mystery" (here equivalent to fantasy) even in a purportedly real setting:

> After long and patient research I am still unable to give the reader of these Chronicles the exact date of the times that they tell of. Were it merely a matter of history there could be no doubts about the period; but where magic is concerned, to however slight an extent, there must always be some element of mystery, arising partly out of ignorance and partly from the compulsion of those oaths by which magic protects its precincts from the tiptoe of curiosity. (CR vii)

In other words, Dunsany is not yet ready to renounce the realm of fantasy. He comes very close to it in *The Blessing of Pan*, but in the end even that novel celebrates the triumph of the fantastic over the real.

The King of Elfland's Daughter seems to represent a glorious return to that jewelled manner typical of the early short stories; it could well be considered a novel-length prose-poem. In its juxtaposition of a fantasy world (Elfland) with the real world, with a presumed exaltation of the former and the denigration of the latter, it could also be said to hark back to the scorn of the real and the glorification of pure fantasy that we saw in such things as "Idle Days on the Yann." And yet, Dunsany's stance is more complex than these simple dichotomies suggest.

The ruler of a small corner of the real world, Erl, is told by his parliament that the people wish to be ruled by a "magic lord" (KED 1), and so he urges his son, Alveric, to go to Elfland, which lies just to the east of his realm, and win the hand of Lirazel, the daughter of Elfland's ancient king. He does so, assisted by a magic sword fashioned by the witch Ziroonderel. But Lirazel, although she gives birth to a half-human, half-elfish son, Orion, cannot become accustomed to the ways of earth, and when she and Alveric quarrel, she returns to Elfland. Alveric, shattered by the loss, undertakes an arduous quest to win her back, spending years on what seems to be a hopeless errand. But Lirazel herself starts to yearn for the fields of earth, and she ultimately persuades her powerful father to engraft the little realm of Erl within the fabric of Elfland, so that she can enjoy both the eternal charm of Elfland and the variegated charms of earth, and so live in tranquility with her husband and son.

It does not require much erudition to know that Erl is German for "elf": already the distinction between Elfland and the real world becomes very problematical. Erl itself, a placid rustic realm, is close to Nature, and its people engage in activities that unite them with the natural world: "They went back to their ancient crafts, to the fitting of iron to the hooves of horses, to working upon leather, to tending flowers, to ministering to the rugged needs of earth; they followed the ancient ways . . ." (KED 1–2). The names of the people of Erl—Narl, Nehic, Vlel, Guhic (KED 37)— are suggestive not of London or New York but of Pegana or Babbulkund. Time in Erl "moved gently, not as in our cities" (KED 34). When Alveric takes little Orion hunting in a wood in Erl, they find that the wood has a wonder of its own: "There seemed to be a magic all round that fire of big logs quietly smouldering in the woods upon Autumn's discarded robe that lay brilliant there; and it was not the magic of Elfland, nor had Ziroonderel called it up with her wand: it was only a magic of the wood's very own" (KED 112). The very sword fashioned by the witch for Alveric, a sword that of all objects of earth has the power to subdue the forces of Elfland, has the magic "that is in English woods" (KED 8).

If Erl is such a magical place, what then is Elfland? It is simply an intensification of our own (natural) world:

Know then that in Elfland are colours more deep than in our fields, and the very air there glows with so deep a lucency that all things seen there have something of the look of our trees and flowers in June reflected in water. And the colour of Elfland, of which I despaired to tell, may yet be told, for we have hints of it here; the deep blue of the night in Summer just as the gloaming has gone, the pale blue of Venus flooding the evening with light, the deeps of lakes in the twilight, all these are hints of that colour. (KED 17–18)

When Dunsany adds that "our painters have had many a glimpse of that country" (KED 18), and that the flowers and lawns of Elfland are "seen only by the furthest-travelling fancies of poets in deepest sleep" (KED 31), he makes an important connection between Elfland and art—as if Elfland is really that quintessence of Nature all genuine artists are seeking to express. Elfland, like art, is timeless:

Now it is thus with time in Elfland: in the eternal beauty that dreams in that honied air nothing stirs or fades or dies, nothing seeks its happiness in movement or change or a new thing, but has its extasy in the perpetual contemplation of all the beauty that has ever been, and which always glows over those enchanted lawns as intense as when first created by incantation or song. (KED 49)

And yet, what is art but the distillation of memory? Elfland is Nature, it is art, but it is also all those memories of our past, specifically our childhood, that have been burnished with wonder and longing; it is the essence of our imaginative lives. When Lirazel returns to Elfland, leaving her husband and child, her father sweeps away Elfland and carries it off away from Erl; but little tokens get left behind:

Next Alveric saw lying there on the flat dry ground a toy that he yet remembered, which years and years ago (how could he say how many?) had been a childish joy to him, crudely carved out of wood; and one unlucky day it had been broken, and one unhappy day it had been thrown away. And now he saw it lying there not merely new and unbroken, but with a wonder about it, a splendour and a romance, the radiant transfigured thing that his young fancy had known. (KED 84)

But even before Lirazel has seen earth—or, as Dunsany phrases it throughout the novel, "the fields we know"—she longs for some sight of it. Does she find the stasis in Elfland, its frozen perfection, a little tedious? Alveric boldly invades Elfland with his sword and meets Lirazel, saying to her, " 'I come from the fields that are mapped and known.' " "And then she sighed for a moment for those fields, for she had heard how life beautifully passes there, and how there are always in those fields young generations, and she thought of the changing seasons and children and age, of which Elfin minstrels had sung when they told of Earth" (KED 26–27). Perhaps the inhabitants of Elfland find our world as fascinating as we find theirs.

One of the most persistent criticisms of Dunsany is his supposed failure to deal seriously with human emotions. I think this criticism is entirely misguided, first as applied to his early work—which deliberately demotes the human from prominence and vaunts the cosmic and the nonhuman realm of Nature in its stead—and second as applied to much of his later work, which does deal movingly, but wholly unsentimentally, with love, loss, pain, and death. The growing cleavage between Alveric and Lirazel as the latter fails to conform to earthly standards—"In those days Alveric learned that she would never now grow familiar with earthly things, never understand the folk that dwelt in the valley, never read wise books without laughter, never care for earthly ways" (KED 43–44)—is depicted with exquisite poignancy; and her decision to leave her husband and child and return to Elfland, after Alveric has made some particularly harsh and unjust criticism of her, is perhaps the most moving passage in all Dunsany. She loves Orion deeply: "And there all day she stayed and played with her child . . . and, merrily though she played at whiles, yet there were strange calms in her eyes, which Ziroonderel watched while she wondered. And when the sun was low and she had put the child to bed she sat beside him all solemn as she told him childish tales" (KED 74). But she cannot resist the love of her father, embodied in a rune that will summon her back to Elfland:

And whatever magic there was in the rune, . . . the rune was written with love that was stronger than magic, till those mystical characters glowed with the love that the Elf King had for his daughter, and there were blended in that mighty rune two great powers, magic and love, the greatest power there is beyond the boundary of twilight with the greatest power there is in the fields we know. (KED 75)

It is incomprehensible to me how C. N. Manlove, in speaking of this novel, can remark that it "is a beautiful book, and one that moves the reader with longing: but it does not move very deeply, largely because it has not really faced pain and evil."[5] Perhaps Manlove misses some tidy moral polarization between good and evil in this novel; but Dunsany rarely opts for easy solutions of this sort. Lirazel, Alveric, and the King of Elfland are all acting in accordance with what their emotions tell them is true and right, and Dunsany depicts each of their sentiments sympathetically and realistically.

If there are any villians in *The King of Elfland's Daughter*, it is the people of Erl, specifically their rustic parliament. It was this body of twelve old men that urged their lord to send Alveric on his quest to begin with; then, when he returns with Lirazel, the parliament finds all sorts of dissatisfactions with her. Alveric, influenced by the narrow doctrinal teachings of the Freer, criticizes his wife for her worship of stars and the smooth flat stones that lie in the riverbed, even though she in her innocence is trying to worship as she imagines a Christian would:

Now of all things that men feared in the valley of Erl they feared most the arts of the heathen, of whom they knew nothing but that their ways were dark. And he spoke with the anger which men always used when they spoke there of the heathen. And his anger went to her heart, for she was but learning to worship his holy things to please him, and yet he had spoken like this. (KED 73)

This incident is, indeed, the principal reason for her return to Elfland. When Orion, now grown, summons the trolls to accompany his hounds, the parliament now finds that there is "too much magic" (KED 261) in Erl, even though this is what they wished at the outset. In a mordant satire on democracy, the parliament, after Orion and his hounds capture and slay a unicorn that strayed into Erl from Elfland, soberly votes that it was in fact not a unicorn: they yearn for magic, but cannot come to terms with it once it is actually in their midst.

The Freer, who of all the characters in the novel is portrayed entirely without sympathy, is urged by the parliament to curse the realm of Elfland after it has engulfed the land of Erl; and his brand of intolerant Christianity does indeed have an effect after a fashion:

And within the dark circle in which the Freer stood making his curses were no unhallowed things, nor were there strangenesses such as come of night, nor whispers from unknown voices, nor sounds of any music blowing here from no haunts of men; but all was orderly and seemly there and no mysteries troubled the quiet except such as have been justly allowed to men. (KED 271)

The King of Elfland's Daughter is very close to the pinnacle of Dunsany's novelistic achievement; in its unparalleled beauty of style, its emotive power, and its complex interplay between Nature, art, and religion, it rightfully takes its place as a masterwork of fantastic litera-ture. It also remained one of Dunsany's personal favorites: thirty years after its composition he told Hazel Littlefield, "I shall never write so well again" (L 84).

The conflict between Nature and civilization, fantasy and reality, beauty and ugliness, is for Dunsany also a conflict between paganism and Christianity; and if that final polarization is not the focal point of *The King of Elfland's Daughter*, it is very much at the forefront of *The Blessing of Pan*. This novel is notable for being the first to be set wholly in the real world, with only the most subtly introduced supernatural element; but it nonetheless presents the victory of Nature, fantasy, beauty, and paganism that we have seen as the dominant motif in all Dunsany's work. And in a wholly different way from *The King of*

Elfland's Daughter, *The Blessing of Pan* contains some of the most well-modulated and expressive prose Dunsany ever wrote.

Elderick Anwrel, a vicar in the small English community of Wolding, is increasingly disturbed by a haunting tune he hears on a nearby hill, on the top of which is a megalithic site called the Old Stones of Wolding. The tune, played by a young boy, Tommy Duffin, from some reeds he took from a marsh, seems to be exercising some unwholesome influence: first all the young women of the town, then all the young men, are compelled to follow Tommy up to the hill and dance around the Old Stones. Finally all the inhabitants of Wolding become entranced by this tune—even, at long last, Anwrel's own wife, Augusta. Anwrel seeks help from the bishop and others in the church hierarchy, but they provide no assistance at all, having no conception of the gravity of the situation. Finally, being unable to hold out any longer, Anwrel himself goes to join the citizens on the hill, performing a pagan sacrifice and leading the community into a repudiation of modern life.

The quiet but cumulative intensity of this novel makes it unique in Dunsany's work. In a sense it could be read as a sort of reworking, perhaps even a subtilization, of *The King of Elfland's Daughter*: the place of Erl is now occupied by Wolding, while the tune is all that is left of Elfland. Once again it is important to Dunsany's purpose that Wolding, and Anwrel himself, be depicted as close to Nature. The very opening image—Anwrel pondering the idle buzzing of a blowfly—is symbolic of his ties to the natural world. Unlike the Freer, Anwrel is an intimate part of his community: "His daily, week-day work may be said to have been concerned with all the times of intensity that his neighbours knew; not only when they mourned or when they wed, but when the cricket-team won a notable local match or when they were badly beaten" (BP 31).

That community itself, adhering to the old ways and having not yet succumbed to mechanization, represents a relatively benign triumph of civilization over Nature. In a final plea from the pulpit, Anwrel seeks to draw his congregation back to the simple life they are abandoning:

And he spoke to them of their own gardens, of lanes they knew and the hedges all white at the end of May, the wild rose in the midst of the year, then the hazel nuts on the uplands, and the journey that the stream made all the while, going quietly on through Wolding like the ages, the stream on whose banks the white-haired farmers there had all sat once on a time angling for minnows. (BP 226)

Gardens, lanes, hedges—these seem to be the mildest human inroads upon untamed Nature, but they are enough to drive the community to the unadulterated Nature represented by the tune and the Old Stones. It was, indeed, inevitable that Pan (in the figure of Arthur Davidson, Anwrel's predecessor, who planted the seeds of Pan's victory) should have chosen Wolding as the site of his return, for Wolding had held out against the machine age longer than others. Anwrel, bitterly wondering why his community has been singled out for this recrudescence of paganism, fails to take note of this fact:

For he gave no thought to a factory here, a factory there, and a whole new town in the next place; and villas going up on hill-side after hill-side, arising out of no feeling in any human mind and reflecting no feeling back, brief monuments to pretentiousness, that would be down in two hundred years; and everywhere machinery with teeth and claws of steel getting its grip on the earth, that had belonged but a while ago to Man and his poor relations. There were not so many valleys, after all, that were unspoiled like this one. (BP 218–29)

The tune, which is first described as "piercing the air like a moonbeam" (BP 2), is the essence of the pagan and the natural:

[Anwrel] wondered how the tune affected others; whether the strangeness that seemed to have come over the parish before he came there absorbed it and made it seem natural; whether minds a little coarser than his were less easily swept afar by it, or whether the plainer minds being closer to natural, even to pagan, things responded to the marvel of that enchantment with an abandonment unknown even to him. (BP 25–26)

And yet, the tune does more than affect the emotions: there is some great mystery for which it seems to provide the explanation. Tommy Duffin, feeling the call of the hill, felt that "there all his puzzles might be explained, by the sudden discovery of some purpose that none seemed to know in the village" (BP 37). He makes the reed pipe and begins to play on it; and the tune "was the answer to all things" (BP 41). What is that answer?

What those clear notes said to him he could never put into words; perhaps no man could. But while the music thrilled from his pipes, and while the echoes haunted the air, all his longings were gathered in peace before one enormous answer, and nothing seemed strange or perplexed him any more, and all the mysteries over the ridges of hills seemed near and familiar and friendly, and he knew himself one of a fellowship to which the hush of the night, the deep of the woods, or mysteries bold in the moonlight or hidden by mist, reported all their secrets. (BP 48)

This sort of mystic pantheism—reminiscent of Algernon Blackwood or Arthur Machen—is relatively unusual for Dunsany; and yet, this is perhaps the prototypical passage embodying his central theme of unification with Nature.

Tommy himself is a scarcely conscious participant in this entire scenario, and it is made clear that some great force is using him to effect the townspeople's repudiation of civilization. At one point he takes his boots off, because "[s]omehow in his bare feet he felt a little closer to that mystery of which the pipes were the clue" (BP 50). The tune itself makes all the tokens of civilization—small talk, card games, parlor ornaments—seem "trivial" and "pointless" (BP 53).

The conversion of the townsfolk to the pagan tune is handled with great subtlety and dramatic tensity. The young women of Wolding are the first to be affected, following Tommy up the hill "almost as wild things might" (BP 5). Later the young men of the town, initially hostile to Tommy, make quasi-military plans to destroy the pipes, but Tommy overcomes them: "And then he played a tune that was utterly new to him, and strode away up the hill. They [the young men] looked to each other to ask if they should follow: none gave the word, none spoke. All followed. It was not strange that they followed; for the new tune that Tommy Duffin was playing was the march of the things of the wild" (BP 111). The older inhabitants, in whom the habits of civilization are most ingrained, are the last to go, but in the end they go too. A farmer fails to gather his hay; the postman ceases to deliver mail; Anwrel's maid does not clean the coffeepot; and in one striking scene Mrs. Duffin, the schoolteacher, is overheard by Anwrel giving a lesson that sounds as if she is saying, "Egg, oh, pan, pan, tone, tone, lofone, R. K. D.," but in fact she is teaching the children the Greek line *ego Pan panton ton lophon Arkadiou basileus* ("I, Pan, the king of all the Arcadian slopes"; BP 215).

Anwrel's wife, Augusta, holds out the longest. On one occasion, when Anwrel returns home, he finds Augusta reading (BP 135)—the epitome of civilized life. After Anwrel's great final plea from the pulpit, all the townsfolk leave the church when they hear Tommy's tune; Augusta is the last, but finally she goes too. Returning home later, she apologizes ("But she was not apologising for anything she had done. . . . She was only sorry for him" [BP 251]) and adds poignantly, "I stayed till you finished" (BP 251).

Anwrel is, indeed, the focal point of the entire novel, and all the events are seen through his eyes. Dunsany's portrayal of him is sympathetic, perhaps to a fault; we are meant to empathize with his earnest concerns about the triumph of paganism over his brand of mild, benevolent

Christianity, but we can sense that Dunsany's true sympathies are on the other side. And yet, Anwrel's anguish at being rebuffed at every turn in his quest for help is searing:

Why not go too? Why not go over the hill to the grey old stones, and hear that golden music beat against their ancient silence? There would be no perplexities amongst their calm, no weariness in the hold of that splendid music. Why not go too?

Yet if he went, who would stay? What would be left if he went? And in the end duty held him.

When that was decided the tune had gone over the hill; and an old man stood alone, a little weary, very cold, and in tears. (BP 129)

Those who find this a little sentimental cannot rightly criticize Dunsany for failing to involve human emotions.

Anwrel's final yielding to paganism is anticipated ingeniously. He has a collection of eoliths and palaeoliths, which he gathers as a harmless amusement (BP 72). It requires little knowledge of etymology to realize that "palaeolith" is Greek for "old stone"; but what relation is there to the megaliths on the hill? Anwrel has classified his palaeoliths: "every one [was] numbered on a little square piece of sticking-paper, and a note-book with date and place against every number" (BP 201). He is striving by means of science and rationalism to impose control and order upon these tokens of a primitive past; but the attempt is fruitless, for when he does give up the battle and agree to lead the final ritual on the hill, he fashions the largest of his palaeoliths into a crude but powerful axe and uses it to sacrifice a bull.

If Anwrel is not exactly the hero of the novel, he is by no means its villain either; if there are villains, they are the members of the church establishment who fail to comprehend the situation and cannot be bothered to lend assistance. At the outset Anwrel has hopes that the bishop might give valuable advice; he is, after all, a "man of the world" (BP 10). This is in fact a pun, for the bishop is simply a man of our (civilized) world who has no cognizance of the pagan, natural world revealed by the pipes. He may know London and the Athenaeum Club (BP 26), but this knowledge is useless against the primeval knowledge of the tune. All the bishop can do is urge Anwrel to take a holiday. Anwrel does so, but comes back to find nothing changed. Later it occurs to him to query his replacement, a noted scholar, to see if he saw or heard anything odd during his stay. But the man heard nothing (BP 149): he is deaf to the spiritual hopes and fears of the people.

The only help Anwrel can find comes from an apparent madman whom he encounters by chance, a man named Perkin. Perkin gives him some peculiar advice: "'Keep your illusions, man; keep your illusions'" (BP 173). Christianity is Anwrel's illusion, but he knows that maintaining it requires a communal effort, and it is exactly that effort which is breaking down. Toward the end Perkin comes to Anwrel:

"But what shall I do? What shall I do?" cried Anwrel.

"Why, what does one need but illusions?" answered Perkin.

"They're gone. I've lost them," said the vicar. "One can't hold them all alone." He spread his hands to the emptiness of his room. "I've none to help me now."

"Plenty of friends over there," said Perkin, pointing to Wold Hill. "Plenty of illusions."

"But," gasped Anwrel, "but they're the enemy's!"

"They're yours if you want them," said Perkin. (BP 250)

Much earlier Perkin had remarked, in response to Anwrel's horror at yielding to the pipes of Pan, "'[W]hy, Pan was always friendly to Man'" (BP 175): human beings and Nature were always meant to be in harmony. This is, indeed, the final message of *The Blessing of Pan*, as Dunsany makes perhaps a little too clear when he notes how Wolding, now wholly converted to paganism, is consciously rejecting modern civilization:

Tommy Duffin's curious music that lured one away from the present, and that then seemed to wake up old memories that nobody guessed were there, seems to have come at a time when something sleeping within us first guessed that the way by which we were then progressing t'wards the noise of machinery and the clamour of sellers, amidst which we live today, was a wearying way, and they turned from it. And turning from it they turned away from the folk that were beginning to live as we do. (BP 274)

The Blessing of Pan is remarkable in Dunsany's work for being a tightly knit fabric of symbols; every action, every utterance is symbolic of some aspect of the conflict between paganism and Christianity, Nature and civilization, that is at the heart of the novel. It contains some of his most careful, heartfelt writing, and it quietly builds to a powerful and cataclysmic conclusion with the sacrifice on the hill, an event as rich with awe and wonder as anything in his earlier work. Its single-minded focus on Anwrel, whose torment and despair grow as he struggles vainly to defend his values, makes it as delicate a character study as any of his plays. And the extreme tenuousness of its supernatural phenomena—the magical power of the tune, the suggestion (rather implausible and even a little ridiculous) that Davidson was some sort of faun or satyr, or even Pan himself—paves the way for *The Curse of the Wise Woman* and Dunsany's later renunciation of fantasy. *The Blessing of Pan* has been curiously ignored even by Dunsany's advocates, but it is a focal novel in his entire output.

All four novels discussed here can be counted relative successes, guardedly in the case of *The Chronicles of Rodriguez* and *The Charwoman's Shadow* and unreservedly in the case of *The King of Elfland's Daughter* and *The Blessing of Pan*. With the exception of the first, which tends to meander and has some inessential episodes, these works are fully novelistic in conception and in richness of character development, but only the last has a genuinely powerful and satisfying climax; in the others the resolution of the central conflict occurs perhaps a little too easily and without sufficient emotional preparation. And yet, all the novels contain fine writing and moments of great emotive and imagistic power, and no one need regret Dunsany's virtual abandonment of short-story writing in this period. If these four novels in varying ways emphasize unification with Nature, they do so very differently from works of this and a slightly later period; for all these works conclude with a symbolic harmony between human beings and Nature, something Dunsany felt to be increasingly unlikely as the juggernaut of industrial civilization continued on its relentless course. In subsequent tales, plays, and novels the growing alienation of human beings from the natural world comes to the forefront, and it is these works of Dunsany's middle and later period that we will now study.

NOTES

1. Darrell Schweitzer, *Pathways to Elfland* (Philadelphia: Owlswick Press, 1989), 66.
2. *Times* (London) No. 42,637 (5 February 1921): 8.
3. Rebecca West, *Time and Tide* 2, No. 23 (10 June 1921): 554.
4. Schweitzer, p. 84.
5. C. N. Manlove, *The Impulse of Fantasy Literature* (Kent, OH: Kent State University Press, 1983), 134. Vernon Hyles, parroting Manlove, ventures still further into fatuity by noting that Dunsany's works "are beautiful and moving, but they do not move us deeply as do Tolkien's because they do not face evil and pain, central Christian issues for Tolkien as well as [C. S.] Lewis" ("Lord Dunsany: The Geography of the Gods," in *More Real Than Reality: The Fantastic in Irish Literature and the Arts*, ed. Donald E. Morse and Csilla Bertha [Westport, CT: Greenwood Press, 1991], 221). I hardly imagine

that Dunsany ought to be held responsible for failing to deal with moral issues in a suitably Christian way, since by all accounts he was not a Christian; and Hyles's earlier remark that Tolkien's durability is vindicated by the existence of "Saturday morning television cartoons" based upon his work had, I think, best be passsed over in merciful silence. My admiration for Tolkien's work is high, but cartoons are not going to convince me of its substance.

4

The Nonhuman Perspective

A shift of focus occurs in Dunsany's Nature theme during the late teens, a shift caused either by or a consequence of his gradual renunciation of pure fantasy as the foundation of his work. Whereas, in the early tales, an imaginary realm and its denizens served as symbols for human renunification with Nature, works of Dunsany's middle period, set wholly in a recognizable "real" world, underscore the Nature theme by what might be called "the nonhuman perspective." Specifically, this refers to a mode of narration—in novels, stories, and plays alike—that compels us to look at the world from the point of view of an animal or other nonhuman entity, such creatures being always more in harmony with the natural order than civilized human beings. This development is, in a sense, an outgrowth of the antihumanism of Dunsany's earlier "cosmic" perspective, whereby the value and importance of human achievements were devalued in light of the relative insignificance of human beings in the cosmic framework. With this framework, as well as imaginary-world fantasy, now largely abandoned, Dunsany's antihumanism takes the form of a stark contrast between the artificiality of human civilization and the "naturalness" of the rest of creation. Accordingly, there develops in the works of this period an increasing polarization between human beings and Nature, as if Dunsany is coming to realize that industrial civilization has progressed so far that a sloughing off of our dependence on machines is now beyond any hope of fulfillment.

This subtheme is commenced, somewhat flippantly, in an early essay or prose-poem, "From the Mouse's Point of View" (1911). This brief piece does little save to show us the world from the perspective of a mouse, as it contemplates the huge house within which it roams and the terrifying and ever-present danger of the cat: "Let us picture a tiger thrice the size of an elephant yet with feet so padded, so soft, that were he to come upon you in the daylight, which he does not, he would come no noiser than his shadow." This essay is, of course, anomalously early, coming in the midst of Dunsany's imaginary-world period, so that it is not surprising that the trope was not developed for several more years.

The first significant contribution occurs in the rare play *The Old Folk of the Centuries*, written in 1918 but not published until 1930. It does not appear as if this play has ever been performed, probably because of the difficulty in staging some of its supernatural phenomena; it is, in any event, a relatively slight work. A dithering scientist, Sir Joseph Wundle, has come upon a species of butterfly that is entirely new to him. A little girl, Pansy Simpkins, thinks that it may be a human being—perhaps a prince—upon whom some witch has cast a spell; and she knows that the way to restore the prince to his true form is to talk to him as if he were a prince. Sir Joseph and Pansy attempt to do this, but nothing happens; losing patience, Pansy cries out angrily to the butterfly: "I believe you are a nasty, dirty, vulgar little boy" (OF 22). Instantly the butterfly turns into a boy, "with bits of the green cage crammed on to his head and pieces of it on his shoulders" (OF 22).

The boy tells the story of how he was wandering in a nearby forest—Golden Wood, which has the reputation of being inhabited by a witch—and eating the apples that grow in abundance there. Some old lady comes to him and says he is eating the apples of the Old Folk of the Centuries and promptly turns him into a butterfly. He is grateful to be a boy again, although he rather liked being a butterfly; but when Mrs. Tweedle, Sir Joseph's maid, sees him, she insists that he must be sent off to school—specifically "Messrs. Birchem, Crammem and Wurriam; Birch Grove, Canington, London" (OF 34). The boy doesn't like the school at all and eventually flees; he goes back to Golden Wood and makes the witch turn him into a butterfly again. Pansy, who has grown fond of him, persuades the witch to transform her also, and the two butterflies go fluttering off together.

This is not, as I say, much of a play, but some touches are uncommonly fine. The portrayals of the bumbling Sir Joseph and the ignorant and insensitive Mrs. Tweedle are full of clever strokes, although the caricature of a grammar school is a little too broad to be effective. The importance of the play comes in its expression of two critical topoi to which Dunsany returns time and again in his works dealing with the nonhuman perspective: first, that animals live a life of natural comfort because of their harmony with their surroundings; and second, that animals have perceptions and sensations different from, and perhaps finer than or superior to, those of human beings.

The little boy describes his first transformation:

She stamps her foot and says two dreadful words at me. Dreadful they was, and biff,—I was flapping about in the air, a bloomin' great butterfly . . . but it was jolly. Up over the trees I went, and the whole of the top of the wood was down beneath me. And I danced about on the air and enjoyed myself some. And I danced all day. And night comes and the stars pops out, bigger nor ever you'd think. And I finds a warm place in some moss on a tree, and I sits down in it and begins to go to sleep. . . . And when the sun gets high next mornin' up I gets too. Whew! it seems to lift you. When the air gets warm you can sit on it, without no effort you can; when it's cold it lets you down some'ow. (OF 25)

"Without no effort"—this could be the boy's motto for his entire life as a butterfly, and no doubt that animal was chosen by Dunsany as an emblem for the carefree, uncomplicated, effortless life of the animal world in contrast to countless burdens of human life in the industrial age.

Later the boy attempts to describe to his schoolmates some of his sensations as a butterfly; he has difficulty in doing so, not so much because he is an ill-educated Cockney but because the phenomena described are not within the range of human sense perception. As a butterfly, for example, the boy can hear a wood singing:

Kind of a—kind of like a nurse singing, singin' soft you know, like when they've got a kid. All the leaves singing like. Bit of a breeze comes, not what you'd notice much, but to a butterfly it's like wot 'ud start ships on their journey, wot 'ad sails. Bit of a breeze comes, and every leaf turns a bit and makes a sort of sigh, very faint, wot *you* wouldn't notice. All doing it together, like, they sort of makes a song. (OF 43–44)

No, we human beings wouldn't notice: our senses are too coarse.

It was a brilliant device to narrate these anomalous sensations through the crude patois of a boy who had previously known nothing but the streets of London, so that the greatest possible contrast could be provided between his previous existence and his new life as the natural inhabitant of an ancient wood. The device is scarcely less effective when adapted to the gruff language of a retired officer in *The Strange Journeys of Colonel Polders* (1950).

Lord Adrian (written in 1922–23 but not published until 1933) exhibits a more antagonistic view of the relation between human beings and animals: they are now seen to be actively hostile to each other and even to be plotting each other's extermination. The play appears to begin as a social satire, as the aging Duke of Fenland and Arden expresses great disapprobation at his grandson Lord Sandborough's breaking off of his engagement with Bessie Branson; the duke wants to disown him, but realizes that under his father's will he cannot leave his property to anyone but a direct descendant. He then stumbles upon an advertisement for "a surgeon who makes people young again by grafting a gland of an ape" (GHL 292). He is initially incredulous, and thinks it "horrible" that any "animal quality" (GHL 293–94) might be passed on to him by means of such an operation; but he gradually warms to the idea as a means of providing an unobjectionable heir to whom to leave his estate. He marries Bessie himself and begets a son, Lord Adrian.

It is at this point that the play lapses woefully. The premise is ingenious, but the execution is crude and obvious to the point of caricature. Adrian, although entirely human-looking, develops a fierce loyalty to the animal world in opposition to humanity, uttering such self-important pomposities as "Everything we own is built up on the slavery and slaughter of animals" (GHL 320), "I don't love man" (GHL 326), and "I regard the domination of all life by man as the greatest evil that ever befell the earth" (GHL 336). There is only a single sharp satiric stroke, when Adrian is fervently expounding on his devotion to animals and his sweetheart, Nellie, replies with fatuous conventionality, "I'm awfully fond of animals too" (GHL 321). But it is not enough to save this play, easily the worst of Dunsany's major dramatic works. Adrian is killed as he is trying to teach the animals in the nearby wood the secret of fire, since he knows that this is what gave human beings their domination over the rest of creation.

Vastly superior is *The Use of Man*, which similarly stresses the entire animal kingdom's hostility to the human species. Dunsany has taken a lackluster story of 1931 and turned it into a scintillating little play, one that must have been highly effective when read over BBC radio in 1933. We are invited to the mansion of Lord Gorse at Bowton Grange, "in the middle of the hunting season" (PEA 51). Lord Gorse is complaining that his horse nearly fell because of a patch of earth upturned by a badger: "I'd kill every badger in the whole country" (PEA 51). What, after all, is the use of badgers? Indeed, it seems as if—from the human perspective—very few animals are of much use. Exceptions are, of course, made for horses, cows, pigs, poultry, and dogs—and the heads of stags look very nice on one's walls, and elephants provide ivory. But what of crows, or rabbits, or—perhaps worst of all—mosquitoes? "Can't think what he was ever invented for" (PEA 56).

The party retires. Mr. Pelby, the master of foxhounds, is roused in the night by what seems to be a spirit, who commands Pelby to follow him to a congregation of the spirits of animals in the depths of space. The spirit asks him peremptorily: "What is the use of man?" (PEA 58). Pelby, who—unfortunately for our species—"[doesn't] *do* a great deal of thinking" (PEA 59), finds it a little hard to supply much of a rationale. He cites cities, roads, harbors, and the like, but the spirit pointedly notes: "That is only for man" (PEA 59). How can man justify his existence in the context of the rest of creation? Perhaps one of the spirits of animals will speak up for him.

The dog does so promptly, but his remarks are so servile and unreflective that they do not count for much: "He is man: that is enough. More is not needed. More could not be needed. All wisdom is in him. All his acts are just; terrible sometimes, but always just. No use can be asked of him, only to be man. Man he is. He is man. The supreme perfection of which life is capable. Man! Man! Man!" (PEA 59). This sort of brainless sycophancy, reiterated throughout the play, does not carry much weight with the other spirits, who have not profited as the dog has from man's rulership of the earth. Some animal other than the dog must explain the use of man, else the presiding spirit will destroy the entire human race. What of the crow? He doesn't like man's guns. Bears are locked up in zoos. The mouse doesn't like man's traps. The self-centered cat seems to have had a nice time in man's houses, but was so offended that the mouse was asked her opinion first that she refuses to speak for man. What of the horse, cow, and pig? Here are animals that will surely defend man, but the horse merely titters stupidly, the cow stares into space, and the pig claims that he does not like being closed up in pens. Birds hate man's cages. In an echo of the "Prayer of the Flowers" theme, the animals, seeing that no one will come to man's assistance, look forward to his extinction from the planet (PEA 60). Finally, at the last moment, the mosquito speaks for man—he is its food (PEA 71).

It is precisely because this play is meant to appeal only to the aural, not the visual, imagination that it is a success. The actual spectacle, on a stage, of a congregation of animal spirits in space might appear even more ridiculous than the lumbering presence of one of Dunsany's gods or idols from his early plays; but in adapting his tale to the medium of radio Dunsany could play off stereotypical conceptions of animals for comic effect. Hence the elephant is introduced as "the large gentleman in the frock coat" (PEA 62), the mouse is "that lady who has . . . run so quietly to her place" (PEA 63), the horse is "that silly fellow that's always surprised when anyone moves" (PEA 66), and so on. Pelby himself is a rather silly fellow, one singularly ill-equipped for the unenviable task of defending the use of man among a gathering of creatures who have only been used by him.

A number of stories, early and late, emphasize the nonhuman perspective without adding much to the overall conception; but they are clever tales nonetheless. In "Ardor Canis" a man has been injected with a secretion from the brain of a dog as a cure for his listlessness; he immediately begins acting like a dog, rushing about with unseemly enthusiasm at every moment. This tale is largely a social satire on the conventional reticences required of "dignified" behavior, but much is also made of the fact that the man's sensations and emotions are now keener and less inhibited than a human being's:

Then Tabbener-Worbly went into the reading-room and ran, or at any rate moved with a very unnecessary display of energy, to an arm-chair in front of the fireplace, and sat gazing into the fire with the most absurd delight. The beauty of it seemed absolutely to enthral him. And I daresay that the fire is a beautiful thing. In fact, it certainly is, but we are brought up for some reason or other to conceal our feelings to some extent, even when we are especially delighted with something; and our habit of not noticing things very much, perhaps rather limits the number of occasions on which we are so delighted. (MAP 207)

"A Witch in the Balkans" (1951) is the amusing but insubstantial tale of a man who has been turned into a cat by a witch and his ultimately successful attempt to escape from this peculiar predicament. Then there is "As It Seems to the Blackbird" (1951), in which a scientist has devised a means of transferring the thoughts of a blackbird into the mind of a man, and vice versa. As with *The Old Folk of the Centuries* (and also *The Strange Journeys of Colonel Polders*, as we shall see later), the result is a nearly ineffable perception of the glories of the natural world, here expressed through the metaphor of music:

And all the great trees were singing their solemn song to the dawn, with low murmur of deep voices, and every one of their leaves which had only lately emerged into a world that was new to them, so that there was a touch of wonder in all their songs, a wonder of which I have only words to tell but which music can make so clear, the art that seems to begin where the art of words has ended.

A trilogy of works—the play *Mr. Faithful* [1922], the short novel *My Talks with Dean Spanley* (1936), and the novel *Rory and Bran* (1936)—

probes the relationship between human beings and dogs, largely in a comic manner. Dunsany was, of course, a great lover of dogs—they were invaluable on his hunting expeditions, especially in Ireland—and late in life he wrote a very touching essay, "Tales about Dogs" (1951), on the dogs he had owned over the years and the distinctive personalities of each of them. When he came to write about dogs, therefore, he knew his territory. A useful place to begin this discussion is an exquisite short story, "The Cut" (1936). Here a man teaches a dog tricks of increasing complexity; in particular, he places a penny in the dog's mouth and has him fetch the newspaper from a local newsagent, causing the dog to gain an inkling of the value of money. The dog puts this knowledge to use, leaving his owner and selling himself to another man, who gives him five pounds for himself. With this money the dog begins to buy clothes, first a collar—not a dog collar, but a starched one (MAP 150)—then a full suit with walking stick. The inevitable occurs: the dog starts "giving himself airs" (MAP 152), and when he passes a man with no collar, he cuts him: ". . . no one that has not seen a man being cut by a dog can perhaps quite appreciate the sickening drop that that is to one's self-esteem" (MAP 153). While this tale, like "Ardor Canis," is fundamentally a satire on the artificiality of social etiquette, it also suggests that distinctions between humans and animals in civilized society are also similarly rooted in inessentialities.

This theme is, in part, the foundation for *Rory and Bran*. It might be thought that this is nothing more than a novel-length joke—the joke being that Bran, although a dog, is never described as such and might be taken by many readers to be simply a rather silent human companion to Rory O'Cullen as he takes twelve cattle to the county fair. Dunsany himself relished the joke, remarking: "I did not state what Bran was, because I considered it unnecessary: every act of Bran throughout the book was, so far as I have been able to observe, what one in his place would have done" (SiW 32). This is, of course, entirely disingenuous, and Dunsany knows it; he can't resist adding: ". . . not all readers seemed quite agreed about Bran, and one of them complained that he was *rather* silent for an Irishman" (SiW 32). This remark was evidently made in a review, although I have not found it; the joke may be on Dunsany, for the reviewer was perhaps noting obliquely that he saw through the ploy. Of the four British reviews I have seen (the American reviews don't count, since the dust jacket depicted a boy and a dog on the cover, thereby ruining the joke), three—the *Times* of London (October 16, 1936), the *Times Literary Supplement* (October 17, 1936), and the *London Mercury* (November 1936)—were clearly aware that Bran was a dog, while the fourth—by

J. D. Beresford in the *Manchester Guardian* of October 16, 1936—was neutral on the subject: "So they [the parents] sent Bran with him [Rory]."

There are, of course, more serious things going on in *Rory and Bran* than concealing the identity of a dog. Dunsany considered it "unnecessary" to reveal that Bran was a dog because he, even more than Rory, is a natural component of the Irish landscape. One passage at the very beginning emphasizes this point ingeniously: Rory asks Bran what time it is, and "Bran took no notice" (RB 13)—an action that simultaneously fosters the deception of the reader as to Bran's identity and underscores his greater closeness to Nature, for Rory learns from Bran's silence that "the time of day is not one of the essential matters" (RB 13) of life. A later passage noting that Bran takes no interest in gold (RB 30) is of similar import.

And yet, it is hard to deny that some of Dunsany's contortions in concealing Bran's canine status are labored and deceitful. A piquant character encountered by the pair along their journey, the O'Harrigan, refers to Bran as "that lad" (RB 40); shortly thereafter Bran makes his first and last utterance: "Oh-ho" (RB 42), evidently a yawn. On the other hand, other details all but reveal, sometimes through mere omission, the true status of Bran. At one point "Bran looked *up* to Rory full of understanding" (RB 112; my italics), something he would do only if he were very much shorter than his companion. Bran later becomes unusually interested in a tinker's dog (RB 116). Still later it is said that "the tinker and Rory had tea" (RB 227)—but not Bran. At the very end Dunsany finally lets the cat, as it were, out of the bag, although only by Rory's acknowledgment that Bran has fleas (RB 319). This novel is, of course, worth considering in greater detail for its Irish theme and for its delicate portrayal of the romantic dreamer Rory, and I shall do so in a later chapter.

Mr. Faithful might at first glance seem to be exactly contrary to *Rory and Bran*, but a more careful analysis reveals that it emphasizes the same point—a dog's closeness to Nature—from a different perspective. This play, among the best of his comedies, presents another of Dunsany's magnificently preposterous premises. A young man, Captain Dick Johnson, has had trouble getting a job after the war; in order to win Sir Jonas Grapt's approval to marry his daughter Betty, he must hold a bona fide job for at least six months, simply to show that he can do so. At his wit's end, he answers an ad placed by Sir Walter Wample: he will be Sir Walter's watchdog. After all, he is a man, and he is tired of seeing "these damned dogs going about in comfort doing a job that I could do better" (MF 26).

It might be thought from this premise that Dunsany is simultaneously negating that unity with Nature which both Rory and Bran achieved and subverting his entire nonhuman perspective by presenting the grotesque and humiliating spectacle of a man reduced to impersonating a dog. In fact, an opposite conclusion could be reached: while the scenario allows for predictable puns (Johnson says, "I was ready to live a dog's life for six months if they'd let me" [MF 17]; he insists on having a *white* dog collar [MF 44]), the brutal truth is that Johnson *cannot* perform a dog's function better than a dog: his actions (chasing cats up trees, biting a man who is trying to swindle Sir Walter, howling at the moon) are absurd not because of their apparent degradation of human dignity but because a human being is performing actions that are wholly natural to dogs but not natural to humans.

The play is, like "The Cut," a social satire, and beneath the surface levity is an undercurrent of incredible bitterness and cynicism regarding the postwar world of narrowed job opportunities. When Johnson is told that he must, like a normal dog, live in a barrel lined with straw, he thinks nothing of it: "*I've* lived in a *trench*" (MF 28). Indeed, as Sir Walter gradually overcomes his incredulity at Johnson's proposal and realizes that Johnson is serious, he thinks Johnson may be suffering from shell-shock (MF 26). But there are too many delightful comic moments to allow us to pause very long over the socioeconomic significance of the play. And as with Dunsany's best dramas, *Mr. Faithful* presents a resolution at once startlingly unexpected and wholly satisfying.

My Talks with Dean Spanley, written just prior to *Rory and Bran*, is another of Dunsany's comic gems. Dunsany admits its humorous import in *The Sirens Wake*, mentioning that in the preface to the work "I put the solemnity that it usually amuses me to put into a preface, but the joke of this book required that the preface should be even especially solemn" (SiW 31). In this preface the narrator speaks of the "meticulous detail" of Dean Spanley's recollections of being a dog in a previous life as proof of their veracity; indeed, the narrator will "stake my reputation as a scientific writer" (MT 5) on it. All this recalls the owlish prefaces to Dunsany's Jorkens tales, where similar deadpan claims are made as to the contributions toward the advance of science represented by those accounts. Here the notion becomes an actual thread of the plot, as the narrator repeatedly plies the dean with Tokay (*in vino veritas*, and all that) to elicit this remarkable tale; and various points in the dean's story are held up as demonstrable proofs of the truth of reincarnation, as when the narrator, hearing of the dean in his dog state drinking foul water (" 'There is no such thing as bad water. . . . There is interesting water and uninteresting water'" [MT 40–41]), expresses disgust but states that "I decided that in the interests of science it was my duty to get all the facts I could" (MT 41). The mere fact that the dean would speak of all these matters, so undignified from the perspective of an elderly and respected cleric, is for the narrator the clinching argument that the tale in fact is true.

The title of this short novel seems to involve a double pun—a play not only on "spaniel" (actually mentioned at MT 31) but on Arthur Penrhyn Stanley (1815–1881), the celebrated Dean of Westminster. Beyond this, however, the tale reinforces many of those features by which, in *The Old Folk of the Centuries*, the life of animals is shown to be superior to that of human beings. The selection of a dog to bring this out is of some significance: if this most subservient and even sycophantic of animals can be seen to have virtues not granted to our species, still more might that be said of other creatures. In his dog state the dean always refers to his owners, and to human beings in general, as the "Wise Ones," the "Great Ones," and so on; and yet he is filled with a sort of dazed pity that human beings are so slow, that their sense of smell is so bad, and even that their sight is not as keen as his. But his is not to question, only to obey. Even in so small a matter as a tick, the dean states: "'The Wise Ones, the Masters, can get them out. Nobody else can'" (MT 48).

The wholly unreflective state of being a dog, the lack of any worrisome self-doubts or even self-consciousness, is emphasized by the simple statement, "'It is undoubtedly the most perfect form of enjoyment that can be known.'" He elaborates on the point: "'Where else shall we find those hourly opportunities for sport, romance and adventure, combined with a place on the rugs of the wisest and greatest? And then the boundless facilities for an ample social life. One has only to sniff at the wheel of a cart to have news of what is going on, sometimes as much as five miles away'" (MT 66). "There is no completer life than lying and watching the fire" (MT 97), the dean says later.

But of course the true charm of *My Talks with Dean Spanley* comes from its seemingly uncanny insights into the mind, emotions, and outlook of a dog. When the dean says that a rabbit is best to eat when it is "hot" (MT 19), he is of course not referring to its being cooked but to its being hot from being chased. He speaks with endless contempt of the habit of cats running up trees when they are chased: ". . . to see a four-footed animal in a tree is a sight so revolting and disgusting that I have no words in which to describe it" (MT 39). And the dean's "fatalistic attitude to a tick," cited earlier, assists appreciably in convincing the narrator that the entire account is true, since it is "so strangely different from the view that we take ourselves" (MT 48). In an entirely different way from *Rory and Bran*, this short novel is one long joke—but it is a joke once again directed at the reader, whom Dunsany dares to disbelieve him even though everyone knows the whole story is pure imagination.

The Strange Journeys of Colonel Polders (1950) might be called a sort of *editio maior* of *My Talks with Dean Spanley*, for here we are presented with a Hindu member of an exclusive English club who, insulted by Colonel Polders, casts a spell over him and compels him successively to inhabit the bodies of a vast array of animals. It is the summation of Dunsany's nonhuman perspective, and also one of the finest comic fantasies, or fantastic comedies, ever written. This novel's purpose is nothing less than the systematic display of the complete superiority in every respect of animal life over human life.

The first thing Dunsany wishes to establish is the perfect comfort and contentment of the animal world. As a fish Polders is " 'entirely content' " (SJ 12) as he glides along in the sea, where " 'the scenery is marvellous' " (SJ 13). In a later transformation Polders finds that he was " 'lying very comfortable in a good fur coat in a dim, but rather pleasant light' "; in fact he is a fox, and " 'I discovered that the little room which seemed so exactly suited to my needs was in reality nothing more than a hole in the ground' " (SJ 43). It is important for Dunsany to show that this comfort is a natural, instinctive result of a fox's very being, not a product of the cumbersome intellect:

Well, I lay there contemplating the beauty of the world; the air, the light, the damp earth, the whole feel of it. No, contemplating is not the right word. I did none of that. I just enjoyed it. And something more than that. I was a part of it all, if you understand me. No, certainly I did not contemplate. Do you know, I find contemplation, as we do it, rather fatiguing, compared with the immense comfort of just feeling it. (SJ 43–44)

When he becomes a cat, Polders reflects, " 'The cat may be called a specialist in the matter of comfort, probably the greatest student of it in the world' " (SJ 115).

In many other ways is animal life preferable to human life. As in *My Talks with Dean Spanley*, Dunsany stresses the superiority of animals' senses, particularly the sense of smell. As a dog Polders finds, " 'The street was full of smells' " (SJ 17); and, in spite of his adoration of his human master, he is filled with an overwhelming sorrow for his physical limitations: " 'For his inability to smell, which made it impossible for him to understand half of what was going on, and his slowness of movement, which prevented him from taking any part in it all, I had the most profound pity. And, as it appeared to me at the time, he was very hard of hearing. . . . And, about this, as about all his defects, I felt the very deepest sympathy'" (SJ 19). A dog feeling sorry for humans! How low can we sink? Later Polders even loses patience with the human race, expostulating when he is a butterfly, "'How blunt our senses are!'" (SJ 107).

But what of our great accomplishments in civilization—language, literature, great cities? One by one Dunsany demolishes them all, asserting that the animal world's achievements are fully equal to the human, or even superior. As a pig "'I found that I could express quite as much as I can now. I didn't merely say honk, as you people suppose. Every grunt had a different tone to it. Men may not have understood me. But that was not my fault'" (SJ 84). As for the song of the lark, "'I think no pen but Homer's would have been able to write it. Shakespeare's perhaps. But even he was born too late for that song'" (SJ 143). What of our houses as compared to that of a snail? "'They are as dull as the paths leading up to them'" (SJ 172).

As in *The Old Folk of the Centuries* and the later "As It Seems to the Blackbird," the incommunicability of animal perception is repeatedly stressed. If, in the earlier play, we thought that it was only the mental and linguistic limitations of an ignorant Cockney schoolboy that precluded our full comprehension of the psychology of animals, what are we to think when a well-educated colonel cries out in despair, "'How many things I cannot describe to you!'" (SJ 98)? This is both because the minds of animals are so alien to ours and also because our own minds and sensations are dull, heavy, and imperceptive: "'We are wonderfully ignorant of things that there are in the world'" (SJ 108).

Polders, like Gulliver, finds as a result of his occupation of animal bodies that he is developing an increasing hatred for the cruelty and savagery of human beings. *The Strange Journeys of Colonel Polders* is the summation of Dunsany's antihumanism, a tendency that we saw originating in his early work and one that is a constant undercurrent in all the tales of the nonhuman perspective. When, as a fish, he is caught and put in a tank, he gains a "'distaste for the human race'" (SJ 13). This sentiment increases with each successive incarnation, although he expresses it to the other club members with a certain awkwardness and embarrassment ("'We so seldom hear any criticism from any other race'" [SJ 70]). In a recrudescence of the "Prayer of the Flowers" theme, he learns of a prophecy held by Barbary sheep: "'And we had another prophecy too, very odd and curious. I don't know what it meant. It was that the Barbary sheep would outlast men, and come to the green fields again. For there was a memory among us of green fields long ago. I don't know who handed down the prophecy, or what it meant: mere conceit, I expect'" (SJ 103). But the camels have a similar prophecy, which "'foretold that camels would one day be free'" (SJ 153)—free, that is, of human control. Even the frogs believe they will outlast the human race (SJ 192).

Like all the tales of this type, *The Strange Journeys of Colonel Polders* is remarkable for its apparently unerring awareness of the mental and emotional states of animals. How perfectly Dunsany captures the unconscious self-centeredness of a cat when he finds the cook repeatedly preventing him from lapping a jug of cream: "'She can't have known what she was doing'" (SJ 118). As a swallow he finds that flies are delicious (SJ 38). And in one of the most stirring tableaux in the novel, Polders finds himself a fox that is chased in a fox hunt—"'There is,'" he concludes with dry understatement, "'no other experience exactly like it'" (SJ 76).

As humor this novel is scarcely surpassed in the entirety of Dunsany's work. We are first arrested by the bluntness with which Polders notes his various incarnations: "'To make a long story short, I became a fish'" (SJ 12); "'In fact I was a dog'" (SJ 15); "'I found that I was a fox'" (SJ 43); "'I was a pig'" (SJ 84); "'He made me a tiger'" (SJ 96); and on and on. Our credulity is then strained to the limit when Polders says that he became a djinn (SJ 163). "'But are there such things?'" says one listener. Why shouldn't there be? A fifth of the human race accepts the principle of transmigration of souls, and they also believe in djinns; if they are right about the one (and they appear to be, if Polders's account is believed), then they may be right about the other. But the comic pinnacle is reached when Polders, as a stag in the Scottish Highlands, is shot by a hunter; this creates an exceptionally anomalous situation at the club:

It was simply this: Chindery-Podson, a member of our club, had gone stalking in Scotland only last autumn, and had been talking to several of us about what he had got, and I now remembered that one of his heads was a royal. . . . But what if that head should have been the very one that was Colonel Polders? And what if he did what many sportsmen do, who are members of the Electors, and presented it to the club! Suppose then that the colonel recognized it? Am I wrong in saying that perhaps such a problem never confronted a man before? (SJ 131–32)

Polders's feelings must be taken into consideration: "'. . . I should like to ask my reader how he would feel, himself, sitting in a club under a wall on which other members had put up his own skull'" (SJ 132). But

Chindery-Podson is persuaded not to present the head to the club, and this extraordinary awkwardness is averted.

The imaginative vigor shown by Dunsany in *The Strange Journeys of Colonel Polders*, written when he was past seventy, is a remarkable testament to a fifty-year writing career that exhibited one triumph after another. His last two undistinguished novels, *The Last Revolution* (1951) and *His Fellow Men* (1952), must be forgiven and forgotten, for the *Strange Journeys* not only culminates his tales of the nonhuman perspective but brings to a close a thirty-year span of novel writing that began so tentatively with *The Chronicles of Rodriguez*. The novel may seem formless, but its kaleidoscopic display of successive animal incarnations, each designed for maximum contrast with its predecessor, is all the structure a work of this sort requires. It is one of the lost masterpieces of weird fiction.

An entirely separate series of works that may be studied here focuses specifically on human alienation from Nature as a result of industrialization. Two brilliant plays, *Cheezo* [1917] and *The Evil Kettle* (1925), belong to this class, and they are among the strongest of Dunsany's more obviously didactic works. We have already noted his general opposition to overt didacticism, but he himself made an exception in the case of *Cheezo* when he remarked in the preface to the American edition of *Plays of Near and Far*: " 'Cheezo' is a play of Right and Wrong, and Wrong triumphs. Were not this particular wrong triumphing at this particular date I should not have thought it a duty to attack it, and were it easily defeated it would not have been worth attacking" (PNF v).

The wrong, of course, is adulterated food, augmented and encouraged by false advertising. It is a very modern theme, and this play ought to be looked upon with favor by the nutritionist and environmentalist movement. The play interweaves two threads in such a way that both achieve their denouements simultaneously, one as a result of the other. The first thread is the attempt by Sladder, "a successful man" (PNF 108), to market a synthetic replacement for cheese, which he has named Cheezo; the second thread is the attempt of a humble vicar, Charles Hippanthigh, to persuade Sladder to let him marry his daughter Ermyntrude. Sladder is disinclined to approve of the union because Hippanthigh does not appear to have a sufficient amount of spunk or drive: he has been a vicar for years, and his prospects for promotion are not good. The sticking point is his disagreement with the bishop over the matter of eternal punishment: Hippanthigh cannot conceive of such a thing, and his failure to yield on this issue has left him in his lowly state. But Hippanthigh and Ermyntrude are genuinely in love—so what are they to do?

It is here that the resolution of the first plot thread comes into play. In a devastating satire on advertising, Sladder and his publicity agent, Splurge, discuss marketing strategy over the new product, coming up with wildly exaggerated claims as to its miraculous nutritious capacities ("There is a hundred times more lactic fluid in an ounce of Cheezo than in a gallon of milk" [PNF 117]), crassly appealing to sentiment ("Cheezo makes darling baby grow" [PNF 117]) and even to the prurience of common people:

I've rather a nice little poster being done, sir. A boy and a girl looking at one another with a rather knowing look. There's a large query mark all over the girl's dress. Then over the top in big letters I've put: "What is the secret?" and in smaller letters: "I've got a bit of Cheezo." It makes people look at it, the children's faces are so wicked. (PNF 121)

Sladder knows that advertising is the key: "I'll rub their noses in it" (PNF 120). With such a massive and ubiquitous advertising campaign, the product is bound to be a success; after all, people "eat everything that's advertised" (PNF 126).

There is, unfortunately, one drawback. A sample of Cheezo has been fed to Ermyntrude's pet mice; at first they take to it readily enough, but later they are found dead. It seems a fatal setback to Sladder; but the crafty businessman is only momentarily defeated:

So they would beat Sladder, would they? They would beat Sladder. No, that has yet to be done. We'll go on, Splurge. The public shall eat Cheezo. It's a bit strong perhaps. We'll tone it down with bad nuts that they use for the other cheeses. We'll advertise it, and they'll eat it. See to it, Splurge. They don't beat Sladder. (PNF 163)

Hippanthigh hears this, and then says, "suddenly with clear emphasis": "I THINK I *DO* BELIEVE IN ETERNAL PUNISHMENT" (PNF 163).

Cheezo is the most vicious and unrestrained satire in Dunsany's entire corpus. The character of Sladder is as unrelenting a broadside against the "business mentality" as we are likely to find, and—as with such a later play as *The Raffle*—Sladder applies his business sense to all facets of life, remarking on Hippanthigh's disagreement with his bishop: "I don't care a damn about eternal punishment one way or the other. But a man who quarrels with the head of his firm's a fool. If his bishop's keen on hell he should push hell for all it's worth" (PNF 143). The portrayal of Splurge, the sycophantic toady who commends Sladder's every decision, is equally ruthless. Only in the character of Hippanthigh himself does *Cheezo* suffer: he is meant to be the one admirable figure in the play, but his moralistic priggishness sounds naive and at times even self-parodic; it is clear, however, that Dunsany intends him as the mouthpiece for his point of view and as the honorable foil for Sladder.

The Evil Kettle is a still more searching satire on the very foundations of industrialism, as Dunsany recounts the celebrated anecdote of James Watt's discovery of the power of steam. We are asked to envision the home of the young Watt in the early eighteenth century. As his mother boils a kettle of water for tea, he notices the lid lifting up and down, and his quick mind begins to work: "I've been thinking that if steam can do that it might move a rod, mightn't it? And the rod might move a wheel. . . . And if we could set wheels moving we could do all the work men have to do without ever using horses" (A 120). His mother is incredulous, but we all know that this is the origin of the industrial age.

Dunsany makes it clear, however, that Watt is not to be held accountable for the horrors that industrialism has brought in its wake. As the play opens he is looking out the window, and he remarks: "How lovely the hills are, mother" (A 117); and as he ponders the uses of steam power, he thinks, "All the work of the world would be done in the morning, and men could walk about the beautiful hills all the rest of the day" (A 121). Machinery has, in Watt's mind, the ability to liberate human beings from unceasing labor and to bring them sufficient leisure for the appreciation of natural beauty.

But Mrs. Watt's casual remark, in answer to one of her son's endless questions—"Satan just makes the ugly things" (A 119)—is the catalyst for the rest of the play. Satan suddenly appears to Watt, although his mother cannot see him; he shows him a world dominated by machines: "At the window Satan waves his left hand a few times upwards. Smoke as of factories rises up covering the entire landscape. The noise and clangour are heard of the twentieth century. The smoke lifts and a factory city appears in all its devilish ugliness" (A 122). The symbolism here is very obvious—steam = the smoke of factories = the fires of Hell—but it is made all the more hideous when Satan "slaps [Watt] on the back with cheerful encouragement" (A 122). Watt reels in horror, unable to believe that his simple idea of steam moving a wheel could lead to such a nightmare scenario. He falls ill, vowing repeatedly that he will never do what Satan wants him to do; but Satan casts a spell over him to make him forget what he has seen, and we know what the outcome of the play, and of history, will be.

The Evil Kettle is a little masterwork of fantastic drama, and displays how shrewdly and tellingly Dunsany can introduce the supernatural for aesthetic, moral, and political ends. The phantasmagoric image of Satan drawing back the curtains of the window to reveal the dark, Satanic mills of the eighteenth century's future—somewhat similar to the spectacle of World War I seen by Don Rodriguez in the house of the professor of magic—emphasizes, as no other dramatic effect could, the fatal historical consequence of the young Watt's seemingly innocent discovery, a discovery whose beneficent purpose has, for Dunsany, been perverted by the relentless advance of the machine age.

Dunsany was rarely as successful in later works in portraying the evils of industrialism as he was in *Cheezo* and *The Evil Kettle*. Several stories treat the idea in a somewhat lighter vein. "The Honorary Member" (MAP) tells of a very unusual new member of a club: it is Atlas, who has given up his task of holding up the world because it has grown too scientific. I am not sure that "The Policeman's Prophecy" (1930) should be discussed here, but it is such a delightful tale that I cannot forbear comment on it. Extrapolating from a policeman's remark to a reckless driver, "You'll kill yourself and everybody else" (MAP 93), Dunsany imagines what the world would be like with no people in it: Nature, of course, would rejoice, and all the animals would reclaim the territory they have lost from the dominance of the human race. This tale is not so much an attack on industrialism as a piquant expression of the "Prayer of the Flowers" theme: "What a noise we made! But it will all be forgotten" (MAP 95). In "The Traveller to Thundercliff" (1950) a man travels to the edge of Elfland to gain respite from the machine age: "there he rested, perhaps for an afternoon, perhaps for ages and ages"—a statement that makes us recall that time works differently in Elfland and in our world, and also that the imagination is similarly not under the rulership of clocks. Finally, the very late tale "The Ghost of the Valley" (1955) brings this entire topos to a fittingly poignant conclusion. A man meets a ghost in a rural valley; there is no horror in the encounter, only pathos as the ghost, who is "little more than a thousand years [old]" (GHL 92), tells of his imminent departure:

"Times are changing," it said. "The old firesides are altering, and they are poisoning the river, and the smoke of the cities is unwholesome, like your bread. I am going away among unicorns, griffins, and wyverns."

"But are there such things?" I asked.

"There used to be," it replied.

But I was growing impatient at being lectured to by a ghost, and was a little chilled by the mist.

"Are there such things as ghosts?" I asked then.
And a wind blew then, and the ghost was suddenly gone.
"We used to be," it sighed softly. (GHL 96)

This is a fine conceit: the departure of the creatures of the imagination is a potent metaphor for the loss of wonder and mystery in the industrial age.

The Last Revolution is Dunsany's most exhaustive treatment of the subject; but this tale of machines revolting against human control and attempting to gain rulership of the earth is crippled by ponderous moralizing, implausibility of plot and character development, and a simple failure to understand the complexity of the issues involved. We are asked to believe that an inventor, Ablard Pender, has suddenly and with little apparent effort devised a mechanical brain out of "quantities of wire, and little electric currents like what cause thought in our own brain and which stimulate nerves which move muscles" (LR 7), a conception that reveals a staggering lack of awareness of the scientific difficulties involved in artificial intelligence. But Dunsany, who even in his odd science-fiction tales (e.g., "Our Distant Cousins") never troubled himself about the plausibility of some new device or advance of science but was only concerned with the playing out of a scenario based upon it, merely wants to frighten us with the prospect of a world in which machines no longer obey our commands.

Pender encases the wire brain in a steel case and fashions an anomalous crablike body for the creature, endowing it with a hundred hands. Initially it seems merely a mechanical wonder, beating the narrator, Pender's friend, at chess (which leads him to believe that "I was facing a superior intelligence" [LR 19]) and running all sorts of useful errands around the property. It begins building copies of itself and is able to control them hypnotically with its mind. But trouble starts when the narrator notes that the machine is clearly jealous of Ablard's fondness for his girlfriend, Alicia, and eventually it manages telepathically to influence Alicia's motorbike such that the latter literally kidnaps her by driving her along at a hectic pace and refusing to obey her commands. By a tremendous effort she leaps off the bike and runs for shelter to the small cottage where Pender built the creature; here she, Pender, the narrator, and later a group of policemen find themselves besieged by the machine and its cohorts, and the bulk of the novel tells of their efforts at escape.

All this might have been an entertaining science-fiction adventure story if Dunsany did not pepper his narrative with labored ruminations like the following:

Would the time come when Man's cleverness would get ahead of him, when the inventions that it had created would be too much for their creator? Had it come already? Our civilization was getting more and more complicated before Pender's time; more and more machines upon which we all depended were understood by fewer and fewer, as their intricacies increased. And now Pender's invention. Was this the thing that was to dethrone us, as Zeus dethroned Chronos? (LR 31–32)

This sort of thing will not place Dunsany in the company of Max Weber. And yet, Dunsany is at least aware by now that machines have become an inextricable part of our civilization and that their elimination would cause more misery than it would alleviate:

For what is our civilization? It is something as intricately connected with machinery as an American cotton-plantation was once connected with slavery. To remove machinery from our civilization now would be an uprooting that would result in the starvation of millions. So what we had to defend against the machine was something of which the machine was a very large part. (LR 124–25)

In an irony that Dunsany may or may not have perceived, the combating of the domination of machines is itself aided by machines: trench mortars are brought in by farm carts. The surface reason given for this is that cars and other machinery, affected by the revolting machine's telepathic commands, are no longer obeying human beings, so that the army must revert to the tools of preindustrial agriculture; and no doubt Dunsany imagines that these farm carts are somehow emblematic of our continuing ties to Nature and hence our moral superiority to machines— but those trench mortars are still there. And yet, they turn out to be useless: in a conclusion that was very likely influenced by Wells's *War of the Worlds*, the machines perish not through the onslaughts of human weapons but through rust.

And a still more pervasive irony rests in the very actions of the machines: it is exactly at the point when they (somehow) gain human emotions—jealousy, anger, vengeance, resentment—that they become a danger to human beings. It is hardly worth remarking that Dunsany does not provide even the faintest plausible account of how wires and electricity could gain such emotions; he seems, more significantly, wholly unaware that this very link with humanity virtually negates the contrast between humans and machines that he is so keen to establish. In lamely denying that we ourselves are somehow the enemies of Nature because of our constant destruction of it—we are only Nature's "harsh master"

(LR 159)—Dunsany attempts to paint a foreboding picture of the rule of machines:

We and the tiger might be allies some day. Neither we nor the tiger blot out all life around us. But the machine, what would that spare? Sometimes we sing, and the birds sing; often we play; and the birds play, but the machine is without mirth as it is without pity. What hope for Earth if this revolution succeeded? It would be the worst and the last. (LR 159–60)

In all this Ablard Pender, like James Watt, is held relatively blameless; for not only are his motives noble—he too wishes merely "to give to the human race a leisure from which our civilization should be led to higher levels" (LR 43)—but the narrator realizes that someone else would have invented the artificial brain if Pender had not. Pender himself remarks: "Things have been shaping that way for a long time. Watt and Stevenson [*sic*] were at it long before me" (LR 85), establishing a more or less direct link with *The Evil Kettle*. It should be no surprise that, when the machines are subdued, Pender and Alicia wholly renounce machines and establish a farm in the country, doing all the work themselves with a simple plough and farm animals. And yet, the narrator is aware that the last revolution— last because "no race . . . that was ever superseded ever got back" (LR 121)—may still come: "These slaves of ours are not likely to be content to serve us any longer, when they are given the cunning that Pender gave them to use their enormous strength. There are machines that could easily crush a hundred men, if only they knew how to escape from obedience to the hand of a single man" (LR 184).

The Last Revolution is without question the worst of Dunsany's fantasy novels; as with *His Fellow Men* (1952), we feel his authorial hand guiding us at every turn, and it is too clear which side he is on. The battle against mechanization was one Dunsany had been conducting since the beginning of his career, but when he finally chose to confront it plainly instead of by metaphor and symbol, he failed utterly.

The works studied here are among the more solid novels, tales, and plays of Dunsany's middle period; and if the comic is prevalent in such works as *Mr. Faithful*, *My Talks with Dean Spanley*, *Rory and Bran*, *The Strange Journeys of Colonel Polders*, and others, there is sufficient tartness, and even bitterness, in *Cheezo* and *The Evil Kettle* to demonstrate how seriously Dunsany regarded the conflict of human beings and Nature, and what little hope he saw for its ultimate resolution. Humor continues to predominate in the Jorkens tales and those works of comic fantasy which we are about to study, but their increasingly sharper satiric edge underscores Dunsany's belief that our civilization has somehow gone astray, a belief he had encapsulated as early as "Romance and the Modern Stage" (1911): "I know of the boons that machinery has conferred on man, all tyrants have boons to confer, but service to the dynasty of steam and steel is a hard service and gives little leisure to fancy to flit from field to field."

5

Jorkens

Dunsany's canonical statement on Joseph Jorkens, the clubman whose tall tales fill five collections from 1931 to 1954, occurs in *While the Sirens Slept*, as he tells of his return from a hunting expedition in Africa.

It was from material gathered on this journey that on 29th and 30th March, 1925, I wrote a tale called *The Tale Of The Abu Laheeb*. There was in this tale more description of the upper reaches of the White Nile or of the Bahr el-Gazal than I have given here; indeed the whole setting of that fantastic story may be regarded as accurately true to life, though not the tale itself. I mention this short story and its date, because it was the first time that I told of the wanderings of a character that I called Jorkens. He was my reply to some earlier suggestion that I should write of my journeys after big game and, being still reluctant to do this, I had invented a drunken old man who, whenever he could cadge a drink at a club, told tales of his travels. When in addition to his other failings I made him a liar, I felt that at least there could be nothing boastful about my stories. (WSS 78)

This statement is full of interesting details, the most interesting of which is the blunt confession that Jorkens is a "liar": for it is exactly the secret of these tales' effectiveness that, however much they strain one's credulity, there is no single point at which they can be proven definitively false. This is what Kipling was referring to when he wrote to Dunsany about "Mrs. Jorkens," a tale of Jorkens marrying a mermaid: "For sheer 'cheek' the Mermaid yarn is the best. I am not thinking for the minute of anything except the audacity of it" (Am 227).

That Dunsany used the Jorkens tales as vehicles for writing not merely of his physical travels around the world but also of the sensations he derived from them is abundantly clear. It is perhaps the clearest instance of his renunciation of otherworldly fantasy—tales of peculiar adventures in fabulous but emphatically real corners of the world, corners Dunsany himself had visited and from which he now drew inspiration. Only someone who had been to the Sahara could have written the following: "Baked earth, he said, rather than sand, and sprinkled with little rocks, as though colossal spadefuls of gravel had been thrown at it from a far planet; and very occasional tufts of dwarfed bushes growing. The whole desert he described as being like a gravelled drive carelessly weeded, of infinite breadth and leading to nowhere" (TT 25). A lengthy description of Abu Simbul in "The Ivory Poacher" is prefaced by the following: "when I saw Abu Simbul I felt that whatever brought me there fulfilled some higher purpose than poaching ivory, for to have seen Abu Simbul is an event not only in a lifetime, but one that is worth waiting for through three or four lifetimes, if the guess that the Hindus make at what none of us knows should turn out to be right" (JH 317). In a late article, "Nine Wonders" (1950), Dunsany notes that Abu Simbul ought to be added to the seven wonders of the world (the ninth is the airplane).

And yet, if we take note of the actual settings of the 127 Jorkens tales in the five collections (excluding at least six or seven uncollected stories), we find that by far the most take place in the United Kingdom—either England or Ireland. Here is a breakdown:

United Kingdom: 54

Africa: 26

Asia: 11

Outer space: 7

The Mediterranean (including Greece and Egypt): 6

The Americas: 6

Europe: 5

The Middle East: 4

Russia: 2

Pacific Ocean: 1

Unspecified: 6

(The above breakdown totals 128 because "A Mystery of the East" [JRA] deliberately contrasts magic from India and the Sahara.) Every one of these places—except, of course, outer space—was visited by Dunsany at some point in his life, but the predominance of England as a setting is still surprising. Hence, although Terbut, Jorkens's bête noire who is continually trying to detect some flaw or deception in his tales, says querulously, " 'Let's hear of England this time . . . I'm tired of the ends of the earth' " (JRA 277), his complaint is not a legitimate one. Jorkens manages somehow to find exoticism within the very center of civilization, as the narrator of "The Invention of the Age" attests: ". . . one of his most extraordinary experiences [occurred] from somewhere no further away than Cavendish Square" (JH 271).

The feat Dunsany must perform in each of these tales is to present a fantastic, a bizarre, or simply an odd or implausible scenario but to resolve it in such a way that things return pretty much to normal at the story's end. Remoteness of setting—which precludes clear disproval of seemingly supernatural phenomena—is only one device by which this trick is performed. In other tales Jorkens meets individuals who have produced fantastic inventions, which are either lost or destroyed at the end or whose phenomena are attributed to other causes. Elsewhere Jorkens, who shows a marked inclination to make a quick buck, gains and loses many fortunes, in diamonds, gold, or cash. Still other tales (mostly the later ones) are simply written-out jokes, as Jorkens bamboozles other members of the Billiards Club or individuals he encounters along his travels, oftentimes by mere verbal trickery.

All this raises the question of Jorkens's believability, something Dunsany confronts in a seemingly direct but in fact roundabout and tongue-in-cheek way in the preface to *The Travel Tales of Mr. Joseph Jorkens* (1931). Here Dunsany (if indeed the "I" of the preface is Dunsany) claims to have set down these tales in order to fill "a gap here and there amongst the experience of travellers"; but he continues with a second motive:

I even hope for these tales that they may at certain points advance the progress of Science, and establish our knowledge upon a firmer basis; yet should they fail to do so, I feel that they may at least be so fortunate as to add something of strangeness to parts of our planet, just as it was tending to grow too familiar, and so to help put our knowledge back on to a foundation on which it rested once, so airily shaky as to possess some interest for all that find any charm in the queer and elusive. (TT v)

These tales will add either to "knowledge" or to "strangeness"—two more contrasting goals could hardly be conceived. We shall, Dunsany is saying, either know more about the world—or know less; and the latter seems clearly preferable, since by this means we shall restore to the world a little of the wonder of the unknown which the advent of science and machinery has been steadily diminishing.

The very first Jorkens story, "The Tale of the Abu Laheeb," lays the groundwork. The first-person narrator (who may or may not be Dunsany) meets a man named Murcote, who tells him of the Billiards Club, one of whose chief attractions is that " 'one heard tales there . . . ; very odd ones sometimes' " (TT 1), many of them told by one Joseph Jorkens. Jorkens has, Murcote says, " 'seen a lot of the world' " (TT 1), but Murcote is quick to warn the narrator " 'never to believe one of his tales nor any part of them, not even the smallest detail of local colour' " (TT 2). When the narrator says, " 'I see . . . a bit of a liar' " (TT 3), just as Dunsany would say in his autobiography, Murcote backs off; the true situation is this: "It wasn't Jorkens' fault; he didn't mean to be inaccurate; he merely wished to interest his fellow-members and to make the evening pass pleasantly; he had nothing to gain by any inaccuracies, and had no intention to deceive; he just did his best to entertain the Club, and all the members were grateful to him" (TT 2). All, of course, except Terbut, who had "never . . . travelled much beyond Paris" (JRA 58) and whose own tales "were too dull to be worth recording" (JB 173). It is either the cause of science or of entertainment that Jorkens is seeking to serve.

The most interesting of the Jorkens tales, from a weird perspective, are those that tread the very borderline of the supernatural but never quite cross it, failing to do so precisely because the weird phenomena seen or recounted by Jorkens cannot be confirmed. "The Tale of the Abu Laheeb" speaks of a new species Jorkens discovers in Africa, which alone of all animals knows how to use fire; Jorkens, keen on fostering the advance of knowledge (and to make a name for himself in the annals of science), wishes to name the creature Prometheus Jorkensi (TT 16). In "Mrs. Jorkens" (TT) the raconteur not only confirms the existence of mermaids but actually marries one—but she swims out to sea at the end. "What Jorkens Has to Put Up With" (JRA) tells of Jorkens hunting the unicorn. In all these cases Jorkens is either the sole witness for the events or else the supernatural entities elude notice, sometimes in the midst of London, until they escape into the unknown.

But the question of Jorkens's veracity is constantly raised, sometimes by Jorkens himself. In "The Walk to Lingham" he says, " 'One man even compared me to Munchausen, compared me favourably I admit, but still he made the comparison' " (JRA 42); this may actually have occurred in a review of the first volume. Jorkens claims to be pained at the comparison and blames the narrator for it: " 'It's the way you told those tales; they were true enough every one of them; but it was the way you told them, that somehow started those doubts' " (JRA 42). Later the narrator asserts: "Tales that Jorkens has told me, and that I have written down, have now been before the public for some while, and, though doubts about parts of them have been occasionally noticeable, no proof has been even offered, far less established, against the accuracy of any of them" (JRA 138). This is at best a negative virtue: the absence of definitive proof against the tales' veracity should at least cause us not to dismiss them out of hand. And yet, even the narrator's credulity becomes strained in "A Doubtful Story," which begins bluntly: "Frankly, I disbelieve this story" (JH 184); but he is quick to add that there is no falsehood on the part of Jorkens. What has happened in this case, the narrator explains, is that Jorkens has become so annoyed at the doubts cast upon his tales that he has said to himself: " 'If they are so damned incredulous I'll give them something to be incredulous about' " (JH 184). This is the closest the narrator comes to declaring outright that Jorkens is a liar. Jorkens himself turns the tables on his skeptics in "The Bare Truth," replying to a sarcastic query by one club member, " 'Jorkens, have you ever told the truth in your life?' " (JRA 84), with an unfazed " 'Yes, once' " (JRA 85), going on to say how his very telling the truth on one unfortunate occasion lost him a fortune.

It need hardly be remarked, of course, that all this is done with tongue in cheek: Dunsany knows that these tales are preposterous, and he knows that we know it; a great part of the charm rests in witnessing the deftness with which Jorkens anticipates and counteracts the doubts that any normal readers would have if they were reading these tales as plausible narratives. In some cases it is as if Dunsany has made a sort of wager with himself to contrive as bizarre a scenario as possible; hence, "The Charm against Thirst" (TT) tells of a man who drowned—in the Sahara.

The many tales involving wondrous inventions are among the most clever of the cycle. "The Invention of Dr. Caber" (JH) is the first of three stories about this ingenious doctor, who has devised a drug that makes one, not younger, but older. Who would want such a drug? Who but a criminal who wishes to make himself older so that he will not be recognized by the police? The two sequels—"The Strange Drug of Dr. Caber" (FBJ), telling how Caber did in a spy during World War II, and "The Cleverness of Dr. Caber" (FBJ), in which Caber devises an antigravity machine—are less interesting. "Making Fine Weather" speaks of a man who has invented a machine that controls the weather: " 'You may remember that year, when all the oats in England were laid flat'" (FBJ 12). Here there is no supernaturalism as such; instead, an unknown cause is attributed to a natural, if anomalous, phenomenon.

Some tales are merely improbable adventures, with nothing remotely supernatural or weird about them. One of the best of these is "The Escape from the Valley" (JRA), which tells of how a man, trapped in a valley with unscalable cliffs on all sides, captures a sufficient number of ducks so that they airlift him to safety. "How Ryan Got out of Russia" (JRA) is the bizarre tale of a man whom the Russians capture and attempt to blast out of a cannon to the moon; but he lands in England instead. In "The Correct Kit" a man finds himself taken prisoner by a bunch of cannibals; they are all wearing evening dress, taken from some previously captured group, as they are under the impression that this attire "'sanctified everything'" (JRA 245). This story turns out to be a satire on social etiquette: the man escapes by claiming that their bow ties actually go on their shoes, with the result that the cannibals cannot pursue him for fear of dislodging their newly positioned shoe ornaments. Later the man remarks: "'. . . they daren't do anything without their evening dress. Lots of people are like that'" (JRA 247).

There are also any number of stories about criminals, but they are no ordinary criminals. Dr. Caber thinks he can extort money out of the nations of the world by threatening to free the moon from its path with his antigravity machine. Other criminals encountered by Jorkens have similarly vast ambitions. "A Drink at a Running Stream" (TT) tells of a man who uses an old riverbed to import vast amounts of whiskey from Canada to the United States during Prohibition; in "The Ivory Poacher" (JH) a man smuggles an enormous quantity of ivory out of Africa by building a ship out of ivory and painting it to look like wood; "Jarton's Disease" (FBJ) is the rather grim story of a man who thinks he can get rich by inventing a new disease and developing a cure for it, but he ends up succumbing to it himself—because he could not invent his patent-medicine cure fast enough. Jorkens adds, however, "And yet it was not so much the ingredients that troubled him, as the advertisements which had to be written to make it attractive and to give it that dominant hold on the imagination without which it could never be possible for it to cure an imaginary disease" (FBJ 66). One is reminded of an acerbic passage in *The Old Folk of the Centuries*, where Mrs. Tweedle says: "They're up-to-date folks in Canington. There's where I learned about Quack's Quick Pills for Kidney Trouble, and took 'em ever since. Not that I've ever had no trouble of that sort, nor don't want to, thanks be to Mr. Quack" (OF 35).

Perhaps a subclass of tales about criminals might be those in which characters make pacts with witch doctors or the Devil himself for the purpose of gaining some sort of superhuman trait or other advantage. "How Jembu Played for Cambridge" (TT) is one of the most delightful of these, telling of an African who prays to his local god to gain prowess in cricket; the god, however, decrees that he must score no more than fifty runs lest some dire fate overtake him. Inevitably, Jembu finds himself at bat during a test match down by just more than fifty runs, and must find some other way to win without running afoul of the god's commandment. This tale is the first of a whole series of cricket stories in the Jorkens cycle, and one of the last ones, "The Unrecorded Test Match" (JB), is of a man who does not give up his soul to the Devil for mastery of cricket—that would be too high a price—but merely one of his virtues: that of telling the truth. This is a clever play on the "All Cretans are liars" paradox; unfortunately, Dunsany repeats the joke in a non-Jorkens story, "Told under Oath" (1952; GHL).

Jorkens himself occasionally skirts the law, usually in an attempt to make a quick fortune; but even when he makes the fortune, he invariably loses it through mishap. In "A Large Diamond" (TT) Jorkens comes upon a diamond in Russia the size of a lake (the result of a meteorite crashing into a mass of coal), but it sinks into the earth from an earthquake before he can retrieve it. "The Pearly Beach" shows Jorkens discovering an island in the Indian Ocean which is littered ankle-deep in pearls; but he wisely puts the pearls back because he senses that certain guardians of the island may not look kindly on his pilfering. In "The Jorkens Family Emeralds" Jorkens appears to come away with a fortune in emeralds, but loses it in some mysterious fashion: " 'I invested it in a way. You know the way one does. And a lot of things happened. I'll tell you about them some day' " (JH 99).

It should already be evident that Dunsany uses the Jorkens tales to underscore some of his central themes—the triumph of Nature, hatred of advertising, folly of political maneuvering, and the like. In particular, the topos of human beings against animals or against Nature as a whole is developed with ingenious variations in story after story. The very first Jorkens tale, "The Tale of the Abu Laheeb," is of this type: Jorkens cannot shoot the Abu Laheeb because he senses a profound link to humankind in its ability to handle fire. As it senses Jorkens's presence and flees, it utters "gusts of human-like laughter" (TT 18). "On Other Paths" is a striking late tale in which an African god shows Jorkens what the state of affairs would have been if human beings had not secured domination over animals: " 'It was very likely a nearer thing than we think, our getting the domination.

We had to beat the mammoth and the tiger. It might easily have gone some other way'" (JB 37). What if dogs had gained superiority over humans? Jorkens is shown a vision of dogs in charge—"'self-satisfied, condescending, patronizing'" (JB 38). Is this not our own attitude toward animals?

"Our Distant Cousins" is a queer science-fiction story that hammers home the same point. A man, Terner, makes a fabulous (and wholly implausible) trip to Mars in a rocket-powered airplane and finds that there is a quasi-human race on the planet; it is, in fact, "'rather more refined than the best of our people'" (TT 85). The surface reason given for this is that Mars cooled earlier than Earth and therefore a civilization must have developed there earlier than here; but Dunsany's real motive for such an exaltation of the Martian race is so that its fall can be the greater—for Terner discovers to his horror that "'[m]an isn't top dog there'" (TT 90), but that some loathsome and amorphous entity dominates Mars and uses the quasi-human creatures for food. Perhaps our own rulership of this planet is not entirely secure.

Two comic stories show animals getting the better of their human pursuers. In "The Showman" (TT) a man goes to Africa to capture apes for his circus, but the apes capture him instead and put him on display for their amusement. "Elephant Shooting" (JH) tells of a hunter's attempt to shoot an ancient and highly intelligent four-tusked elephant by an elaborate trap by which a string will pull the trigger of a gun; but the elephant sees through the ploy and shoots the hunter. The titles of both stories, of course, are delicious puns.

The entire natural world develops a hostility to humanity in the gripping tale "The Walk to Lingham," as close to a pure horror story as Dunsany ever wrote. Jorkens, walking along a road in England, has idly praised the skill with which some lumberjacks have cut down a row of poplar trees; but, when night falls, he senses pursuit behind him, and comes to feel that it is those very poplars that he has insulted by his thoughtlessness:

I heard the clod clod of the steps, and a certain prolonged swish, but never a sound of breathing. It was fully time to look round, and yet I daren't. The hard heavy steps had nothing of the softness of flesh. Paws they were not, nor even hooves. And they were so near now that there must have been sounds of large breathing, had it been anything animal. (JRA 47)

Those trees are not exhibiting the "'respect that is due to man'" (JRA 49) on account of his supposed mastery of Nature. Finally Jorkens reaches an inn and finds that there are no pursuing poplars; he comments in a significant political metaphor: "'I knew at once that there had been no revolution'" (JRA 53). The plant world has not (yet) rebelled from human domination.

Two stories focus more centrally on the lack of harmony between human civilization and Nature. "The Development of the Rillswood Estate" involves a satyr who has strayed into a new suburban community because the nearby wood has been cut down—a transparent metaphor for the loss of mystery and wonder resulting from the ongoing destruction of the natural realm and the advent of bourgeois culture. The satyr comes to the home of a Mr. Meddin and his sister Lucy; although they take the satyr in, they are anxious to preserve their respectability and—in a tableau that brings "The Kith of the Elf-Folk" to mind—dress the satyr and attempt to force him to conform to the standards of their middle-class life. The conclusion of this story is too clever to be revealed here.

"A Doubtful Story" seems in some ways a deliberate parody of *The Blessing of Pan*: Jorkens brings Pan himself from Greece to London, since Pan has evinced a desire to be at what is the center of things nowadays. But this comic scenario, in which Jorkens, like Meddin, wrestles with the difficulty of dressing Pan ("'I knew he wouldn't like boots, but morning dress with hooves was simply out of the question'" [JH 200]), turns poignant when Pan begins to whimper in the middle of London:

> "'What do you want?' I asked him sharply again.
> "'Green things. Green things,' said Pan.
> "'Not so loud,' I said.
> "'And quiet,' added Pan." (JH 197)

Finally Jorkens leaves Pan in the wild moors of Yorkshire, since this region "'is far from the centre of things, far from our loud noise and far from our complications'" (JH 204). Pan, as always in Dunsany, is a symbol of Nature, and the irremediable conflict of Nature and civilization has rarely been expressed more keenly in his work than here.

Some stories deliver the same message a little more flippantly. "Jorkens Handles a Big Property" (JH) is another of the Jorkens-tries-to-get-rich-quick tales, as he makes bootless efforts to sell the Gulf Stream to various parties in England; but his motive for doing so is to preserve spring in England, as a man Jorkens has encountered in New Orleans plans to redirect the flow of the Gulf Stream so that its temperate waters do not reach England. "The Lost Invention" (JB) tells of a man who devises a machine that will make sheep and cattle obsolete, but he destroys it when he hears the bleating of a sheep—he cannot bear to lose such a thing from the English countryside.

Then there is "The Electric King," which Dunsany declared flatly to be "my best story" (WSS 148). It is certainly one of his most peculiar. An American businessman, Makins, who has made a vast fortune in electricity finds himself harried by a recurring nightmare of a rat that seems on the verge of pouncing on him. He seeks aid from sages in the monasteries of India and Tibet, who finally solve his problem with a prayer wheel. Makins returns and builds an electrical plant with huge dynamos that turn a single gigantic prayer wheel—the only way to keep the rat at bay. I would like to think that this is some sort of parable on the futility of industrialism, but I confess not to knowing what this long, meandering story's import really is.

Some of the Jorkens tales are political satires, but not many of these are very effective. The best of them, perhaps, is a late story, "A Life's Work," a brief tale that has some staggering implications. An unnamed individual is appointed by one of the two leading political parties in some unspecified country to demolish a hill that is obstructing the capital city's view of the sea. This party scorns the old ways and believes only in practicality. The man accordingly spends thirty years with a pick and shovel levelling the hill. But by this time the other party—which "was for the old things that always had been" (FBJ 102)—has gained power, and it wishes the hill to be put back because everyone had got accustomed to the sight of it; and so the man spends thirty years shovelling the hill back into place. Jorkens ironically hails this man as the one " 'who's done the most work of all the people' " (FBJ 101) he has met: " 'He has spent a hard, hard life, a model for all of us' " (FBJ 104). In this story the surface satire on the futility of political action gives way to a broader and more withering satire on the futility of all human effort.

Other political tales do not amount to much. The satire on evil communist Russians in "How Ryan Got out of Russia" is too obvious to be interesting; "Jorkens in High Finance" addresses the Depression, as Jorkens and others conceive the plan of capturing all the gold in the world and burying it in the sea so as to return to "much simpler methods of exchange" (JH 110); "Jorkens Looks Forward" (JH), published in 1938, is a rather frivolous tale in which Dunsany makes clear his expectation of an imminent European war; "The Strange Drug of Dr. Caber" deals with spies during World War II. There is a whole group of stories in *Jorkens Borrows Another Whiskey* (1954) dealing with the atomic bomb—"A Conversation in Bond Street," "The Two-Way War," "The New Moon," "The Gods of Clay," "The Greatest Invention"—but they all convey too bluntly and clumsily Dunsany's horror at this new threat to world civilization.

Dunsany after a time clearly began to use the Jorkens tales as experiments in tonal variation. It is not the case that all the stories are merely lighthearted jeux d'esprit: a large proportion of them do indeed adopt that dryly comic tone which we find in the bulk of Dunsany's later work, but we have already seen that "The Walk to Lingham" is as grimly terrible as any story in his entire corpus. There is also a tremendously potent atmosphere in the wood in which Jorkens stumbles in "The Witch of the Willows":

I went into the solitude of the willows, and no sooner had I come than all that they seemed to portend with their ancient limbs in the dusk and their frozen motionless fingers, all that they seemed to whisper with shadows, or plot with the ice and the gloaming, was suddenly multiplied; and I seemed to have strayed once more to the tryst of an unseen company, silently planning things that were not all well for man. (TT 281)

In the harrowing late story "Lost" (FBJ), a man finds a talisman that allows him to double back upon his own past; but as a result, he becomes a different person and goes insane because he cannot reconcile his old personality with his new one.

Conversely, an atmosphere of pathos fills "In the Garden of Memories" (JRA), as Jorkens stumbles upon the garden that, because of its seclusion, preserves the memories of those who have walked in it. "The King of Sarahb" is very reminiscent of Dunsany's early tales of otherworldly fantasy, telling of a man who suffers hallucinations while wandering in the Sahara:

Amongst the lakes was a city all of white marble, with a flush of pink in it as faint as late sunlight, wandering amongst the towers, and here and there the flash of thin veins in the gold. And the beauty of that city shining in the soft water, in a light all of its own, that had nothing to do with the wild glare of the desert, touched his heart as neither dawn nor music nor memory had ever touched it before; and he stood before its battlements by the edge of its lakes and wept. (TT 27)

Another tale that recalls his early manner is "A Daughter of Rameses," in which Jorkens encounters the spirit of the title, from whom he derives the following ponderous moral: " 'it's better not to make gods or demons smile: they don't laugh at the same jokes as us' " (TT 204).

It is also worth considering the Jorkens tales as experiments in narration. A serial character—especially one that appears in more than a hundred tales, even if written over a thirty-year period—is in constant danger of becoming tedious or repetitious, as readers of detective fiction can attest. Moreover, within the compass of the short story—the longest of the Jorkens tales is no more than ten thousand words—there is relatively little opportunity for character development, as there would be in the novel. Dunsany must accordingly devise increasingly ingenious venues for the introduction of one of Jorkens's adventures, and as the series develops he resorts more and more to clever narrative variations.

An oft-repeated motif is the presence of what the narrator calls an "envious clique" (JB 151) within the Billiards Club who are determined to preclude the possibility of a Jorkens narrative by resolutely discussing subjects in which he cannot take any conceivable interest. The trick invariably backfires, simultaneously displaying Jorkens's wide experience in matters beyond simple travel and Dunsany's ingenuity in introducing a story from an unexpected angle. "The New Moon" opens:

Punctuation is of course of considerable importance in writing a story, but nobody can imagine a story being made *out* of punctuation; and it was for this reason, if so wretched a device can be dignified by the name of a reason, that that clique in the Billiards Club, of which I am tired of complaining, adopted punctuation as a topic for discussion as Jorkens came into the dining-room. (JB 151)

Other implausible subjects that lead to Jorkens tales are etiquette (JRA 107), alchemy (JRA 186), singing (JH 67), transmigration of souls (JH 115), free will (JH 250), consistency (FBJ 109), spiritualism (FBJ 133), proverbs (JB 64), influenza (JB 81), and absentmindedness (JB 246). Once again one senses a certain bravado on the part of Dunsany himself, as if he had dared himself to concoct plots from such unlikely sources.

Sometimes Jorkens himself becomes reluctant to tell a tale—or at least to do so within the confines of the skeptical Billiards Club. In "Our Distant Cousins" Jorkens and the narrator must visit Terner in his flat, and he tells the story only after receiving assurances that the narrator is not one of the " 'sneering fools' " (TT 69) from the club. "The Lost Romance" begins: "All through the summer Jorkens had told us no story" (JRA 1). Finally, after much cajoling, his tongue is loosened not by a request to tell of some far-flung voyage, but by the query: " 'Have you ever failed . . . in any affair with a lady?' " (JRA 2).

By the time we come to "In the Garden of Memories," we see Dunsany flexing his narrative muscles. The tale begins boldly: "I never heard the beginning of this story. I never heard exactly how it happened, and Jorkens never referred to it again. Jorkens was already talking as I came into the

Club" (JRA 158). This is because the reason for Jorkens's arrival at the house with the garden of memories is entirely supernumerary, so that the narrative device of commencing in medias res is aesthetically justified. This device is carried further in a later story, "A Royal Dinner": "One day as I entered the Billiards Club I found Jorkens in the midst of a story. I remember his actual words as I came in: 'I said to him, "The moon will be much annoyed if you do"'" (FBJ 165). With this opening Dunsany sets for himself the challenge of filling in the background of the story while simultaneously carrying the narrative forward—and all within about a thousand words.

Toward the end of the cycle Jorkens increasingly sheds his role as storyteller and becomes a listener or an inciter of others' stories. "The Sultan, the Monkey and the Banana" (JH) is similar to the early "Why the Milkman Shudders When He Perceives the Dawn" (LBW) in that the tale suggested by the title is never actually told; this story and the one immediately following it, "Pundleton's Advice," are also not told by Jorkens. In "The Greatest Invention" (JB) it is Jorkens who plies another man with wine to coax the tale out of him, just as the narrator and others have frequently lubricated Jorkens's tongue with whiskey. In the very last story in *Jorkens Borrows Another Whiskey*, "Greek Meets Greek," Jorkens's nemesis, Terbut, finally gets to tell a story—and a sorry one it is. Even here Jorkens gets the last word. This whole tendency reaches its reductio ad absurdum in an uncollected story, "Fatal Mistake" (1955), in which Jorkens sleeps through the entire narrative, only waking up at the end to utter some random and apparently irrelevant remarks.

The supernatural quotient of the Jorkens tales very gradually and unsystematically decreases as the cycle continues. Every one of the tales in *The Travel Tales of Mr. Joseph Jorkens* (1931), with the exception of "A Drink at a Running Stream" (the story of smuggling whiskey from Canada into the United States through an old riverbed), involves the supernatural, assuming for the moment that Jorkens's accounts are true. But *Jorkens Remembers Africa* (1934) opens with "The Lost Romance," in which Jorkens is merely tricked by a nun whom he hopes to steal away and marry. The opening story of *Jorkens Has a Large Whiskey* (1940), "Jorkens' Revenge," involves a bet between Jorkens and Terbut as to whether the distance between Westminster Bridge to Blackfriars Bridge is longer than the distance between Blackfriars Bridge and Westminster Bridge; Terbut takes up the bet, and loses. There is nothing remotely weird or supernatural about this story. Later Jorkens tales become rather slight, frivolous, and contrived, as in "Out West" (FBJ), in which Jorkens tricks some American soldiers on a train as to when they have left the Western

Hemisphere (they have just passed Greenwich), or "On the Other Side of the Sun" (FBJ), when Jorkens declares that he can prove he was on the other side of the sun (he was, six months ago, along with the rest of us). These are, in effect, written-out jokes.

Nevertheless, the cycle remains vigorous to the end, and Dunsany's narrative drive and fecundity of imagination make these stories compellingly readable. H. P. Lovecraft, lamenting the passing of Dunsany's early manner, is at liberty to dismiss them as "tripe,"[1] but they are all written with such verve, ingenuity, and deadpan humor that they remain fresh and distinctive. They seem a peculiar combination of Kipling, Wodehouse, Poe, and Conan Doyle, but in the end they remain uniquely Dunsanian.

NOTE

1. Lovecraft, letter to Fritz Leiber, 15 November 1936; in *Selected Letters*, ed. August Derleth, Donald Wandrei, and James Turner (Sauk City, WI: Arkham House, 1976), 5: 354.

6

The Comic Fantastic

Of his commencement as a writer Dunsany made the rather odd assertion that it was "guided, as ever since, by two lights that do not seem very often to shine together, poetry and humour" (PS 111). He did not explain this utterance, and it is the more puzzling in that it is made specifically in reference to *The Gods of Pegāna*, in which the element of humor can be detected only obliquely in the owlish ponderousness by which an ersatz theogony is established. But Dunsany is correct in thinking that much of his entire output is comic, although it takes widely differing forms—satire, irony, cynicism, parody, farce. We have already seen that humor is a central component of the Jorkens stories, of novels such as *My Talks with Dean Spanley* and *The Strange Journeys of Colonel Polders*, and of tales as early as "The Highwayman" (SW). In general, however, Dunsany found that the drama was particularly felicitous in accommodating humor of various types, and even the high seriousness of such plays as *The Gods of the Mountain* and *The Queen's Enemies* are leavened with doses of humor ranging from low comedy to acerbic satire. Several of the *Plays of Near and Far* (1922) are avowedly comic, as are all the *Seven Modern Comedies* (1928) and nearly all the *Plays for Earth and Air* (1937).

There are perhaps three broad subdivisions into which Dunsany's humor and satire fall: social, religious, and literary. Each reflects some central component of Dunsany's philosophy: his social satire pokes fun at artificialities in class distinctions and etiquette; his religious satire criticizes the hypocrisy and intolerance of religion, specifically the Christian religion; his literary satire both ridicules stolid bourgeois imperviousness to art and jeers at freakish avant-garde tendencies in art and literature. Dunsany's pervasive satire on the business mentality is perhaps an aspect of both his social and his literary satire, as the objects of attack are those hardheaded middle-class businessmen whose hostility to art because it "does not pay" seals their doom. These three categories rarely occur in isolation in any given work, but it may still be profitable to treat them separately.

I have noted how *The Lost Silk Hat*, written in 1912 and published in *Five Plays* (1914), seems anomalously early as a light comedy of manners amid the plays of gods and men of Dunsany's early period; but it should be borne in mind that Dunsany's very first play, *The Glittering Gate* (1909), is the real anomaly in its use of Cockney dialect—at a time when Dunsany was still devoted to Biblical prose-poetry—and in its many fine touches of pungent humor. Where *The Lost Silk Hat* gains its relevance is in its being entirely non-fantastic. In this play a man hails a series of passersby on the street and asks each of them to fetch a hat he has inadvertently left in someone's flat. He cannot get the hat himself because he has quarreled with the woman in the flat, his former lover, and has melodramatically declared to her that he has "sworn to join the Bosnians and die in Africa" (FiP 99); he is accordingly unwilling to spoil this exit line and ignominiously retrieve his silk hat.

This play is simultaneously a satire on social etiquette and on the pomposities of romance. This well-dressed gentleman cannot possibly be seen on the street without his hat: "It can't be done," since "being decently dressed in London seems pretty essential" (FiP 100) to him. And yet, this play may actually be the first inkling of that renunciation of fantasy which we shall shortly examine: what is being made fun of is not merely romance in the conventional sense of the term, but romance in Dunsany's sense also; and it is not much of a step from poking fun at romance (fantasy) to giving it up altogether. In this sense the critical character in the play is not the caller but the poet who is accosted by him and urged to fetch the hat. One might suppose that the poet embodies Dunsany's views on wonder, but the fatuous bombast of his utterances makes him as much of a buffoon as the hatless caller. The poet indeed ridicules the caller's hidebound social convention ("A hat is not one of the essential things of life" [FiP 100]), but in pleading with the caller not to return to the flat and ruin his glorious exit, he himself lapses, perhaps self-consciously, into bathos: "What is a hat! Will you sacrifice for it a beautiful doom? Think of your bones, neglected and forgotten, lying forlornly because of hopeless love on endless golden sands. Lying forlorn! As Keats said: what a word. Forlorn in Africa. The careless Bedouins going past by day, at night the lion's roar, the grievous voice of the desert" (FiP 102). Well, the caller is not going to get much assistance from this fellow. In fact, when the poet says that he will himself comfort the lady ("I'm damned if you do," retorts the caller hotly; "I do not mean it in that way," the poet assures him [FiP 103]), the caller decides to eat humble pie and retrieve the hat himself, and it leads inevitably to a reconciliation, leaving the poet lamenting on the death of romance: "You will marry. You will sometimes take a ticket with your wife as far as Paris. Perhaps as far as Cannes. Then the family will come, a large, sprawling family as far as the eye can see—I speak in hyperbole— you'll earn money and feed it and be like all the rest. No monument will ever be set up to your memory . . ." (FiP 104).

A rather slighter but quite amusing play on somewhat the same idea is *The Hopeless Passion of Mr. Bunyon*. Here a humble clerk is about to be dismissed from his job because he spends all day peering out the window and gazing at the wax figure of a woman outside the shop; it has, he tells his boss, become "the romance of my life, sir" (SMC 175). In a pungent satire both on romance and on women's vanity, the clerk speaks with rapture about the beauty of the statue: "Fashionableness, sir. That's what's the matter with her, *it* I should say. Fashionableness. She's got more fashionableness than anyone in the world. There isn't a queen so fashion-able. Look at that sort of affected way she stands, and that simper, sir, if I may call it so; all pure fashionableness. I've never seen anyone like her" (SMC 176). Bunyon, like so many naive and sequestered young men, simply wants romance—but it has to be a *hopeless* romance, a romance that by definition cannot be fulfilled in actuality and can remain safely in the realm of the imagination. After all, "there've been scores of cases of what's called hopeless passions. There have really, sir. Men have loved queens, sir; they really have. Just ordinary men, sir" (SMC 177). And, as is typical of Dunsany's later plays, there is an added fillip when the statue turns out to be merely a live but lower-class woman ("Ow, reely, Mr. Bunyon" [SMC 180]) who has been hired by Bunyon's boss; both are fired and both go off together, Bunyon "almost kneeling, stretching out adoring arms" (SMC 181).

A much more devastating satire on romance is *Atalanta in Wimbledon* [1927]; it is one of Dunsany's strongest later plays. The title is clearly a parody of Swinburne's poetic drama *Atalanta in Calydon*, and the whole play is a blistering parody of the very idea of poetic romance in the modern age. Marjorie Dawk, an unmarried young woman, has been reading William Morris and has derived a plan from him; after all, Marjorie thinks, poetry "doesn't seem much good" (SMC 11) if you can't act upon it. She has taken out an ad in the paper challenging any man to a Ping-Pong match (in Dunsany's modern bourgeois world, everything is done on a lesser scale: it is Ping-Pong, not tennis, at Wimbledon): if the man wins, she will marry him; if he loses, he must die by the sword. This extremely simple scenario is fraught with complex thematic resonances: the deflation of high romance; the stolid literal-mindedness of the bourgeoisie in regard to poetry; the bland amoralism of the smart young generation; even, perhaps, a satire on the vast and spurious importance attributed to sports, a satire highlighted by a devilish pun on "sudden death" (SMC 28). Each of the characters—Marjorie; her father; Mr. Jinks, a man who takes up the challenge; and Bill, Marjorie's bashful lover who has not had the courage to confess his feelings to her—is vividly realized, and we can forgive Dunsany a somewhat contrived resolution (Jinks has to withdraw from the match because he is told by the secretary of the World Ping-Pong Amateur Association that he would forfeit his amateur status if he wins) in light of the crisp dialogue and perfect pacing of this pungent little play. Very surprisingly for Dunsany, the play ends on an amusing sexual innuendo as Bill takes up Jinks's place in the match:

Dawk: . . . Why, they seem to have stopped.

Constable: That's what they've done, sir. They've stopped.

Dawk: I hope she's not overtired herself.

Constable: No sir. I don't think so, sir.

Dawk: You think not.

Constable: No, sir. I remember me and my missus. My girl she was then. Her father had a licensed house out at Bromley, and a nice little lawn at the back. My girl and I we used to go there of an evening to play a bit of bowls. A fine set of bowls he had.

Dawk: Did he really?

Constable: Yes, sir. He did, the old chap. And we usedn't to play much bowls.

Dawk: Oh. You didn't?

Constable: No, sir. (SMC 43–44)

Three plays—*The Raffle*, *A Matter of Honour*, and *Mr. Sliggen's Hour*—represent a transition from social to religious satire, although each contains a substantial dose of both. *A Matter of Honour* is an extraordinarily vicious play. An old man, Sir John, is on his deathbed, and anxiously awaits the arrival of two old friends, Sir Algernon Griggs and Mr. Smew; he must resolve something before he dies. Finally the two arrive, and they have this enigmatic exchange:

Sir John: You remember that Bishop's wife?

Sir Algernon: He-he-he. She beat you old boy. (*To Smew.*) It was his only defeat wasn't it? But she beat you. Even the greatest conquerors you know. . . .

Sir John: No, I won it [the bet] really.

Sir Algernon: You won it?

Sir John: Yes, she's dead now, I read that she died three years ago; and I won it really. (PEA 15–16)

What is the bet that Sir John has won? What else can it be but a bet that he could seduce the bishop's wife? And his confession of the deed is not some unburdening of a guilt-ridden conscience but a vital clarification of the facts of the case, as Sir Algernon explains: "Well the spirit of the arrangement was that you should tell us what really happened in order to get the money. When you let the money slide you were free of your obligation" (PEA 17–18). Now that the situation is clear, Sir John can "die a man of honour" (PEA 18). I do not know if Dunsany intends any significance by setting this play in the "late 19th century" (PEA 13): is the pious hypocrisy of the Victorians the target of satire?

A little less pungent is *Mr. Sliggen's Hour*, in which Mr. Sliggen, the vicar, makes a deal with the Devil that his sermon "may move all who hear it to tears" on condition that "within an hour your sermon shall be derided by all who heard it" (PEA 24). Sliggen accepts the bargain, finding it inconceivable that a sermon that had brought tears to its listeners' eyes could ever suffer derision within an hour. But this is exactly what happens; and the faultless modulation of the play—as a group of people, among them the bishop and his wife, the chaplain, and the squire, all discuss the sermon and gradually come to the conclusion that it was spurious, contrived, and manipulative—is the key to its effectiveness. This play could also be considered a literary satire, as the characters all subject the sermon to increasingly searching criticism of its substance, its rhetorical tricks ("Was he right, do you think, to use that pause that he made, in order to get his effect?" [PEA 29]), and its general theatricalism. I am not sure whether a general condemnation of the hypocrisy and duplicity of sermons is intended here, but such a subtext could easily be derived from the play.

The hypocrisy of religion—or, at least, of those who purport to be its custodians—is the focus of *The Raffle* [1926], another of Dunsany's great later plays. Here again a deal with the Devil triggers the action: Sir James Elford, who now regrets having offered £2,500 for a raffle on his estate, accepts the Devil's offer of £2,000 for the soul of the Rev. John Biffins, although this will require Sir James to persuade Biffins to give his soul up;

and Biffins, as Sir James remarks querulously, is "the sort of fellow who'd set a lot of *store* by his soul" (SMC 60). Nevertheless, Sir James sees a "probable margin of profit" (SMC 61) in the transaction. When Sir James summons Biffins in and, as squire, demands that he give him his soul, Biffins reacts not with horror or outrage but with a sort of sycophantic reluctance, and finally yields: "But I still have the greatest compunctions. But to oblige *you*, Sir James, only to oblige you" (SMC 69). Sir James buys Biffins's soul for £1,250.

It is at this point that the play becomes still nastier. The bishop bursts in, having heard of the transaction, and is outraged. But when Sir James says to the bishop that he will sell back Biffins's soul to him for £3,500, the bishop begins to demur: is Biffins's soul really worth that much? "You see, I've been a bishop for some years now. And I necessarily have a certain amount of experience. And if I were to begin, only to *begin*, to pay more for anything than its reasonable value, I should in a very short while have nothing left, like any other spendthrift. A bishop *cannot* give reckless prices" (SMC 75–76). After all, "a diocese requires as much *savoir faire* as perhaps any business" (SMC 79)—a remark that makes us think immediately of the business mentality being urged upon Hippanthigh in *Cheezo.* As if this twist—Sir James and the bishop crassly haggling over the price of a man's soul—were not enough, Dunsany adds yet another one by making us pause to wonder whether Biffins indeed deserves to get his soul back: he had already demonstrated spinelessness in giving it up so readily; and when, by a series of accidents, he gets it back by way of the raffle, he is seen to be utterly frivolous and empty, "running and skipping" (SMC 81) like a schoolboy. Perhaps, we are forced to consider, Biffins's soul isn't worth that much after all. This is one of several Dunsany plays in which every single character is made the butt of ruthless and mordant satire: Sir James for his coldblooded desire for profit; the bishop for his cynical calculativeness in spiritual matters; Biffins for his brainless buffoonery; even Sir James's snobbish and dictatorial sister (when asked by the bishop how he could have made such a deal, Sir James replies: "if you had a sister like mine, she'd drive you to it" [SMC 73]). And the Devil's remark at the outset that he "rather like[s]" (SMC 63) church bazaars could not be a clearer suggestion of the boundless hypocrisy to be found, in Dunsany's eyes, at such an event.

The Jest of Hāhalābā [1926] is, among other things, a satire on business, and has become one of Dunsany's better-known plays: it served as the partial basis of the French film *C'est arrivé demain* (1944; released in this country as *It Happened Tomorrow*) and was made into a chamber opera by Morris Cotel. The scenario is somewhat reminiscent of *If*, as a strange alchemist from the East comes to the home of Sir Arthur Strangeways on the last day of 1928 and, presumably in exchange for some benefit Strangeways has bestowed upon him, gives him the formula for conjuring up a spirit. The alchemist is terrified of the entire proceeding, urging Sir Arthur not to summon the spirits of Death, of Fever, or of Terror. When Sir Arthur decides to call up Hāhālābā, the spirit of Laughter, the alchemist is still more alarmed: all these spirits are "at enmity with man," and Hāhālābā is "the worst of all but one" (SMC 191–92). But Sir Arthur persists and, having summoned Hāhālābā, asks him to supply copies of all the 1929 issues of the *Times*. Sir Arthur intends to "make millions" (SMC 196) and to "play hell with the Stock Exchange" (SMC 199) by learning of stock results ahead of time (the play was obviously written years before the stock market crash of October 1929); but he must read all the papers before dawn the next day, as they will by then disappear. As he begins to read the paper, making furious notes on stock prices and race results, he comes to the last one; it is the paper for the next day, as Hāhālābā has arranged the papers in reverse chronological order. The paper announces Sir Arthur's own death.

All this may be both contrived and predictable, but the treatment is very effective. Sir Arthur's death is anticipated when he reads in the paper of October 27 that a friend, old Perrot, has died: "He should have kept himself fit: he was no older than me" (SMC 198). He has scribbled down the winner of the Derby, Aurelian, on a slip of paper; when his butler finds Sir Arthur dead at the end and sees the slip of paper, he remarks scornfully: "Aurelian for the Derby. *He's* no good" (SMC 204). As with *If*, the mystery of Time, and our ineffectual struggles against it, are at the foundation of the play.

Golden Dragon City (produced 1934) leads us from Dunsany's social to his literary satires. I have remarked that this play is an adaptation of the early story "The Wonderful Window" (BW); in the process the basic thrust has been transformed from the wonder to be found in the midst of mundane reality to a satire on bourgeois insensitivity to the imagination. The principal vehicle for this transformation is the addition of a fatuous young girl, Lily, who joins the fatuous young man, Bill, and his fatuous landlady, Mrs. Lumley, in regarding the wonderful window—which looks magically down upon a dream city of pinnacles and minarets—as a transient parlor amusement. Bill and Lily decide to "spend an hour up on those chairs after tea, instead of going to the pictures" (PEA 127): in spite of the absence of sound, the view from the window seems rather more engaging than a movie, although apparently not much different in kind. A single exchange between the three characters is sufficient to convey the import of the play:

Bill: Won't you take another look at your city, Mrs. Lumley?

Mrs. Lumley: Not now, thank you, sir. I've a few things to do. I'll take a good look later. I'm glad we've got it down there. Come to think of it, I really am. I'll be going now, sir.

Bill: Well, Lily, when you've finished your muffin we'll take another look at the city.

Lily: (*mouth full*) Yes. (PEA 129)

Mrs. Lumley cannot pause from her household chores to contemplate a violation of the natural order; Lily has to finish stuffing her face before she can do so. Mrs. Lumley is one of several lower middle-class characters whom Dunsany portrays harshly for their stodginess and imaginative stultification; this sort of satire is not looked upon favorably in our democratic age, when only the wealthy and the upper class can be made fun of, but Dunsany handles it brilliantly. Bill's tiny rooms are, according to Mrs. Lumley, not mere flats but "residential chambers" (PEA 117); and she doesn't care much for "those foreigners" (PEA 118), from one of whom Bill got the window. And when Bill urges her to keep an eye on the city, lest it come to harm, she counters: "Well, I will, sir, when the cat's-meat-man has come. He comes this morning, and I mustn't miss him, you know" (PEA 132). And yet, "I wouldn't like any harm to come to it, with all those nice towers and all" (PEA 132).

Dunsany's several plays in which art is the focus—*Fame and the Poet, If Shakespeare Lived To-day, The Journey of the Soul, Fame Comes Late, The Seventh Symphony*—are all marred by a sort of blunt transparency, and only a few are worth studying in detail. All these plays are satires on the lack of respect accorded to poetry, literature, and music, and some of them are quite embarrassingly bad. The early prose-poem "The Assignation" (FOT 9–10) sets the tone for this entire topos, and Dunsany would have been better off had he written nothing more in this vein. In this brief tale Fame is seen "singing in the highways, and trifling as she sang, with sordid adventurers"; a poet seeks her but is repelled, and he chides her for "laugh[ing] and shout[ing] and jest[ing] with worthless men," at which Fame replies: "I will meet you in the graveyard at the back of the Workhouse in a hundred years."

The personification of Fame works in this simple parable, but in the plays it borders upon absurdity. It is true that Dunsany has a good deal of fun with the conception: the whole point of *Fame and the Poet* is that Fame, when she finally comes to the earnest poet Harry de Reves ("Harry of Dreams"), turns out to be a Cockney-spouting harridan. Although

Fame is dressed according to custom in a "Greek dress with a long golden trumpet in her hand" (PNF 238), her first words are arresting:

Fame: You're a bit of all right.

de Reves: What?

Fame: Some poet.

de Reves: I—I—scarcely . . . understand.

Fame: You're IT. (PNF 239)

Fame goes on to shout out the window, to an adoring crowd, what Harry's favorite color is, what he has had for breakfast, and the fact that he plays golf. All this is emphatically not what de Reves expects or wants, but Fame concludes the play with an ominous "I've come to stay, I have" (PNF 245).

This is a clever enough satire on celebrity making, but one wonders whether there is an autobiographical connection. This play was written in the spring of 1917, at close to the height of Dunsany's own fame. De Reves, like Dunsany, writes with a quill pen (PNF 242); prior to Fame's entrance he complains: "Ten years' work and what have I to show for it? The admiration of men who care for poetry, and how many of *them* are there?" (PNF 237). The mob, of course, cares nothing for the sonnet de Reves has just written, but only wants to know what he had for breakfast. Is Dunsany complaining that his own fame is restricted to externals of this sort, and that few care for or understand his actual work?

The later play *Fame Comes Late* reverts to the central conception of "The Assignation." Here a poet, Perdins, is visited by Fame, but she is old and tired; as he explains to his girlfriend, Angela, she has walked a long way and "the road's a bit damp to-day" (PEA 7). Perdins lets Fame rest in the next room, but the strain of her arrival, after long years, takes its toll on him and he himself falls ill and dies. At that point Fame suddenly revives and "lifts her trumpet and sounds peals from it" (PEA 10). Once again the point that genuine fame arrives only posthumously is made a little bluntly.

Still less worth notice is *If Shakespeare Lived To-Day*, whose title gives away the idea before the play has even started. Here two stodgy members of the Olympus Club debate whether they should admit a dubious character named William Shakespeare. It is all rather laborious: Shakespeare's plays are really not very suitable, they are full of blood and supernaturalism, they are lascivious, etc., etc. There is only one good joke in the entire play:

Sir Webley: What else does he say he's done?

Trundleben: Er—er—there's an absurdly long list—er—"Macbeth."

Sir Webley: "Macbeth." That's Irish.

Neeks: Ah, yes. Abbey Theatre style of thing. (PNF 201–2)

This remark itself suggests that this play, like *Fame and the Poet*, may have an autobiographical undercurrent: Trundleben notes that "I believe they [Shakespeare's plays] were acted in America, though not of course in London" (PNF 208), something Dunsany was always acerbically fond of pointing out about his own work.

I would very much like to believe that *The Seventh Symphony* is meant parodically, but it does not seem as if it is. A young musician, Mr. Territ, is gravely ill, but insists on listening to a radio performance of Beethoven's *Seventh Symphony* (one of Dunsany's favorite works [WSS 67]). Just prior to its commencement the spirits of Beethoven, Cervantes, Milton, Shelley, and Herrick all come to him and ask him if he wishes to come with them and "stay with us the Immortals" or "wake and go back to the world" (PEA 105). Each of these great artists is portrayed in what amounts to a crude caricature of the most distinctive features of their work—Beethoven the irascible genius, Shelley the ethereal dreamer, Cervantes the lover of jollity, Milton the stern moralist, Herrick the languid lover—and it is here that one would like to detect parody. But the focus of the play is elsewhere. Territ's landlady turns the radio on, but to the wrong station: jazz comes out of it and drives the spirits away. Beethoven remarks as he leaves: "We can't walk upon these notes. They hurt our feet" (PEA 111).

One final play is somewhat more amusing. *The Journey of the Soul* is a sort of metadrama in which actors are rehearsing the play of the title. They fail utterly to understand its import, since it is nothing like the shallow musical comedies they are accustomed to acting. Fortunately, Dunsany rescues his play from heavy-handedness by poking fun at the ponderous bathos of the play being rehearsed. One exquisite bit of dialogue between the author of the play, Pollit, and the leading actress shows how Dunsany's satire cuts both ways:

Pollit: Well, it's called "The Journey of the Soul."

Phyllis: Oh?

Pollit: Yes; you see the Soul sets out accompanied by Hope to find the Celestial Heights. Well, then, he meets Despair and Remorse, and—and Temptation; and—and all that sort of thing.

Phyllis: (*unhappily*) Oh.

Pollit: Yes; and after that he meets Sin.

Phyllis: Oh, does he?

Pollit: Yes; and then—of course I'm not *telling* it very well—then he comes at last to a sort of place where he meets one with an inexpressibly beautiful face, and . . .

Phyllis: (*slightly interested*) Oh?

Pollit: Yes; and he . . .

Phyllis: (*bored again*) Oh, it's a he?

Pollit: Well, it's a sort of angel, you know, really. They aren't any particular sex, I think.

Phyllis: (*very bored*) Oh. (SMC 91–92)

And Phyllis does seem to get to the heart of the matter when she complains, "But does anything *happen* at all?" (SMC 92). One senses nevertheless that Dunsany's sympathies are generally on the side of the naive but beleaguered poet and not with the preening and aesthetically insensitive actors and stage manager. There are some fine comic moments in *The Journey of the Soul*—as when a bumbling actor and the stage manager debate whether to read "reckon" or "beckon" in one passage, deciding, wrongly and over the playwright's objections, on the former—and this play is perhaps the most successful of Dunsany's literary satires.

Several short stories continue the theme. "The Club Secretary" is a delightful Jorkens tale in which the traveler stumbles upon a very exclusive club in a rural corner of England—it is a club for poets, one whose qualifications are so rigid that Alexander Pope is only a hall porter. Full membership belongs only to the genuinely great poets of history, but an honorary membership can be obtained by writing one great line, something the secretary encountered by Jorkens has done: "A rose-red city half as old as time" (JRA 283). The implication, of course, is that Pope has not written even one imperishable line. Awkwardly enough, Dunsany later discovered that this line (from John William Burgon's *Petra* [1845], although Dunsany never mentions either the poem or the author by name) was a partial plagiarism of Samuel Rogers's "By many a temple half as old as time," so that he was forced to write a sequel, "The Expulsion" (1941; FBJ), in which the secretary meets Jorkens again and relates disconsolately that he has been dismissed from the club for thievery. This is all good fun, and "The Club Secretary" in particular is simply a fictionalization of Dunsany's own critical evaluation of world poetry.

A great many of Dunsany's later tales skewer the pretensions of modern art, literature, and especially poetry. One of the best is "A Fable for

Moderns" (1951; GHL 115–18). The object of attack is T. S. Eliot, although he is never mentioned by name. A bank clerk named Sperkin reads an example of modern poetry—

> The infinite is inexplicitude,
> The final is finality,
> The beginning is the end.
> Shaboo. Shaboo. Shaboo.
> Nip.

—and determines to free himself from those "little tyrants," numbers: "Why should the old dogma that two and two make four be binding upon us forever?" He is, of course, fired from his job, and one would think that his life is ruined; but not so: "He took at once to writing modern verse and won a substantial prize in America, and in Britain enjoys very wide popularity, though he uses a nom de plume. And my reader would be surprised to learn who he really is."

Even better is "Darwin Superseded" (1952). The narrator encounters a friend, Pozzet, who has been working on the theory of evolution. "But didn't Darwin discover that?" the narrator remarks. "Ah, but he was going the other way," says Pozzet, who has determined that modern poetry—and, more importantly, the apparent acceptance of it by intelligent people—is a clear sign of our regression back to apedom. He cites a bit of modern verse: "'I have been carefully analysing the lines, and I estimate that, between the intellect of man and that of the ape, they are just about midway. . . . In fact, if my theory is sound, as I feel sure it is, this should bring us back to the trees before the end of this century.'"

From a slightly different perspective, "That Suprasensical Lear" (1953) exquisitely dynamites the pomposity of modern poetic criticism with a ponderously learned but entirely ridiculous explication of a nonsense lyric by Edward Lear, who is referred to as "the founder of the poetical school of our age."

It should be no surprise that Dunsany extended his critique of modernism to other arts as well. "A Fable for Moderns" points out that "[w]ords, sculpture, and painting had freed themselves from the wearisome bondage of meaning already" (GHL 116); Pozzet in "Darwin Superseded" notes that "'I have been studying some modern plays as well . . . I got more from modern sculpture.'" Modern art is the object of a devastating brief squib, "The Art of Longjuju" (1956), in which a crude stick-figure drawing (drawn by Dunsany himself) is claimed as a masterpiece by the neglected artist Longjuju: "The doors of the Metropolitan are open. Let this picture be carried through." "The Awakening" is the simple tale of a man who is secretly ashamed because he does not understand modern music and who, while at a country house, hears a piece of music and attempts to comprehend it; gradually he thinks he can grasp its essence and its profundity, only to be told (what the reader can hardly have failed to guess): " 'O, the musician. . . . He won't be here for another half hour. That's the piano-tuner.' "

Many of the plays and stories studied here are comic but not fantastic—or, at least, not supernatural. It is, however, one of the distinguishing characteristics of Dunsany's work that he was able to employ the supernatural for comic purposes without poking fun at it. To be sure, there are a few tales where the supernatural is itself made the butt of jest—such as "Biding His Time" (1940), a spoof on the ghost story, or "The Ghosts of the Heaviside Layer" (1955), in which a scientist has invented a device for expelling all substances from a room, including any annoying ghosts that may happen to be there—but these tales are on the whole quite insubstantial. Dunsany also manages to avoid the feeble whimsicality that renders such works as Wilde's "Canterville Ghost" trivial and frivolous: the surface tone may be mild, but the satire is frequently pungent and biting. If Dunsany reached the apex of the comic fantastic in *The Strange Journeys of Colonel Polders*, then the many plays, stories, and novels of the previous forty years that prefaced it are themselves noteworthy for their richness and variety, and for the successful union of "poetry and humour" that was Dunsany's earliest literary goal.

7

The Renunciation of Fantasy

Dunsany is clearly to be identified as a writer of fantasy, if the overall scope and direction of his work are taken into consideration; but one of his many distinctive traits is his ability to infuse an air of weird fantasy into works whose surface plots have nothing of the fantastic or supernatural. A considerable body of his work, early and late, could be classified as purely mainstream, and would be so classified had it been written by anyone other than Dunsany. Among these are such of his writings of World War I as *Tales of War* and *Unhappy Far-Off Things*, as well as three later mainstream novels, *Up in the Hills* (1935), *Guerrilla* (1944), and *His Fellow Men* (1952).

But there is more to it than this. It is not simply that Dunsany occasionally wrote mainstream work; it is that there is, over the course of his career, a perhaps unsystematic but consciously conceived renunciation of fantasy. By this is meant a clear indication that events that are perceived by the characters to be fantastic are not violations of natural law but are in fact delusions, hallucinations, or simply an ignorance of the true state of affairs; there is accordingly a shift of philosophical perspective from an ontological dichotomy (fantasy vs. reality) to a psychological one (delusion vs. reality). The terminus of this transformation is *The Story of Mona Sheehy* (1939).

Of course, Dunsany did write several purely mainstream stories, some of which are very affecting even if they do not, strictly speaking, contribute to his eventual renunciation of fantasy. "Mrs. Mulger" (1932) tells of an elderly keeper of a lodging house who overhears two of her tenants discussing a now-classic poem, "Ode to a Rose." She intrudes with the remark, "You know, my name's Rose"; the men dismiss her peremptorily, but it turns out that "that ode had been written to her" (MAP 109). This brief and delicate tale is surprisingly complex, simultaneously suggesting a woman's loss of youth and attractiveness, the anguish of artistic creation (the poet had committed suicide after writing the poem, perhaps out of unrequited love for Mrs. Mulger), and the class-conscious snobbery of the intellectual elite. It is not surprising that the tale was selected for Edward J. O'Brien's *Best Short Stories of 1932*.

"The Romance of His Life" (1952) is one of the strongest and most bitter stories of Dunsany's late period. A man named Terrup finds himself alone in a train car with Lucy Fells, a famous actress renowned for her beauty. To her profound irritation, Terrup fails to take any notice of her; this is a situation not to be borne ("Supposing a tiger striding out of the jungle came on a herd of gazelles, and they all went on quietly feeding"), so Lucy unleashes all the charm of her personality to win him over. The inevitable occurs: "Albert Terrup was at last at her feet, a tremendously happy, though abjectly conquered, heart." Terrup makes wild suggestions about getting married, to which Lucy half acquiesces ("For a conqueror cannot refuse to accept a surrender"). But when she leaves the train she forgets all about Terrup; nevertheless, for him this brief train ride was the romance of his life. What is remarkable here is the repeated imagery of violence and militarism employed by Dunsany in what purports to be a love story, imagery that underscores the brutal self-centeredness of the celebrated actress:

She had won the hearts of big audiences in great cities in far less time. It took her much longer than she felt that it ought to have taken, but she did not grudge a minute of it; for this conquest had to be made. She could not have anyone holding out against her like this, at the height of her glory. What would Alexander have done if some little village of India had ignored him utterly? No, such a thing could not be.

More relevant to the renunciation of fantasy are a series of tales in the 1930s that explore the form of non-supernatural horror called the *conte cruel*. Lovecraft ably defines this as a tale "in which the wrenching of the emotions is accomplished through dramatic tantalisations, frustrations, and gruesome physical horrors," and describes its prototype, Villiers de l'Isle Adam's "The Torture by Hope," as "the tale of a stake-condemned prisoner permitted to escape in order to feel the pangs of recapture."[1] Tales of this type frequently occupy that nebulous borderland between the horror tale and the tale of suspense, but their distinguishing feature is a horror that is wholly non-supernatural. Hence in Dunsany's "The Sultan's Pet" (1931) we seem to see a sultan reflecting on his lost love while contemplating his pet crocodile, but the final sentence not only makes us understand the true state of affairs—the sultan has murdered the woman and is feeding her to the crocodile—but compels us to reread the entire story in a wholly different light, especially the opening lines: " 'Beautiful fingers, beautiful fingers,' said the Sultan, as he looked at the delicate curve of the shining nails, all faintly tinted with pink" (MAP 87).

Not exactly a *conte cruel* but more on the order of psychological horror is "The Finding of Mr. Jupkens" (1932), a harrowing tale in which an ordinary businessman, Mr. Murblethwaite, hunts down and finally kills a Mr. Jupkens because he fancies himself to be the spirit of Rimmon and Mr. Jupkens to be that of Ahrimmon—"the one for the gods, the other against them, and against all harmony whether amongst the spheres or by the firesides of men" (MAP 104). It is exactly because we know Murblethwaite, although outwardly normal, to be a dangerous lunatic, and not in reality the spirit of a god, that the tale gains its potency.

Dunsany's most celebrated *conte cruel* is "The Two Bottles of Relish" (1932). Dunsany actually took some pride in the fact of its frequent rejection—"my literary agent was unable to get any man in England or America to touch it" (SiW 6)—for he knew that its rejection was derived wholly from its subject matter, cannibalism. This tale introduces Dunsany's eccentric detective Linley, as well as the self-effacing Smethers, a "small man" (LT 7) who becomes Linley's Boswell and Dr. Watson. Linley's Moriarty in this tale and several others is the villain Steeger, who the police are virtually certain has killed his wife and disposed of her body, but who had hidden the body such that no one can find any trace of it. Also a mystery is why Steeger spends so much time chopping wood in the front lawn of his house. Finally Linley solves the case, with the unwitting help of Smethers: the latter had sold Steeger two bottles of the relish Numnumo, a relish designed only for meats (LT 9); but Steeger purports to be a vegetarian (LT 10). Linley concludes that buying *one* bottle of this meat relish might have been an accident, but not *two*: what else could he have done but killed his wife and eaten her? But why the chopping of wood? " 'Solely,' said Linley, 'in order to get an appetite' " (LT 20).

"The Two Bottles of Relish" forms a bridge between Dunsany's *contes cruels* and his pure detective tales—although to refer to them *tout court* as detective tales would be an error, for they are simultaneously parodies of the form. The deadpan, even partly illiterate style of Smethers is perfectly suited to archly morbid humor: "Oh, yes, and he [Steeger] bought a big butcher's knife. Funny thing, they all do. And yet it isn't so funny after all; if you've got to cut a woman up, you've got to cut her up" (LT 11). Linley himself eschews the conventional paraphernalia of the detective ("But Linley never even went near the place and he hadn't got a magnifying glass, nor as I ever saw" [LT 12]), preferring to solve nearly all his cases from the comfort of his armchair.

Subsequent tales of Linley and Smethers are not as entertaining as "The Two Bottles of Relish," and many of them unearth—perhaps by design—the hoariest tricks of the detective story. In "The Shooting of Constable Slugger" Steeger shoots the constable with an icicle, which melts in the wound and leaves no trace; in "The Clue" Linley determines the identity of the murderer based upon the latter's responses to a crossword puzzle; and in "A New Murder" (not a Linley story) a man shoots a glass bullet through a window, thereby releasing a flea infected with plague. "The Unwritten Thriller" is somewhat more amusing, and might even be called a sort of metafiction. A man has come up with what he believes to be the scenario for the perfect murder; but rather than write a novel about it, he decides to put it into practice: " 'It's too good to waste' " (LT 181). The final tale in *The Little Tales of Smethers*, "The Shield of Athene," is interestingly a supernatural detective story. A sculptor has begun to make life-size statues that are remarkably detailed and accurate; it transpires that he has uncovered the shield of Athene, bearing the Gorgon's head, and has been turning people to stone. This conclusion is reached by a course of logical reasoning that eliminates every solution except the supernatural one: " 'What other answer is there?' " (LT 226).

Clever and amusing as some of the stories in *The Little Tales of Smethers* are, they leave an impression of insubstantiality: to parody the detective story over and over again does not, in the end, seem a very interesting thing to do. And yet, Ellery Queen at least was one of those who held these tales in very high esteem, noting that the volume "is a 'tec treasure-trove—no less than 26 tales of crime and detection, all illumined by Lord Dunsany's charm and wit, and his highly individualistic style,"[2] and regarding Linley as one of the more interesting minor detectives in the field.

Much better than many of these detective tales, and really quite unclassifiable, is "The Pirate of the Round Pond," a delightful story of boys who rig up a toy ship with miniature torpedoes and take it to the Round Pond in Kensington Gardens to sink the big, expensive toy ships of other boys. Told entirely from the point of view of one of the boys, this tale could, one supposes, have sociopolitical implications; indeed, the leading "pirate,"

Bob Tipling, fancies himself a Robin Hood (LT 118). But somehow it seems better merely to take delight in the story's narration:

the Rakish Craft, heading towards Bayswater, comes right up to within nearly two yards of the side of the gray ship, which is sailing towards Hyde Park; and just as the gray ship passes our bows Bob makes the sign with his elbow, and I presses the button where I am sitting on the grass beside the luncheon-basket, with my finger inside it touching the wireless set. And there is a white fountain against the side of the gray ship, and both boats rock a bit, and the big one goes on apparently unconcerned. . . . For a moment I thought that Bob's game did not work, and then to my delight I saw the big ship's bows dipping a little, or thought I did. Then I saw I was right. She continued straight on her course, but the bows went lower and lower. And all of a sudden her stern went into the air, and she dived right under, and never came up any more. (LT 121–22)

In studying how non-fantasy can turn into anti-fantasy, it may be useful to begin with several tales of the 1930s that specifically parody Dunsany's earlier imaginary-world manner. In "How the Tinker Came to Skavangur" (1931), the humor is clearly at the characters' expense, especially in regard to their belief in the supernaturalism of the phenomena they witness and experience. The pseudo-Scandinavian setting of the story brings Pegāna to mind, but we are clearly in a realm where the gods are *not* present. Among the many troubles of Haarvold the farmer is the fact that the tinker has not come for weeks, so that he and his wife are without a great many necessities. He goes up to the mountain to pray to the gods to send the tinker, and along the way he thinks he actually sees the gods hunting a stag—but Dunsany makes it very clear that it is in fact a wolf chasing the stag (MAP 79). Ironically, the tinker comes to Haarvold's home on the very day he prays to the gods, confirming him in his theology but making it clear to everyone else that it was mere coincidence.

Somewhat similar is "The Descent of the Sultan of Khash" (1930), in which the sultan of the title wishes to believe that he is descended from the moon when it is very obvious that he is not, although his sycophantic underlings bolster his claims with flowery and bombastic flattery. This story has an atmosphere akin to some of the tales in *The Last Book of Wonder* and *Tales of Three Hemispheres*. A much later story, "The Dwarf Holóbolos and the Sword Hogbiter" (1949), returns to an imaginary realm, and does so in an avowedly supernatural manner; but the narrative—full of such things as a magical sword, a quest for the hand of a fair princess, and battles between fantastic armies—is recounted with a flippancy just on this side of parody. Moreover, this tale was written for a children's magazine, suggesting Dunsany's belief that the *Gods of Pegāna* style is now only suited for the young.

Another late tale, "The Story of Tse Gah" (1947), also plays off of Dunsany's early idiom, but the result is a powerful and grim psychological study. A boy is brought up by monks in some Eastern land to believe that he is "an earthly incarnation of Tse Gah," the god of the mountains who "ruled over our land . . . and spoke by the thunder." This scenario is somewhat reminiscent, as we shall see, of Mona Sheehy's culturally induced belief that she is a child of the fairies. The monks are not, evidently, acting cynically in the matter, for they appear genuinely frightened of the boy. This tale, narrated in the first person by the boy, achieves moments of excruciating poignancy, especially when an old monk beats the boy mercilessly when at one point he declares that he will no longer be Tse Gah: "Then he stripped off my clothing and brought out a thick bamboo, which . . . was as long as I, even longer. And then he began to beat me. He beat me with all his might. I cried out, but no one came. Then I screamed louder, but nothing stirred in the temple; not even the gongs were sounded. . . . I have never known such pain. And then I cried so hard that I could not speak." This passage, unparalleled in the whole of Dunsany's work for its nearly sadistic ferocity, has a far greater impact than those of his *contes cruels*, where the loathsomeness of the events— murder, cannibalism, and the like—is tempered by the half-parodic flippancy of their narration.

The boy finally agrees to resume his role as avatar of Tse Gah, but there is one more twist of the knife. Now himself convinced that he is Tse Gah, the boy is nevertheless compelled to flee when "the revolution came" and the people kill all the monks and destroy the monastery; but he will, he believes, gain his revenge: "The air is sultry now, and I feel that it will be easy to thunder. It is very sultry, and the sky is growing black. Now I have reached the peak. I will thunder, and the people shall know. I will. I . . ." That is the end of the story; and we are left with the searing realization that the boy's delusion of godhead has only condemned him to a life of misery and to futile dreams of vengeance he is utterly unable to carry out. "The Story of Tse Gah" is a model of the penetrating psychological analysis allowed by Dunsany's renunciation of fantasy.

Several late tales are simultaneously anti-fantastic and also about Ireland. "The Burrahoola" (1950) is a frivolous story of swindling, whereby one man spreads a rumor about an anomalous creature named the burrahoola and another man follows him by peddling a charm against it. The credulousness of the Irish countryfolk seems to be the target of this faintly malicious satire. "How Mickey Paid His Debt" (1950) is another tale of swindling: Mickey Mulgraby, owing Thady Murragher £50, connives with a wisewoman to create the illusion that Thady has been turned into a goat, which is then sold for fifty guineas. This story is only of interest because it can be contrasted with a still later tale, "A Goat in Trousers" (1953), where the implication is very clear that a man has in fact been turned into a goat by a wisewoman. These tales feature exactly the same scenario, but the implied supernaturalism of the one and the transparent non-supernaturalism of the other result in wholly different generic and satiric effects.

The best tale of this type, however, is "Helping the Fairies" (1947), a remarkably nasty satire which Dunsany for some reason failed to include in any of his later collections. An Englishman, William Smith, comes to Ireland and purchases some property. He wishes to cut down a thorn tree "that the Little People had danced round for ages." Dunsany knew of the importance of thorn trees in Irish folklore, and writes of them in an aside in *My Ireland*:

Thorn-trees, I may say, are particularly sacred to everything that is pre-Christian, and to this day there are few men who would willingly cut a lone thorn on a hill or out in a field, or one showing by any queer twist of gnarled branches, or greyness of age, that it is likely to be sacred to those who were great in their day, before St. Patrick came to trouble them, and who might not quite be trusted to have lost their power yet. (MI 159–60)

None of the countryfolk will help Smith cut the tree, so he does so himself. At this point Timmy Maguire says that the Little People will be revenged on him; but, to the annoyance of the entire community, Smith continues to prosper. The bland first-person narrator declares pointedly that "the Little People are insulted by this man's luck, as though they didn't exist"; perhaps, then, they need some help. A little later Smith is found dead with bullet holes in his body.

Two late stories fail to make explicit whether the supernatural actually comes into play. "The Rose By-pass" (MAP) is about a wisewoman's curse that forces a town council to give up plans for cutting down her hedge of roses to lay down a road; instead, a bypass is made around the hedge. It is remotely possible that the wisewoman is actually capable of fulfilling her curse; but the predominant suggestion is again a somewhat unflattering suggestion of Irish superstitiousness, whereby all the workers appointed to cut down the hedge refuse to do so because of the wisewoman's curse. More genuinely ambiguous, and one of the most touching stories of Dunsany's entire output, is "Autumn Cricket" (1952). Here an old tender of an abandoned cricket field continues to take care of the field, claiming to see the great cricketers of a prior age performing in stirring matches. We are led to believe that this is a delusion, but then the old man goes out one evening and participates in a match, perishing of the cold. His wife tells the tale:

I stayed and watched the whole time, but he wouldn't allow me to bring him home. He seemed to be hitting boundaries, and so did the gentleman opposite to him, whoever that may have been, or perhaps I should say *whatever*, seeing they was all ghosts, but for him. But after he had hit about twenty of them he seemed to get tired and not to be able to hit so far, and then he had to run. I couldn't stop him. And after a while he took off his hat two or three times and looked around him, seemingly very pleased. And I think he had got his century. And that was when it happened. Of course a man of his age couldn't run like he did, and he dropped dead. I could do nothing. (GHL 80)

The wife's account certainly leaves open the possibility that the ghosts of old cricketers did indeed return to participate in one final match with their loyal groundskeeper. But the determination of whether the supernatural comes into play here is in fact a secondary issue: since the tale's focus is the poignant delineation of an old man unwilling to give up his life's work, the supernatural—if it is present—becomes simply a metaphor emphasizing that same message.

"The Man Who Ate the Phoenix" is both prototypically anti-fantastic and Irish (and perhaps anti-Irish). It also provides a useful preface to *The Story of Mona Sheehy*, although it may have been written subsequent to it: I can find no publication of this novelette prior to its inclusion in the short-story collection named after it (1949). Paddy O'Hone thinks he has shot a phoenix, but the omniscient narrator makes it very clear that he has in fact shot a pheasant. Unfortunately for Paddy, who his doctor had decreed should never have alcohol, his mother cooks the bird in sherry, and then insists that Paddy eat the bird entirely himself. Again Dunsany resolutely demythologizes the situation: " 'It has a strange taste, mother,' he said, for he had never eaten any sort of pheasant before, or tasted sherry" (MAP 16). Paddy thinks the strangeness of the taste is a result of the flesh of the phoenix, but we know differently.

The rest of the novelette is a series of visions seen by Paddy—visions that he attributes to supernaturalism, but which the narrator ruthlessly explodes as delusion or hallucination. He thinks he sees a leprechaun—but it is in fact a goat; he sees a ghost—but it is an illusion; another leprechaun proves to be a "queer old man" (MAP 23); a banshee is a heron; a prince disguised as a swan is—a swan; the marching dead are merely wind and twigs. The entire tale becomes one of comic deflation.

The Story of Mona Sheehy could be considered "The Man Who Ate the Phoenix" writ large, with perhaps somewhat greater sympathy extended toward the central character. I have already noted that this novel is a sort of mirror image of the very early tale "The Kith of the Elf-Folk" (SW), a story that is manifestly supernatural in that the Wild Thing is clearly shown to be a creature from the realm of fairy, wholly nonhuman and soulless. Of Mona Sheehy, on the other hand, it is stated emphatically (in the first and last lines of the book): " 'I never saw a more mortal child' " (SMS 1, 334). This novel, accordingly, forms what may be the sole instance (aside from other works of this type by Dunsany himself) of an anomalous new subgenre, one that might be termed "psychological fantasy." Just as the term "psychological horror" denotes non-supernatural tales in which horror is engendered by the display of aberrant mental states (as in Dunsany's own "Finding of Mr. Jupkens"), so "psychological fantasy" here indicates the wholly non-fantastic origin of Mona Sheehy even though she herself believes that she is a child of the fairies.

As in several other works considered here, Dunsany seems to have felt compelled to employ an unusually heavy-handed and intrusive omniscient narration to make entirely clear the true state of affairs: it is not to his purpose to allow even the least ambiguity in the story of Mona Sheehy's birth. Dennis O'Flanagan, coming home late one evening, sees what he thinks is the Queen of the Fairies dancing in the forest. In fact, it is Lady Gurtrim, who, annoyed that the man who had promised to take her to a dance never showed up, decides to dance by herself in a clearing. The sexual coupling of Dennis and Lady Gurtrim is told with incredible obliquity, and we would not know that anything has even happened until an old woman shows up nine months later on the doorstep of the cottage occupied by Dennis and his sister Biddy. She thrusts into their hands a baby, and Dennis thinks the woman is one of the Shee because she spoke "the tongue of the fairy people" (SMS 14); actually, she is an Italian maid of Lady Gurtrim's. Mona Sheehy receives her first name from the nearby mountain, Slieve-na-mona, and her last name from the Shee. The entire community of Athroonagh is convinced of the fantastic origin of the child, and as a result Mona herself becomes imbued with the belief. The priest, of course, knows better, but another, older priest advises him not to attempt to convince his flock of the truth: " 'for they would never believe us. And it's best for us not to be telling them things they would disbelieve. You don't know where they would stop' " (SMS 2). The thin veneer of Christian belief is no force against the substratum of paganism in the Irish character.

Because, however, Dunsany makes it abundantly clear that Mona is in fact not a child of the Shee, the novel becomes entirely a study of character—the character of Mona Sheehy as she is slowly compelled to give up belief in her supernatural origin. Dennis is advised to send her to school like an ordinary child; she goes, but she learns geography "with the aloof interest of one that was not wholly of this world, but who deigned to be amused at its affairs" (SMS 20). This aloofness, even arrogance, proves to be the principal motivating factor of the novel's development.

The Story of Mona Sheehy also toys continually with the dichotomy between fantasy and reality—but not, as in Dunsany's earlier work, to the denigration of the latter. One extraordinarily subtle passage underscores this topos. At one point Dennis, clearly under the delusion that Mona is a supernatural creature, remarks to his sister, "'She is a strange child'" (SMS 27); but when the omniscient narrator echoes two pages later, "She was a strange child surely" (SMS 29), the phrase is meant purely naturalistically, as an encapsulation of the anomaly of her (false) belief in her fairy origin. This is only one of many examples of Dunsany's use of the metaphysical distinction between the real and the fantastic as a tool for the portrayal of character.

This same distinction gains a sociopolitical dimension as the novel develops. Mona, beginning to doubt her fairy birth, comes upon a tramp who reinforces her belief. The fairies, he says, used to be abundant, then became sparse for a while ("'Ah, it was about the time they were making railways and the like of all that'" [SMS 46]); but now they are coming back (for some reason the tramp never explains). This is a conceit we have seen running through much of Dunsany's work, in which the realm of fantasy is a symbol for the preindustrial world; and here the fact that Mona is not an actual member of that realm is insignificant, for belief in fairies is seen as a sort of emotional/imaginative outlet—a means of maintaining ties to the rural countryside and a shield against the encroachments of the machine age.

The critical turning point of the novel occurs when Mona storms out of the town of Athroonagh in rage because she is blamed for the appearance of the Northern Lights on Slieve-na-mona shortly after she has gone up the mountain to seek her fairy mother, who is reported to dwell there. She falls in with some tinkers, Mr. and Mrs. Joyce, and finds great contentment in their wandering life, close to the earth. Dennis tracks her down and is on the verge of taking her back home when Charlie Peever, a self-serving friend of Lady Gurtrim's (who has always maintained a covert interest in her child), convinces Dennis that it would be best to send Mona to London to earn a living—in, of all places, an advertising agency. It is here that the parallel with "The Kith of the Elf-Folk" becomes striking; recall the Wild Thing being sent to work in a factory:

Mary Jane was sent away to a great manufacturing city of the Midlands, where work had been found for her in a cloth factory. And there was nothing in that town that was good for a soul to see. For it did not know that beauty was to be desired; so it made many things by machinery, and became hurried in all its ways, and boasted of its superiority over other cities and became richer and richer, and there was none to pity it. (SW 151–52)

Mona is in a still worse situation. This whole segment of the novel appears on the surface to do little but provide Dunsany an opportunity to wield a cudgel against his bêtes noires, advertising and commerce, but this unpleasant episode in London is necessary for Mona finally to slough off belief in her nonhuman origin—in other words, the aloofness that caused her to be a self-created exile in her Irish community and also to scorn the unaffected love of a villager, Peter O'Creagh—and to realize that the reality of her life in Athroonagh was superior to her dreams of being a fairy princess:

She saw now too late that a house on the Harahanstown estate, by the side of the big woods, with the people of Athroonagh round about her, and the sounds and the sights she knew, were better than the court of a dynasty that had forgotten her, on the cold slopes of a mountain, or in any unfulfilled dream; better too than that to which she had fallen, while trying to climb to the clouds, that rode all heedless of her over Slieve-na-mona. (SMS 246–47)

For Athroonagh, and the rural environment generally, in truth possess all the magic that Elfland is reputed to hold, a fact that is made abundantly clear by many metaphors and similes comparing the Irish countryside—particularly the mountain of Slieve-na-mona—to the land of fairy: "As she drew nearer, the very presence of the mountain seemed to hint of enchantment. . . . Glancing again at the far mountains she saw that shadows and sunlight had changed. It was like watching an assembly of giants frowning and smiling" (SMS 89). It is also made clear by a piquant if simpleminded anthropology of fairies offered by Dunsany when Mona is with the tinkers:

And all the way sang the birds, as though they recognized in the girl with the bundle of tins, a daughter of the Queen of that people that was nearer to them than to man; so much nearer that the story of many a fairy, many an elf, is probably but the history of the small things dwelling in woods, altered a little by the eye of man, for he saw them in dim light, altered again by his mind as he tried to explain them, and altered again by frailties of his memories, when he tried for his children's sake to remember the stories that has grandmother told him. (SMS 178)

This not only brings to mind a passing remark in *Rory and Bran*—"The world is full of wonders, and all the wonders that our imagination paints are but the mirage of them" (RB 19)—but those passages in *Patches of Sunlight* where Dunsany admits that his imaginative transmutation of the natural world led to the creation of the imaginary realms of his early period ("the wildest flights of the fancies of any of us have their homes with Mother Earth" [PS 9]).

The denouement of *The Story of Mona Sheehy* is a little contrived— Lady Gurtrim, a passionate race-car driver, dies in a race and leaves all her money to Mona, which allows her to return to Ireland; and the towns-people's objections to the now wealthy Mona marrying the impoverished Peter are removed when Charlie Peever invests her money unwisely and loses it all—but at this point all we are concerned about is the triumphant return of Mona to her simple rural Irish roots, and the consequent spiritual victory of preindustrialism over the maniacal horrors of urban life. It is, of course, a message hammered home in many of Dunsany's works, but rarely so affectingly as here.

The Story of Mona Sheehy is the culmination of his renunciation of fantasy. But there is at least one later tale that perhaps suggests that he was not wholly content with such a renunciation. "By Night in a Forest" (1953) tells of a man who finds himself armed with a lance and a sword riding a horse through a dark forest; he has lost his memory from an apparent fall from the horse. He wonders who and where he is: is he a medieval knight pursuing an enemy? "Clearly something lurked for him, whoever he was, or he would not have been armed like that. Beasts or men? asked his guesses. Beasts or men? And they found no answer. Might there even be a dragon there? he guessed at one time. For he seemed clearly to be in some strange century, and did not know what its creatures might be" (GHL 56). But in fact the man was merely going to a fancy-dress ball. He is, certainly, relieved at this circumstance, but his very regret at the dissipation of the dangers of the forest—"all the hazards of a thousand shadows and that watching for what might lurk in them" (GHL 58)—perhaps echoes Dunsany's own regret at the decreasing quotient of fantasy and wonder in his later work.

It is perhaps for this reason that Dunsany's renunciation of fantasy—in the sense of abandoning the supernatural—is never complete. We return to pure, if comic, supernaturalism in *The Strange Journeys of Colonel Polders* (1950), and the purportedly science-fictional premise of *The Last*

Revolution (1951) is so preposterous that it is virtually supernatural. Many later tales employ the supernatural insouciantly, without a hint of parody.

But what might be called a gradual "desupernaturalization" is evident throughout the whole of Dunsany's career: beginning with a radical, imaginary-world fantasy that scarcely acknowledges the existence of the "real" world, he slowly infuses that real world into his work, first by juxtaposition (*The King of Elfland's Daughter* is emblematic), then by suggesting that the real world is itself a source of fantasy (the Jorkens tales), until the fantasy world becomes a mere delusion. Those works of comic fantasy we studied earlier—especially such wholly non-supernatural plays as *Atalanta in Wimbledon* and *The Hopeless Passion of Mr. Bunyon*—might be thought to transfer the locus of fantasy from topography to psychology: Marjorie Dawk's soberly held wish-fulfillment fantasy of winning a mate by means of a Ping-Pong match—a fantasy that unwittingly parodies the very romantic conventions she has adopted—is perhaps not so far from Mona Sheehy's fantasy of being the daughter of the Queen of the Fairies.

The Story of Mona Sheehy was published in September 1939, at the very outset of World War II. Although Dunsany considered war to be a sort of natural force not very amenable to political negotiation, it is unlikely that he ever considered the possibility of witnessing a second worldwide conflict. But Dunsany's response to this war was very different from his response to its predecessor, and the outpouring of poems, tales, and novels written during and just after Hitler's war deserves separate treatment.

NOTES

1. H. P. Lovecraft, "Supernatural Horror in Literature," in *Dagon and Other Macabre Tales* (rev. ed., Sauk City, WI: Arkham House, 1986), 393.

2. Ellery Queen, headnote to "Near the Back of Beyond," *Ellery Queen's Mystery Magazine* 26, No. 5 (November 1955): 30.

Interchapter: Hitler's War

Dunsany served both as a soldier and as a propagandist in World War I, and both during and after the war he experienced a profound depression that effectively dried up his pen for years. Gradually he began writing again, achieving moderate success with his early novels and great popularity with his Jorkens tales; in the early 1930s he began tapping yet another new vein, writing at long last of Irish subjects in *The Curse of the Wise Woman* (1933), *The Story of Mona Sheehy* (1939), and other novels and tales. But, as occurred a generation before, the course of his literary career was abruptly interrupted by the onset of another World War.

Dunsany, being sixty-one years old at the outbreak of the war, could hardly serve in a very concrete military capacity, although he took great pride and even a certain delight in being part of the Home Guard that kept a lookout in Kent for incoming German planes. What he could do, however, was write, and he was not to be silenced as he was during the earlier conflict. Of the ten books published during World War II or just after it, six deal directly with the war: the novel *Guerrilla* (1944); four books of poetry, *War Poems* (1941), *Wandering Songs* (1943), *A Journey* (1944), and *The Year* (1946); and *A Glimpse from a Watch Tower* (1946), a brief series of ruminations on the end of the war, including the dropping of the atomic bomb. Dunsany's final poetry collection, *To Awaken Pegasus* (1949), also contains a number of war poems, while the third of his autobiographies, *The Sirens Wake* (1945), speaks much of his activities during the war, recounting—as do *Wandering Songs* and *A Journey*—his curious trip through the Middle East and Africa as he was forced to evacuate Greece in 1941 when Hitler invaded.

It is difficult to gauge the effect of the outbreak of Hitler's war upon Dunsany's temperament. He could hardly have failed to take note of Hitler's rise over the six years prior to the commencement of hostilities, but there is no mention of Hitler in *The Sirens Wake* until the actual invasion of Poland. Perhaps because he had been through it all before, this new war did not affect him as apocalyptically as the first one had:

Looking at things that I wrote in those days I see a faith in victory that almost seems to have been too lightly come by, based as it was upon ignorance of so much that has happened to us since. And yet we all had that faith, and was it not that that brought us all the way, till we see victory as clear as we see it now, not yet face to face, as I write in November of 1943, but very close? (SiW 45)

Dunsany goes on to say that he did little writing until the spring of 1940, when he began producing a considerable amount of propagandist verse. This poetry, while not of great intrinsic interest, gives a very clear picture of Dunsany's movements and sensations during the war.

Because this war was a less morally ambiguous conflict than its predecessor, Dunsany's poetry gains a sharper edge as he tirelessly flays Hitler and Mussolini for their tyranny and aggression. And yet, even in some of this verse a brooding and pensive tone enters in; whether it be in something like "Bad News . . ." (WP 47), which suggests that another tyrant will some day emerge even after Hitler is defeated, or "A Song of an L.D.V.," which appears jingoistic in its recounting of what Dunsany might do if he captured a German airman ("Richer for his blood will blow / Kentish flowers which we know"), but then concludes startlingly: "And just the same if he gets me" (WP 76).

Some of Dunsany's most poignant war poetry unites the war with his overriding Nature theme in various ways. On its simplest level such things as "A Bird at Peace" (WP 78) and "Starlight in Kent" (WP 83) contrast the tranquillity of Nature with the turbulence of war; perhaps the most affecting is "The Harmless Wing":

> I saw a sparrow from grey sky
>   Dart down upon his quest for food
> And realized as he flashed by,
>   Bringing a brightness to my mood,
> Not only evil things can fly. (WS 16)

A slight variant on this idea is "The Surprise," where Dunsany notices a
dead butterfly and is amazed that, "even in 1941, / Other things than man
should die" (WP 73).

"The Old Voice" combines war, Nature, and the "Prayer of the Flowers"
theme in a single eight-line poem, remarking how all Nature "seemed to
mark as transient things / The syrens wailing from a town / And drone
of engines upon wings" (WP 16). What heed should Nature take of our
warlike race? Orion's Sword looks down at us, "As though a world at
war / Were nought at all to him" ("The Sword of Orion" [WS 46]). And
yet, it is the very "guns of London" that will bring back, "I know not
when, / Once more a calm and natural Spring" (WP 84).

We will see how the dropping of the atom bomb jarred Dunsany as he
was writing *A Glimpse from a Watch Tower*; and it is not surprising that
his sense of triumph over Hitler, which we see emerging in *The Year*, is
suddenly dampened by the threat to all civilization represented by the
bomb. "At the End of an Era" (TAP 56) and "Nearing the End" are both
wrenching poems on this subject. In the latter we have now entered "the
age of Phaëton / Who so disastrously aspired to follow / The blazing
journey of his sire Apollo"; who can doubt the result?

> And so we hasten onward in our might
>   To that sure end for which old Nature waits,
> And all her wild shy brood that roam the night,
>   When Man's own engines batter at Man's gates
> And cities fall, and quiet will come again
> And all our rails be rust-marks in a plain. (TAP 67)

Dunsany does not seem aware that even animals may not fare especially
well if universal nuclear holocaust ever occurs.

Both *A Journey* and *The Year* unite a number of themes in Dunsany's
poetry, notably those of war, Nature, and autobiography. The former is
a laborious and rather flippant five-canto epic poem recounting his trip
to Greece in 1940 and his subsequent evacuation through Africa following the German invasion. But this work—written, like its successor,
entirely in Byronic stanzas—is only intermittently compelling, as
Dunsany's languid poetic idiom makes many incidents, however dire they
may have been in actuality, sound almost whimsical and frivolous.

The Year is a rather different proposition. Although even longer than *A
Journey*, it is far more interesting for its complex intertwining of many of
Dunsany's dominant themes. Although it purports to be a Nature poem,
describing day by day the beauties of the countryside during the course of

an entire year, it is no accident that the poem was begun on June 14, 1944; for what this poem really is, or wants to be, is a paean of triumph over the fall of Hitler, which Dunsany now feels to be imminent. He in fact expresses disappointment that Hitler was not overthrown on Armistice Day 1944 ("Now comes the day on which I hoped in vain / The war would end" [Y 82]), but gains increasing exultation in the spring and summer as the Germans flee in retreat back to Berlin.

And yet, once again Dunsany's poem is far from naive or jingoistic. The death of Hitler in May indeed inspires Dunsany with a momentary sense of triumph, but he is aware that the end of the war only means that other human evils will come to the forefront:

> The thing is over, and we lose a woe,
>   And our own dangers close round us again,
> Lurking more secretly than did the foe.
>   Man to cheat man will once more work amain,
>   And we, who cannot even grind our grain,
> Must eat instead of bread whatever given
>   And drink strange chemicals, till by some plain
> And barbarous folk we shall again be driven
> To fight for life, more weak than when we last had striven. (Y 160)

This stanza itself embodies the dominant motif of Dunsany's later war poetry—the interplay between war and Nature. War may be over, but the evils of civilization—bred by our increasing distance from Nature—will emerge and eventually overrun us.

By the very nature of its composition—Dunsany wrote anywhere from one to six stanzas every day from June 14, 1944, to June 14, 1945—*The Year* cannot have any sort of aesthetic unity, and its value may derive only from its occasionally poignant evocations of Nature and in its recording of Dunsany's response to world events as they were occurring. In this latter aspect his work is not always successful. Touching as may be his elegies to Franklin Delano Roosevelt (Y 143) and his mother-in-law, Lady Jersey (Y 174–75), keen as may be his shock at the horrors of Belsen (Y 147), he cannot help descending to bathos with his paean to Eisenhower ("Glory to England's arms! Glory to Eisenhower!" [Y 50]) or else seeming merely like a versified newspaper as he recounts the events of the day as he hears of them. Even his Nature descriptions occasionally drag. It may be true that "Nature's white page gleams / With countless stories on a thousand themes" (Y 109), but it is not so clear that Dunsany has the poetic ability to vivify them without monotony. Perhaps it is best to read *The Year* a few stanzas at a time—perhaps, indeed, to read daily those stanzas that Dunsany wrote on a given day. It is certainly an interesting experiment, combining Nature poetry, criticism of industrial civilization, and descriptions of the progress and meaning of the war; but in the end it too will probably remain little read even by devotees of his work.

Many stories written both during and after the war focus on various aspects of the conflict. Dunsany began writing voluminously for *Punch* in 1939, and the stories divide more or less evenly between humorous war stories and stories about Ireland. Few of the former are especially distinguished, but we can take brief note of such things as "Our War Aims Committee" (1939), an amusing tale about Hitler's moustache, and "Very Secret" (1943), which cleverly tells of the deciphering of a message sent in code.

There are some other very odd stories about the war. "Down among the Kingcups" (1940) appears to be an allegory predicting the fate of Hitler. A man in some remote country is caught in a snowstorm and wakes up to find that he is in a monastery, having been rescued by one of the monks. Falling into conversation with a Brother Ignotello, he makes a seemingly innocent remark: "He supposed, he said, that some of them [the monks] had had lives and experiences out in the world quite different to what they now enjoyed with their books" (MAP 189). Brother Ignotello immediately launches into an account of a battle in which he was involved, and in which he commits a tactical error that foils his great ambition—"[w]orld domination" (MAP 192). "A Lapse of Memory" was apparently written after the war, although this curious and poignant vignette of a man who wakes up in no-man's-land with his memory gone may equally be describing World War I or II. Indeed, the tale is the ultimate refinement of Dunsany's earlier *Tales of War* style, here wholly without propagandizing:

> The war had gone on for a long time: he could see that by the strength of the weeds. For what cause, he wondered, was it being fought? Perhaps there had been a vast movement of some large people, suddenly become nomadic; or the war might have come from some definite disagreement between two nations, one of which was his own. Whatever movement there had been, it had been stopped for a while by this line of trenches, and for quite a long while. He wondered which side he was on. (MAP 213)

But perhaps the most powerful of Dunsany's shorter war stories is "The Speech" (1950). Here we are taken back to the days prior to World War I, and old Gauscold, a journalist who narrates several late tales by Dunsany and is a somewhat less self-parodic version of Jorkens, tells of a firebrand member of the House of Commons, Peter Minch, who plans to deliver a speech even though it may trigger a European war. Minch is warned by a nameless organization not to give the speech, but of course he is not about to yield to this insidious curtailment of his freedom of utterance. Tremendous measures are taken to protect Minch's life prior to the day of his speech, but his shadowy opponents do not resort to anything so crude as assassination—not, at any rate, of him. Instead, they kill his father, Lord Inchingthwaite, causing Minch automatically to become a peer and thereby banning him from speaking in the lower house. The peace of Europe is saved. But the tale is not over:

> "So war was averted," said one of us.
> "Well, yes," said old Gauscold. "Not that it made any difference in the end."
> (LT 170)

The Great War came anyway.

Guerrilla (1944), the most significant prose work to come out of Dunsany's war experiences, tells the simple story of a young man, Srebnitz, whose parents are ruthlessly killed by a German major billeted with them and who joins a very small band of guerrillas in the hill near his town, a band organized and under the strict control of one Hlaka. When Srebnitz joins the guerrillas, he is initially unnerved to note that there are only fifteen of them—fifteen against five thousand, as he learns (G 51), a figure perhaps meant to recall the fantastic odds against the Greeks fighting at Thermopylae. An ambush of Germans attempting to capture the band nets a considerable amount of rifles and ammunition, and about fifty more Greeks from the town come up the mountain to carry on the guerrilla war. Hlaka trains them rigorously, and continues to have uncanny success against the Germans: he had fought them before (in World War I, it is implied but never stated), hence knows their tactics very well (G 70). It is to Dunsany's credit that he does not portray the Germans as bumbling—which they by no means were—but merely unaccustomed to guerrilla tactics.

Dunsany was well aware that he could not have his small band of sixty-five hold out indefinitely against the battalion of Germans in the town (and the prospect of an infinitely greater number being brought in if the trouble continued), so the climax of the novel is the attempt of an English airman who has landed on the mountain to assist the guerrillas and some of the villagers who have joined them in reaching a nearby lake, where they can be airlifted to safety. This entire episode is handled with considerable verve and dramatic tension, and upon the successful completion of the mission Dunsany concludes the novel with a predictable but still stirring prophecy of the eventual retaking of "The Land" by those who have rightfully held it for millennia. The novel was reviewed very charitably upon its emergence in February 1944, but with the urgency of its subject matter and of the circumstances of its composition long past, it can now occupy only a modest place in Dunsany's canon.

Similarly modest, but very affecting as a human document, is the series of lectures *A Glimpse from a Watch Tower*, written by Dunsany between July 7 and August 21, 1945, and published early the next year. It does not take a historian to note that these lectures, written with the intention of reflecting upon the state of the world with the imminent fall of the Axis powers, prove to be the unexpected and harrowing testimony of a man whose entire view of the world is altered by the dropping of the atomic bomb on August 6, 1945. Dunsany tries to put a brave face on things: "Strange, strange news came to us today. We have just heard of the atomic bomb. And yet, to me, it does not appear to alter the picture of the future as I have long seen it, however dimly; but only seems to make that picture more visible" (GWT 41). But it is clear, both from this work and from the many stories he subsequently wrote about the bomb, that he was shaken:

It seems that the progress and the wonders of the last hundred years are nearly at an end. Henceforth we are all people with a mission, a strange mission, not to destroy the world. Matter does not care: matter will blow all our cities to pieces. Only the control of matter by spiritual forces, that are lofty enough to have the necessary strength, can have any chance of saving our cities. (GWT 45)

A Glimpse from a Watch Tower begins with predictable hostility toward Germany and a belief that it will promptly rearm itself after the war and try once again to overrun Europe, and continues with still more predictable attacks on mechanization; but the atom bomb causes Dunsany's vision to broaden so as to encompass the future of mankind, as he wonders whether we can control the bomb, whether we can keep it out of the hands of the ignorant, the insane, and the rapacious, and whether in fact some accident might cause the end of civilization and even of the entire race. Dunsany's remark, "Henceforth we are like children in a powder-factory" (GWT 47), betrays his lack of confidence in the maturity of human beings to control this new invention, and—unaware that an all-out nuclear war would end not only the human race but all life on the planet—engages in one more "Prayer of the Flowers" meditation as he pictures the outcome of such a war: "I am told that what wiped out Nagasaki weighed only eight pounds: we can trust the last few years of what we call Progress to increase it to eight tons, and we may turn our eyes away from what that increase will bring, and look to the quieter times that will come after, when more sheep will bleat on the downs and there will be no hooting of motors" (GWT 52). A new human race may then emerge, will develop into a civilization, and perhaps will once again discover machinery: the cycle will begin all over again, and perhaps the next time it will not be merely civilization but the entire planet that will be scattered to the winds; perhaps that is what happened to the fifth planet of the solar system, "so that where that planet ran are now only asteroids" (GWT 53). If nothing else, *A Glimpse from a Watch Tower* is perhaps among the earliest glimpses into the mentality of the nuclear age.

8

Ireland

Dunsany's relations with Ireland and the Irish literary movement were a source of vexation both to himself and to others. We have seen that Yeats, who when staying with Dunsany in 1909 said of him that he "has a very fine style, which he shows in wild little fantastic tales," invited him to write plays for the Abbey Theatre as a way of getting him into " 'the movement.' "[1] Although none of Dunsany's early plays (nor, for that matter, his later ones) are about Ireland, Yeats continued to pursue Dunsany, evidently wishing to put Dunsany's increasing critical reputation to use. In a letter of February 19, 1911, Yeats requested permission to issue the *Selections from the Writings of Lord Dunsany* with the Cuala Press, saying, "It is my way of claiming you for Ireland" (cited in Am 78). But how to claim Dunsany for Ireland if he did not write about Ireland? There is, in fact, a lone exception to the banishment of Ireland from Dunsany's early fantastic tales, and that is "In the Twilight" (1908). In that tale a man who is drowning experiences a series of visions or hallucinations, some involving his past life. One of these is clearly a glimpse of his life in Ireland:

I was back on the Bog of Allen again after many years, and it was just the same as ever, though I had heard that they were draining it. . . . I was glad . . . to see the old bog again and all the lovely things that grew there—the scarlet mosses and the green mosses and the firm and friendly heather, and the deep silent water. I saw a little stream that wandered vaguely through the bog, and little white shells down in the clear depths of it; I saw, a little way off, one of the great pools where no islands are, with rushes round its borders, where ducks love to come. I looked long at that untroubled world of heather, and then I looked at the white cottages on the hill, and saw the grey smoke curling from their chimneys and knew that they burned turf there, and longed for the smell of burning turf again. (SW 167–68)

Perhaps it was passages like this, so keen and unaffected in their appreciation of the Irish countryside, that led Yeats to think that Dunsany might do more work of this sort. But no other such passage can be found in Dunsany's early tales and plays. Accordingly, by the time of the issuance of the *Selections* it was becoming evident that Dunsany would not abandon his imaginary realms of fantasy, and Yeats in his introduction expressed the following pensive regret:

When I was first moved by Lord Dunsany's work I thought that he would more help this change [i.e., the Irish literary revival] if he could bring his imagination into the old Irish legendary world instead of those magic lands of his with their vague Eastern air; but even as I urged him I knew that he could not, without losing his rich beauty of careless suggestion, and the persons and images that for ancestry have all those romantic ideas that are somewhere in the background of all our minds. He could not have made Slieve-na-Mon nor Slieve Fua incredible and phantastic enough, because that prolonged study of a past age, necessary before he could separate them from modern association, would have changed the spontaneity of his mood to something learned, premeditated, and scientific.[2]

This is a remarkably prophetic analysis: somehow Yeats seemed to know that Dunsany would have to renounce otherworld fantasy, at least in part, in order to find inspiration in his ancestral land. And neither Yeats nor Dunsany himself could have known that it would take two to three decades for this renunciation to run its course.

But Dunsany did contribute to "the movement" in other ways. His first periodical appearances were in the Irish magazine *Shanachie*: "Time and the Gods" appeared in the first issue (undated, but 1906) under the title "The Lament of the Gods for Sardathrion," "The Whirlpool" appeared in an issue that was probably published in Autumn 1906, and "The Doom of La Traviata" appeared in the Winter 1907 issue. Two stories by Dunsany were published in the *Irish Homestead*, "The Fall of Babbulkund" in Christmas 1907 (illustrated by AE) and "Poltarnees, Beholder of Ocean" in Christmas 1908. When, in late 1910, James Stephens, Thomas Mac-Donagh, Padraic Colum, and David Houston were founding the *Irish Review*, Dunsany, at Stephens's insistence, managed to find time—in spite of the fact that he was busy writing the *Book of Wonder* stories for weekly serialization in the *Sketch*—to send the prose-poem "Alone the Immortals" for the first issue (January 1911). Many early stories appeared in the *Irish Review*, as well as the plays *King Argimēnēs and the Unknown Warrior* (September 1911) and *The Gods of the Mountain* (December 1911). Dunsany also supported the journal financially.[3] No doubt he was relieved when Stephens assured him, "There will be little or no politics in the paper."[4]

Several of Dunsany's early essays and reviews also champion Irish writers. In "A Note on *Blanco Posnet*" (1909) Dunsany defends both Shaw's play—or, rather, criticizes its banning in England—and alludes briefly to the rioting two years previous at the performance of Synge's *Playboy of the Western World*. Dunsany reviewed a performance of Synge's *Deirdre of the Sorrows* the next year, attributing to Synge that closeness to Nature which was his own distinguishing trait: "Synge is never far away from the fields of men, his is not the inspiration of the skylark remote from earth; our wonder at his fancy is as our wonder at the flight of the white owl low down near beautiful fields." He speaks poignantly of the death of Synge: "I remember the gloom that fell on a small circle in Dublin on the day that he died last year, a gloom out of which his fame has been growing ever since as a crocus grows out of the very shadow of the short days" (*"Deirdre of the Sorrows"*). A review of George Birmingham's play *Eleanor's Enterprise*, published under the title "In the House of Mammon" (1911), refers to Birmingham as "the wittiest writer we have in Ireland," although later he would grant that honor to his friend Oliver St. John Gogarty.

A lengthy review in 1911 entitled simply "Ireland" (with two section headings, "In Myth" and "In Stone") allows Dunsany the opportunity to discuss his views of Irish myth and architecture under the guise of reviewing two books, *Celtic Wonder-Tales* by Ella Young and *Irish Ecclesiastical Architecture* by Arthur C. Champneys. Continuing his anti-civilization diatribe ("a folk has always spoken the truth—lying is taught in cities"), Dunsany speaks of the value of myth:

Tales by a fireside are as true to life as confessions of a death-bed; they are the immemorial heirlooms that the gods gave the ancients, the poor man's legacy to his children. Over the fire of an evening a peasantry weaves, as girls make lace in cottages, the embroidered purple cloak of exaggeration. With this cloak it covers natural and simple Man, or his joyous friend, the Sun.

And although he continues, "Ireland in myth is worth while wandering in; there are wonderful things in its history," the question remains why Dunsany himself did not wander in them until such a relatively late date in his career. He of course cannot address this question in a review, but he similarly fails to deal with it in any of his discussions of his early writing; and we can only fall back on Yeats's assumption that the very specificity of Irish myth would have fettered his imagination. In "Ireland" Dunsany notes:

So, as I wandered through these tales among gods that were mostly new to me, when I read that Mananaun, the god of the Ocean, took the Sun-god, Lugh, in his arms and held him up to say good-bye to Ireland and wrapped him in his cloak and carried him away, then everything became familiar at once and I knew that I was listening to Man again telling of his favourite stories about a sunset.

But he had himself already written his own exquisite quasi-fable about the sunset, "A Legend of the Dawn" (SW), and it is not likely that he could have done much better by adapting the existing Irish myth.

In the summer of 1912 Dunsany received from Francis Ledwidge a copybook of his verses (MI 53), and immediately recognized that a new voice in Anglo-Irish poetry had emerged. Dunsany assisted Ledwidge not merely in the revision of his poetry but in its publication, writing introductions to each of his three slim volumes, *Songs of the Fields* (1916), *Songs of Peace* (1917), and the posthumous *Last Songs* (1918). Some of Ledwidge's verse had, no doubt in part through Dunsany's influence, begun to appear periodically, including a charming tribute to his mentor, "To Lord Dunsany (On His Return from Africa)" (*Saturday Review*, January 10, 1914; reprinted in *Songs of the Fields*). Another tribute, "To an Old Quill of Lord Dunsany's," appeared in *Last Songs*, while a third, "Sonnet on Some Stones Lord Dunsany Brought Me from Sahara," remained unpublished until it appeared in Alice Curtayne's edition of *The Collected Poems of Francis Ledwidge* (1974). Dunsany spoke warmly of Ledwidge at every opportunity—in the introductions to Ledwidge's collections, in a lengthy chapter in *My Ireland* (MI 53–67), and in a later article, "Francis Ledwidge" (1946). As with Synge, Dunsany's highest praise for Ledwidge is as a poet of Nature:

Of pure poetry there are two kinds, that which mirrors the beauty of the world in which our bodies are, and that which builds the more mysterious kingdoms where geography ends and fairyland begins. . . . Mr. Ledwidge gives us the first kind. When they have read through the profounder poets, and seen the problem plays, and studied all the perplexities that puzzle man in the cities, the small circle of readers that I predict for him will turn to Ledwidge as to a mirror reflecting beautiful fields, as to a very still lake rather on a very cloudless evening. ("Francis Ledwidge")

But before the publication of Ledwidge's first book came the Great War. Amid the lengthy accounts of trips to Europe and big-game expeditions in Africa that we find in *Patches of Sunlight*, Dunsany is remarkably silent on the sociopolitical situation in Ireland in the years prior to the war, perhaps because the issues that then seemed so vital—particularly Home Rule—were wholly irrelevant both to the Irish and to the Unionist Dunsany by the time he began writing his first autobiography in 1937. Still, he makes the following pointed remark on the sentiments in Ireland at the outbreak of the war:

Among the currents of feeling that swept Ireland in August 1914, was one of loyalty, and it was believed for a while that bodies of volunteers were ready to take part in the war. I think there was such an intention, and I joined them in that belief for a few days; but nothing came of this, and early in September I joined the 5th Battalion of the Royal Inniskilling Fusiliers. (PS 263)

This is about as close as Dunsany ever comes to criticizing the stance of neutrality that many in Ireland adopted during World War I, and he never refers to the bungled German attempt to aid the Easter Rebellion in 1916. Dunsany was, of course, injured seriously during the Dublin riots, and he tells the story with typical arch understatement. On leave from the 5th Battalion of the Inniskilling Fusiliers, Dunsany was ordered to assist Major Carter at Amiens Street. On the way there his car was ambushed:

I got out and lay down in the road, and many bullets went by me before I was hit. My chauffeur, Frederick Cudlipp, was shot at the wheel, but not fatally. When the volleys went on I saw that there was no use in staying there lying down in front of them at forty yards, so I went across the road to a doorway where I thought I could get cover. . . . The man that took me prisoner, looking at the hole in my face made by one of the bullets, a ricochet, made a remark that people often consider funny, but it was quite simply said and sincerely meant: he said, "I am sorry." (PS 269–70)

Dunsany was taken to the hospital in Jervis Street, where he stayed until the rebellion was put down; he was then transferred to King George V's Hospital. After a month's sick leave he was ordered to Ebrington Barracks in Londonderry, where he wrote the preface to *The Last Book of Wonder* in August 1916 before going to Flanders in early 1917.

We have seen that Dunsany professed to a state of depression after the war, especially after the desultory tour of France in the summer of 1919 that provided the impetus for *Unhappy Far-Off Things* (1919). Dunsany never mentions Ireland at this point in his autobiography, but the fact that upon his return from France he went to his home in Kent (WSS 12) rather than to Dunsany Castle may suggest that he did not feel comfortable in a country that was lurching toward civil war. In this sense, Dunsany's first American tour (October 1919–January 1920) could not have come at a better time. And yet, the moment he arrived in New York he was besieged with questions about the state of affairs in Ireland; some of his responses are recorded in an interview with Montrose J. Moses in the *New York Times* of October 12, 1919.[5]

Dunsany begins by declaring his independence, as an artist, from the pettiness of politics:

Of course, . . . I knew you would ask me what I thought of conditions in my own country, and that's the very thing I want to avoid. Politics are necessary, I suppose, for the governing of a city, just as sewerage is necessary for the health of a people. I think one's drains are perhaps more important. But to an artist politics are dull; they go a shorter journey; they do less of a job for man than art.

When someone comments, "Surely . . . you have not remained outside the turmoil for an Irish republic," and he is asked how he could "escape participation in Irish affairs," he replies: " 'By being an artist first, last, and always. Besides which, at the present time, there is no Irish republic. I'll talk to you about it when it comes'—and he added with a glint and the suggestion of an ironic smile—'if I'm alive.' "

Turning to his literary work, he states bluntly: " 'Perhaps I should say that I am no part at all of the Irish movement in art. No poet should be a part of any movement. . . . I am not interested in depicting Irish condition; what matters with me is the condition of man, not in his relation to governments, as they are, or should be, but solely in relation to Destiny.' " There is nothing especially new here, and Dunsany's assertion of the universality of his work can be inferred from such early pieces as "Romance and the Modern Stage" (1911) and "Nowadays" (1912); but the specific rejection of even an inclination to write about Irish matters is noteworthy.

And it is noteworthy because it is, at this very time, false. "How the Lost Causes Were Removed from Valhalla" (GHL 64–68) was published in the *Smart Set* in October 1919; it was clearly timed to coincide with Dunsany's American tour. It is the first work I know of that is specifically about Ireland. This little squib, scarcely more than five hundred words long, tells how, "in the dawn of time, before peoples began, the spirits of the nations rose up out of their lands and trooped away to Valhalla to be given each a Cause." Each nation thereby gets its cause except the spirit of Ireland. Having nothing left in Valhalla, the gods give the spirit "the lost causes that the other spirits had left." All this is a trifle heavy-handed, but it shows Dunsany's ability to use his *Gods of Pegāna* style for purposes of social satire. Equally obvious but a little more pertinent is an untitled piece that appeared as the first of "Two Sketches" in *Vanity Fair* in November 1919. Here St. Patrick, ridding Ireland of snakes and toads, encounters Satan, who is irked by his wonder-working. He asks him, "What religion are ye at all?" "Sure, I'm a Christian," St. Patrick replies.

"Begob, that accounts for it," says Satan, "for that's a religion I never heard of at all. There's only Catholics and Protestants in Ireland. It's a queer religion you have and it's a queer thing you're doing."
"Sure, I'm only making the country comfortable for Irishmen," says St. Patrick, "the way they'll live at peace in it."

But Satan will have none of it, asserting that if the Irish are comfortable and at peace they will have no "divarsion." In this brief parable we can see the ultimate origin of Dunsany's last novel, *His Fellow Men.*

For the next several years Dunsany shuttled back and forth between Ireland and Kent, but in *While the Sirens Slept* he is still remarkably taciturn about the situation in Ireland. He says a little flippantly that it became impossible to collect a team of cricketers after the treaty (WSS 37), and then very obliquely relates an episode of February 1921 that got wide coverage in the press: Dunsany was brought before a court-martial in Dublin for having an array of weapons "not under effective military control." The report in the *Times* of London goes on to note that Dunsany's solicitor, a Mr. Swayne, pointed out that the offense was a technical one. It concludes dryly (evidently echoing Swayne or Dunsany himself): "He had no sympathy with Sinn Fein."[6] Dunsany relates the episode still more dryly: "The pursuit of woodcock and snipe was not so easy, for in some districts there was a death-penalty for possessing a gun or cartridges, and in others merely imprisonment. I was still a soldier on the active list, although demobilized, and thought that for this reason the order against the possession of firearms could not apply to me. I was quite mistaken" (WSS 37). Dunsany got off paying a fine of £25.

Otherwise, however, Dunsany was in both a social and a financial position to opt out of the civil war of 1920–22 by simply remaining ensconced in the relative safety of Dunsany Castle during quiet moments and staying in Kent or with other friends in England and on the Continent when things threatened to become dangerous. Dunsany never puts forth this rationale for his travels during this period, and in fact never mentions the civil war at all in his autobiography; but his later writings make it clear that he was well aware of the course of the struggle.

As Dunsany turned to novel writing in the 1920s, Ireland was still a subject he refused, or was disinclined, to treat. Indeed, he becomes remarkably silent about other Irish writers, especially such dynamic figures of the younger generation as Sean O'Casey and Austin Clarke. O'Casey's *Shadow of a Gunman* was produced in 1923, only two years after Dunsany's last dramatic triumph, *If*, in 1921, but I find no mention of this play or of any of O'Casey's later work in any writing of Dunsany's I have seen. There is, so far as I can tell, only a single citation of James Joyce in Dunsany, and it proves to be surprisingly charitable given that one would have expected Dunsany to have violently rejected Joyce as an apostle of that chaotic modernism which was destroying his civilization. In reviewing an anthology of fantastic tales, *The Mandrake Root*, edited by Jeremy Scott, Dunsany writes of Joyce's story "The Everlasting Fire" in the *Sunday Times* on June 16, 1946:

It is a thing of extraordinary and astonishing power. I have not been a reader of James Joyce, but had once noticed from a single paragraph which I had chanced to see that he had that last gift of all, rhythm. All else about prose can probably be learnt; but rhythm, transcending reason as it does, cannot be overtaken by our logic, and remains merely a gift. It is abundantly evident in this remarkable story . . . which is no mere empty melody of words, but is a sustained *tour de force* in which the writer has emulated another man's job, and has made a sermon such as in some pulpits and in another age might well have been preached, had any preacher had the power to do it.
So completely does Joyce enter and haunt that pulpit, that it cannot be called a parody: it is the thing itself in a supreme degree, and one sees for the first time, had he lived a hundred years ago, his name would be known to us now as that of one of the great preachers. ("Faint Footsteps")

To praise a writer's prose style is one of Dunsany's highest compliments.

Dunsany had his cadre of literary associates, but they were almost wholly of the generation of Yeats. He had met Lady Gregory at a relatively early stage of his career, and in *Patches of Sunlight* even accuses her of lifting the plot of *King Argimēnēs and the Unknown Warrior* (she had seen it in manuscript a year before it was staged) for her own play, *The Deliverer* (PS 153–54). He thenceforth remained very cool to her, and later (a little unfairly) compared her unfavorably to Synge (MI 262–63). But his friendship with and praise for James Stephens, AE, and Oliver St. John Gogarty remained firm. All three of them returned the favor, although

Stephens only in personal letters. These letters, indeed, are rather embarrassingly effusive: "You have the sharp tang of just before sunrise, the width & horizon of great spaces & the eager curiosity of those children who inhabited the Morning Land— The only example of that clear frankness which I know of in literature is Theocritus. I wish you could rewrite his odes."[7] AE reviewed *Plays of Gods and Men* in the *Irish Homestead* (June 2, 1917) and wrote a sort of joint review of *The King of Elfland's Daughter* and *The Charwoman's Shadow* in the *Irish Statesman* (April 17, 1926), both highly favorable. Dunsany, in a late article, "Some Irish Writers I Have Known" (1952; GHL), expressed regret that AE spent so much time editing these two journals when he could have been writing more poetry. Later scholarship does not appear to have confirmed Dunsany's judgment, for AE is now regarded as no more than a minor poet but his journalism and editorial abilities have been much praised. As for Gogarty, he wrote two eloquent memoirs, "My Friends Stephens and Dunsany" (1951) and "Lord Dunsany" (1955), in the latter of which he makes the following argument for the relative coolness between Yeats and Dunsany:

It would be a mistake to think that the rivalry between Dunsany and Yeats was a literary one. Far from it. Yeats had no rival to fear among contemporary poets. It was not so much rivalry on Yeats's part as it was envy. Yeats, through his descent from parsons, innately loved a lord. He was at heart an aristocrat, and it must always have been a disappointment to him that he was not born one. Not by taking thought could he trace his descent from the year 1181.[8]

Which brings us to 1932. Yeats, with the initial assistance of Lady Gregory, had created the Irish Academy of Letters. What was to be Dunsany's involvement, if any, in this organization? In the *Times* of London on October 3, 1932, appeared an unusually tart letter by Dunsany, saying that he had been told of an article in the *Times* of September 20 in which his name had been mentioned in connection with "Mr. Yeats's academy," and referring to a statement by Yeats in the *Manchester Guardian* of September 19 in which an invitation had been sent to him; but Dunsany concludes bluntly: "I write to say that I have neither accepted any such invitation nor received one."[9] A more extended account appears in *The Sirens Wake*:

Yeats had invented the Irish Academy of Letters and had omitted me, which was no surprise; though his reason for doing so was surprising, which was that I did not write about Ireland.... This then may have been the trifling sting that stimulated my energies. I do not know if it was, but it may have been, because once it seemed that Yeats thought so, for he questioned me very closely as to why I had started the book [*The Curse of the Wise Woman*], and his insight is not likely to have been wrong. (SiW 19–20)

Dunsany is, I fear, guilty of more than a little prevarication. The actual situation was that membership to the academy was divided between "academicians" and "associates"; the distinction is explained in a letter by Yeats and Bernard Shaw (who had agreed to be the academy's first president) quoted in the *Manchester Guardian* article to which Dunsany refers in his letter: " 'We divide our members into Academicians and Associates; the Academicians must have done creative work "Irish in character or subject"; an Associate need not fall within this definition though he must be of Irish birth or descent.' "[10] This article listed twenty-two writers (including Dunsany) to whom invitations to join the Academy had been sent, but the list was not divided into academicians and associates. Another ten members (including Stephens, Gogarty, and AE, who was the academy's secretary) would not be sent formal letters because they had been in touch with Yeats about the organization already and would presumably become members automatically.

It is not surprising that Dunsany overlooked a similar notice in the *Times* of London on September 20, for it was a very brief article that merely listed the writers to whom membership had been extended; this list, however, did divide the members into academicians (twenty-five) and associates (ten, including Dunsany as well as T. E. Lawrence, Eugene O'Neill, and others).[11]

The *New York Times* of October 28, 1932, reported that both James Joyce and Dunsany had refused membership in the academy. (Joyce was to have been an academician.) Yeats, on an American tour, was interviewed by a reporter about Dunsany's refusal: "Lord Dunsany's refusal was 'because he could not endure the thought of being only an associate member,' Mr. Yeats said. Under the rules of the Academy Lord Dunsany could not be offered a full membership any more than could Eugene O'Neill, he said. Mr. O'Neill accepted associate membership, the only American on the roll."[12] This, then, is the true state of affairs. It would, of course, be ridiculous to think that Yeats made the distinction between academicians and associates with Dunsany specifically in mind, although—aside from O'Neill—Dunsany really was the most prominent member on the associates list, and certainly the most prominent native Irishman. Whatever the situation, the result of this contretemps was Dunsany's finest novel.

In *Patches of Sunlight* Dunsany claims that his fascination with the bogs of Ireland began as a boy when he was sent to stay for the holidays at Kilcooley Abbey in Tipperary while his parents were wintering in Egypt.

Here first I saw an Irish bog and, what was almost as important as equipment for a writer, I was told by my aunt how in Galway these heathery wildernesses stretched away for miles and miles, so that in my imagination these strange lands lay ready to be used, if ever my fancy turned homeward from remote places in which it used to travel to find the gods and men of my earlier books and plays. (PS 47)

This passage is a clear nod to *The Curse of the Wise Woman*, but that novel does far more than utilize the bog as a stage setting, even one where fantastic things happen; the bog becomes a symbol for a rural Ireland whose land, people, and imaginative legendry are being systematically crushed by the inexorable progress of industrial civilization.

Charles James Peridore, narrating the tale in the first person, grew up like Dunsany in Victorian Ireland (a passing reference to being "fifty-two years ahead of my story" [CWW 93] sets the tale roughly around 1880); like Dunsany, he is the owner of a large estate near the town of Lisronagh. In an arresting scene that opens the novel, Charles's father flees his manor and the country when political enemies burst into the house:

I saw at once that the men were from the other side of the bog; they were dark and strange and like none of our men. They peered round the room, then one of them looked at me fixedly and said: "There is no one we have a greater respect for than your father, but it is a pity he mixed himself up with politics the way he did; and it's the way it is we want to speak to him, and no one could be sorrier than myself that I have to say it."
Then I knew they had come to shoot my father. (CWW 9)

His mother having died years before, Charles falls in with Marlin, the bog watcher for Charles's father, whose mother is a wisewoman (a term which "was nothing less than a warning that [she] was a practising witch" [CWW 32]). As Charles spends time hunting with Marlin on the bog, he feels he is learning Nature's secrets, and he provides a defense for hunting that we have elsewhere seen Dunsany himself offer: "Indeed, I think we sportsmen are somewhat nearer to the tides and the growth of trees and the light and the morning, and to whatever we call the plan that orders the planets, than many a man that does more useful things" (CWW 47).

Trouble comes when the Peat Development (Ireland) Syndicate, an English corporation, comes to drain the bog and set up a mill on the neighboring river. Mrs. Marlin, who cannot abide any alteration of the land, vows to foil the project, proclaiming, " 'There's a power . . . that is hid in the heart of the bog, that is against all their plans' " (CWW 131). She stands on a high cliff on the bog's edge and rains imprecations upon the workers, who are somewhat annoyed but otherwise unaffected. The destruction of the bog seems inevitable; but then a titanic storm comes and causes the cliff to collapse upon all the machinery of the development company, ending their plans and saving the bog from further spoliation. Charles, meanwhile, has fallen in love with a neighboring girl, Laura Lanley, but, although they remain engaged for several years, the marriage never takes place because she, a Protestant, refuses to give up "what after all is only a heresy" (CWW 219). Charles becomes an ambassador for the Irish Free State and writes of his "memories of an Ireland that they tell me is quite gone" (CWW 5) from an unspecified country in the Balkans.

One of the most remarkable aspects of the novel is the seamless way in which its variegated plot threads are weaved into a unity—a unity that nevertheless exhibits the unyielding polarizations in the Irish character: city vs. country; progress vs. tradition; political stability vs. violence; Catholicism vs. Protestantism (or, perhaps even more broadly, Christianity vs. paganism). Let us consider first the political theme.

We have seen that Charles's father was a landlord, although a Catholic one; what exactly he did to earn the wrath of his political opponents is intentionally left vague, since it is to Dunsany's purpose to suggest that such political violence is always over inessentials. The tables are turned later in the novel when the four men who drove his father away come to Charles and confess that they themselves are now being pursued and require help in fleeing. Charles gives the help, although making them swear that they will not hurt his father. Nevertheless, he learns shortly thereafter that his father had been murdered in Paris; but he is reassured by an old friend of his father's: " 'It was not those men' " (CWW 135). Dunsany ties this thread to the central web of the novel when another terrorist, seeing the threatened devastation of the bog, comes to Charles and says he can arrange to " 'have them out of it in a week' " (CWW 179), presumably by acts of sabotage or even murder. "Never had I known a greater temptation" (CWW 179), Charles confesses, but finally refuses the man's help. The conclusion, where we learn that one of his father's enemies had actually contrived to secure the ambassadorship for Charles, threatens to end the novel on an inappropriately comical note— Dunsany, as we shall see in *Up in the Hills*, regarded the Irish Free State's sending out of ambassadors to obscure countries as a species of low farce—but does not quite do so, and we are still left with a brooding impression of both the tragedy and the grotesqueness of political violence in Ireland.

The religious thread of the novel operates on two levels—the conflict of Charles's Catholicism and Laura's Protestantism, and more broadly the conflict of paganism and Christianity as embodied in the figure of Marlin. Is paganism the true religion of the Irish country folk? Does the triumph of St. Patrick extend only to the externals of religious ritual? Marlin, inspired by his constant nearness to the bog, has developed a longing to attain the mythical realm of Tir-nan-Og; Charles, knowing that is is "purely heathen" (CWW 37), urges Marlin to forget it, to which Marlin replies:

Forget Tir-nan-Og? . . . Forget Tir-nan-Og! With the young men walking with the gold low light on their limbs, and the young girls with radiance in their faces, and the young blossom bursting along the apple-boughs, and all that is young there glorying in the morning, and it morning for ever over all the land of youth. Forget Tir-nan-Og! Not the angels in Heaven could forget it, nor all the blessed saints. (CWW 37)

Later, when Marlin falls ill, he gets up from his sickbed and loses himself in the bog; he has found Tir-nan-Og. Paganism is the religion of those who are close to the soil; what other faith could this old bog watcher have had?

[W]hen I look at the bog shining there in my memories I find it hard to remember the map and to say exactly where its boundaries go; rather I seem to see it crossing the sky-line and narrowing where roads and railways confine it, but a strip of it running on, till it comes to the very sand and shells of the ocean, and across that a little way westward, God help me, Tir-nan-Og. (CWW 44)

For it is the bog, more even than Mrs. Marlin, that is the true focal character of *The Curse of the Wise Woman*. Is it a mere tract of land or some quasi-sentient entity? Have Mrs. Marlin's curses caused the climactic storm, or was it mere coincidence?—or, indeed, was it something in the bog itself that called forth the thunder and rain? Whether the supernatural actually comes into play in this novel is an eternally unresolved question, but Dunsany slyly hints of a potential supernaturalism in the bog. For the bog is certainly one of the "enemies of man . . . a land as different from the fields we inhabit as the Sahara or Indian jungles" (CWW 19). More importantly, and in line with the course of Dunsany's renunciation of fantasy, the bog is explicitly compared to fairyland (CWW 20); it is a "land that had always seemed to me as enchanted as any land can be"

(CWW 151). And yet, perhaps this is a feature that inheres in all Ireland, as Charles discovers when on a fox hunt at Clonrue:

And suddenly above the bare green fields, and clear of hedges and trees, I saw a small town shining on a hill, in light that was flung up there from the last of the sunset. A row of houses below, then two streets running up the sides of the hill; all the town white; and, set among those two streets and the houses below, like an emerald the hill's summit. I did not know that, except in old pictures of Italy, towns were built like this upon hills. Certainly I never thought of seeing one, but believed that they belonged to poetry or romance, or to times long past or countries far away. (CWW 82)

Who can fail to think of Dunsany's earlier story "The City on Mallington Moor" (LBW)? But that city never existed save in imagination; now Dunsany can find its analogue in his native land.

Whatever powers of enchantment Mrs. Marlin may have derive from her closeness to the bog: "I think that living there all her life on that wild willowy land beneath the frown of the bog, that in this flat country seemed to rise up almost like a mountain, the queer haunt had given her whatever powers she had" (CWW 98). Indeed, she herself admits that "'I have to speak with the powers of bog and storm and night, and to learn their will with the men that are harming the heather'" (CWW 155), and Charles echoes her: "Mrs. Marlin had made her compact to protect it, with certain powers that were of the bog itself" (CWW 165). After the spectacular storm that overwhelms the development company, nothing is left but "the top of a meaningless ornamentation that they had built on the front of their factory" (CWW 218); and, as if symbolically to drive home the sense of the bog's utter defeat of industrialism and the triumph of Nature, birds begin using the ornament as a perch.

It is difficult to describe the complex network of sensations to be derived from reading *The Curse of the Wise Woman*, with its unwontedly pensive prose, its rich evocation of the Irish countryside, the ambiguity of its quasi-supernaturalism, and its compact melding of politics, religion, fantasy, and realism. It is at once Dunsany's most unified novel and his most heartfelt plea for the preservation of the natural world, specifically that realm of Ireland whose traditions and legendry, born of the soil, require protection from the relentless march of industrialism. Dunsany claimed that it was "lazy work" (SiW 20) writing the novel, since he was merely writing of what he knew; but he must have felt vindicated when, in April 1934, the Irish Academy of Letters gave it the Harmsworth Literary Award for the best Irish novel of the preceding year.[13] At the awards banquet held in Dublin on December 5, 1934, Yeats announced that Dunsany had now been elected to full membership in the academy.[14]

The Story of Mona Sheehy, as we have seen, in many ways continues the attack on industrialism by vaunting the purity, naturalness, and simplicity of both the Irish countryside and its people. As I have already discussed the main thrust of the novel, only a few points specifically relating to Ireland need be noted here. Dunsany makes clear that the apparent superstitiousness of the people of Athroonagh—in other words, their ready willingness to believe Mona to be a child of the fairies—is in no sense an intellectual or moral deficiency, but rather the product of centuries of tradition and adaptation to the rural landscape. As in *The Curse of the Wise Woman*, this sentiment is regarded as a residue of the pre-Christian paganism of the Irish peasantry—a point underscored by Mona herself in a striking phrase, " 'Sure, we have nothing to do with Heaven' " (SMS 63). But more than this, belief in fairies is one more example of the innate imaginativeness of the Irish mind:

They were a perfectly shrewd people, and knew to a few pence the value of a hundredweight of hay, and might have sold a horse at a profit to a man who came all the way from London; and yet when the mood changed, as it would with a whim of the wind or the flash of a rainbow, they could tell stories of the enchanted people and old kings and heroes that knew them, with as much clear detail, if they would, as they could have used when telling the points of a horse. And, though these two qualities may appear inconsistent, yet the quality of imagination entered often into the sale of a horse, and indeed had to, in order to make the sale truly successful; and the quality of practical detail entered into the tales of the Shee, without which that fairy people would never have been equipped with the clearness of outline and evidence to support them, which has brought them down to our day, through whose perplexing conundrums they still walk. (SMS 56)

As Dunsany noted elsewhere: "Those who do not care for fanciful things have no reason to read about Ireland" (MI 100).

The Curse of the Wise Woman, *Rory and Bran*, and *The Story of Mona Sheehy* all emphasize the need to retain ties to the Irish rural landscape, the first and third by brutal contrast with various forms of industrialism and urbanism. *Rory and Bran* lacks this element of contrast, and therefore becomes in large part a *Bildungsroman*. Rory, though able to read only with difficulty, already scorns the literature of modernism; instead, he is fascinated by tales of old legends and heroes: "So, for the things of every day, Rory read Grimm; while for life's pinnacles, the greater moments, he followed the deeds of Roland, Don Quixote, King Arthur of Britain, or anyone else he could come by who dealt a neat blow with a sword or carried a good lance" (RB 3–4). It is exactly this fervent absorption of fantasy that causes his parents to doubt whether he can do so simple a thing as to take twelve cattle to Gurtnaroonagh sixty miles away.

At the end of his first day's journey, having lost both his cattle and his money, Rory has a dream in which Charlemagne comes to him; the latter tells him not to worry about his loss, for "the splendours of the hills . . . and the splendours of Time . . . [are] enough" (RB 108). This dream, however, is explicitly contrasted by a vision Rory experiences at almost the exact center of the novel, inspired by a song of the tinkers:

Men in old clothes and rain-beaten hats, carrying ash-plants, men with faces lined by the rigours of all four seasons, with mockery at their lips, they might appear, and thus they chose to be known; but Rory would know them henceforth through all their disguises. He knew now who they were. The mighty spirits that strode with ease down the ages were not always content with the bleak spaces of time, nor with the mists and shadows of Slievenamona; they took bodily form when they willed it; and they, that were singing now, had Roland among them, Don Quixote and many a paladin. He would walk the roads to which the song was calling, and henceforth he would know them. (RB 167–68)

From dreams of pure fantasy (Roland, Charlemagne) Rory now invests very real beings with fantastic properties: Rory's growth from naive daydreamer to settled countryman is well under way, as is, simultaneously, Dunsany's renunciation of fantasy. And both developments achieve completion at the end, when Rory and Oriana realize that their own garden—in other words, the earth of Ireland—contains all the wonders they have sought in fairy tales and legends:

In that garden Rory forswore the Irish kings, the knights of Camelot, and Finn, and Roland; he would wander the roads no more, to pierce their disguises; it was enough that they had come to him once on the plain of Gurtnaroonagh; enough that he had dreamed of them long and seen them once. Now he would turn to the world, that had suddenly grown so beautiful. (RB 285)

And yet, Rory remains "a link of a sort between us and Roland" (RB 121): it is he who retains the imagination, nourished by contact with the earth, that we of the cities have lost.

In the midst of what must be called Dunsany's "Irish decade"—comprising four novels (the three discussed above as well as *Up in the Hills* [1935], for which see below) as well as *Patches of Sunlight* (1938), which speaks so eloquently of the literary inspiration he derived from both the

English and the Irish countryside—Dunsany also wrote, at the request of his publisher, Jarrolds, *My Ireland* (1937). The book was the first of the "My Country" series published by Jarrolds, the other titles being *My England* by Edward Shanks, *My Scotland* by A. G. Macdonell, and *My Wales* by Rhys Davies. Lengthy as this reminiscence is, it is only intermittently compelling: it becomes too bogged down with repeated, and repetitive, descriptions of Dunsany's hunting expeditions (for snipe, woodcock, duck, etc.) in Ireland, and, although filled with charming tributes to AE, Ledwidge, and Synge, it fails to deal substantively with the issues it raises. A political polemic structures the entire work, but this is worth considering in the context of a later discussion.

Throughout the last decade and a half of his career Dunsany continued to return sporadically to Irish themes, both in essays and in stories. Almost simultaneous with the publication of *The Story of Mona Sheehy* in September 1939, Dunsany received three stories in manuscript from Mary Lavin. Both Lord and Lady Dunsany would write many letters to Lavin over the next twenty years,[15] and Dunsany wrote a preface to Lavin's first short-story collection, *Tales from Bective Bridge* (1942). Sometime after the death of Joseph Campbell in 1944, Dunsany wrote a sensitive appreciation of his poetry, "A Mountainy Singer" (1946); it was his only contribution to the *Bell*.

Dunsany also had only a few pieces in *Irish Writing*, including "Some Irish Writers I Have Known" (1952) and a review of Geraldine Cummins's biography of Dr. Edith Somerville. A very late piece, "Four Poets" (posthumously published in the *Atlantic Monthly* in April 1958), discusses AE, Kipling, Yeats, and James Stephens, and, although tending to repeat what he had said in earlier works, is still an affecting tribute. One of Dunsany's very latest essays, published two years after his death, is an introduction to a trilingual volume, *Ireland/L'Irlande/Irland: A Book of Photographs* (1959), an introduction that was printed successively in English, French, and German. It is a somewhat discursive rumination on both the urban and rural topography of Ireland and its imaginative overtones.

I have already remarked that many of Dunsany's stories and poems for *Punch* in the 1940s concern Ireland. Two issues seem to predominate in these works: the prevalence of political violence in Ireland and Irish neutrality during World War II. The first is dealt with by Dunsany in a comic manner edged with malice, while the latter earns his wholehearted and stinging contempt.

In "The Judgment of Mullaghagraney" (1940) Dick Leehy has trouble getting a pension from the government until he tells of the "services that he had rendered in the days of the Black-and-Tans"—that is, his having murdered a member of the R.I.C. "A Let-Off" (1943) tells of how a band of Irishmen under "General Michael O'Hara" was all set to invade England in 1920, and would have done so had not O'Hara seen at the shore a redheaded woman, "the unluckiest thing of all." In "The Coming Party" (1946), the bitterest of all these stories, a mother says that she wants to make sure her young son has a future—so she will raise him as a terrorist.

The matter of Irish neutrality during World War II was particularly galling to Dunsany, more so than the analogous position Ireland had adopted during World War I. Perhaps he felt that the stakes were much higher in this conflict, that the moral imperative was much clearer, and that Ireland did not this time have the excuse of severe political turmoil as it did during World War I. Strangely, his attacks are not directed solely toward the government but occasionally toward the Irish citizenry, even though he must have known that a majority of the people supported the Allies. In "Neutrality over Berlin" (1942), the first-person narrator finds a man discussing "Irish strategy" during the war:

> "But I thought Ireland was neutral. Our part of it, I mean," I answered.
> "Most certainly it is neutral," said Muirphaigh.
> "Even though the Germans bombed Dublin last year?" I suggested.
> "That had nothing to do with it," said Muirphaigh.

And indeed, Ireland will, according to Muirphaith, remain technically neutral even if it bombs Germany. "The Higher Neutrality" (1942) is a direct sequel to this tale, telling of Muirphaigh objecting to a man on a bus who said that Hitler was "as damned as Satan." One ought not to slander Satan like that ("'He has never yet written his *Mein Kampf*'"), since one must remain neutral in both politics and religion. As late as 1950, in "A Crime Story," Dunsany was still thrashing the government on this issue, writing of how a swarm of policemen prevented a man from pulling down the flag of the German Legation in Dublin.

And yet, when Dunsany can forget about politics and either write of the distinctive Irish character or mingle the supernatural with Irish themes, he can produce some wholly delightful tales. I have already discussed some of these—"Helping the Fairies," "The Burrahoola," "How Mickey Paid His Debt"—many of which are very tart in their satire on Irish trickery, deceit, and actual criminality. Several others are more innocuous but just as amusing. "An Old Man's Tale" (1945) is one of the best, returning us to the setting of *The Curse of the Wise Woman*, an Irish bog. An old man, O'Hanrahan, tells the narrator that if you step on a green tussock in a bog, you will go down to the King of Elfland, and centuries might pass above ground before you could find your way back. O'Hanrahan ought to know, for it happened to him. How? " 'Sure, I was fleeing from Oliver Cromwell' " (MAP 75). The much-reprinted "Little Tim Brannehan" (1948) involves nothing supernatural, but tells of the villainy of Lord Blackcastle in ceasing to send a pint of milk a day to little Tim—after seventy years of doing so. The sympathy extended from one landlord to another is clearly in evidence here.

"The Widow Flynn's Apple-Tree" (1943) is one more tale of the nonhuman perspective—if, that is, we believe Mickey Maguire, who accounts for his presence under the widow Flynn's apple tree by maintaining, not that he was stealing the widow's apples, but that she had turned him into a gray lag. He spends years in this state (and the mere fact that he makes this statement, so seemingly damaging to his case, paradoxically induces belief in his tale), and at one point a female of his species " 'told me a lot of the old history of Ireland' " (MAP 61), although he does not elaborate on what he learned. The widow refuses to comment on his story, and he gets off.

I have saved discussion of *Up in the Hills* (1935), the second of Dunsany's four Irish novels of the 1930s, for now because it is worth reading it in conjunction with his final novel, *His Fellow Men* (1952), and also with *My Ireland* (1937). The premise of *Up in the Hills* is, by design, entirely ludicrous. A newly liberated country in Africa, Liberissima, having established a treaty with the Irish Free State (UH 5), decides to send a scientific expedition to Ireland to dig up an Irish bog for archaeological remains. The wisewomen of Cranogue, the town neighboring the bog, take great umbrage when human bones are unearthed; accusing the Liberissimans of sacrilege, they begin cursing them lustily. The boys of the town are advised by Old Mickey Ryan to leave town for a while so as to avoid the curses, and Young Mickey Connor (Old Mickey's grandson) decides to form an army up in the hills; perhaps they can have a nice little war there to pass the time until the curses of the wisewomen will have played themselves out. The story, we are told, takes place in 1922 (UH 40), toward the end of the civil war (although Dunsany, again by design, makes no reference to it anywhere in the novel). Ireland is now free, Old Mickey tells Young Mickey; before that time, " '[t]here were unjust laws in the country. . . . And the unjustest law the English ever made was one that said that none might levy war without the King's consent' " (UH 37).

For a time the boys gathered by Young Mickey merely drill and train, laying up provisions and practicing shooting. When, however, they take to foraging on the other side of the hill, they are informed peremptorily by

Patsy Haffernan, a leader of his own gang of boys, that they are forbidden to obtain provisions in his "Brigade area"; this can only mean one thing: "It meant war" (UH 61).

Now the awkward thing is that Mickey's band consists of only eight other boys, while Patsy has close to a hundred. Nevertheless, Mickey employs various ingenious tactics—tactics very similar to those used in deadly earnest in *Guerrilla*—to convey the impression of an army of vastly greater size. When, however, matters come to an actual gun battle, it is abruptly interrupted by a fox hunt passing through:

> "What are they doing?" said the Master to his huntsman, for Mickey's men were still firing.
> "They're only having a battle, sir," came the answer.
> "Well, tell them to stop," said the Master. "We can't draw the covert with all that going on." (UH 87)

This incident is, of course, prototypical, for as Mickey confesses much later, " 'It was a private war and was doing no harm to anyone' " (UH 290). No one gets killed or seriously injured in any of the skirmishes between Mickey's and Patsy's bands, even when Mickey attempts unsuccessfully to steal Patsy's machine gun and is captured in the process (he escapes by a clever ruse).

Things do, however, take a serious turn when both Mickey and Patsy are arrested by the army of the newly formed government led by General James Cassidy. Both are court-martialed for possessing arms—an incident that can hardly fail to remind us of Dunsany's similar experience in 1921—and sentenced to be executed, Patsy the next morning and Mickey the morning after that. Patsy is in fact executed—a rather jarringly tragic note in a novel that otherwise strives for hilarity, even frivolity—but Mickey manages to escape in the very process of digging his own grave. Meanwhile General Cassidy is himself dispatched in a hideous manner while pursuing Mickey: he is *eaten* by one of the African archaeologists, who have been ostracized from the town and are starving for want of food. Dunsany presumably expects us to find all this amusing, for he cannot resist adding the predictable pun that he will at once leave "this distasteful topic" (UH 268); the racist overtones of the entire episode escape him utterly. In any event, after this escape from death Mickey joins the Irish Guards in London.

Up in the Hills is meant to be preposterous, and it was indeed received as a delightful light farce; but the whole notion of boys playing at war in the hills underscores the puerility and political naïveté of the radical, anti-English I.R.A. and similar groups. One passage, a discussion between Mickey and his sweetheart, Alannah, sums up the novel's political satire perfectly:

"What are your politics?" she asked.
. . .
"Just against the government," answered Mickey.
"Which government?" asked Alannah, for the English had only been gone a year.
"Any government," said Mickey. "Sure what's the use of them? No man can be free when there's a government over him." (UH 68–69)

My Ireland picks up the idea. The avowed "subject" of this book is a question Dunsany asks early on and to which he promises a definitive answer: "What the people of Ireland actually think of the new form of government" (MI 33). The first person to whom he puts this question is none other than Old Mickey of *Up in the Hills*. He claims to do this because he wants "some fairly representative man" (MI 33) and thinks that a fictional character might satisfy this criterion better than a living human being. Mickey, however, puts Dunsany off, frustrating his desire for a clear statement on the issue. Later Dunsany claims to take up the matter with a neighbor, who gives him an answer but makes Dunsany promise not to print it; but we can surely infer the answer by Dunsany's comment, " 'It's rather what I thought' " (MI 81). The neighbor picks up the theme much later, in response to Dunsany's plea that both the Irish and his readers want the truth on this issue:

The Irish have got what they wanted and clamoured for. Won't they want you to make it out the finest thing in the world? Of course they will. They'd look like bloody fools otherwise. And the English gave them the Free State. If that was the cleverest thing that the English ever did, won't they want all the credit for it? And mind you I'm not saying that it wasn't. But if it should turn out to be the damnedest silliest thing they ever did in their lives, will they want you to be reminding them of that? It stands to reason they won't. (MI 264–65)

And that is Dunsany's final word.

His Fellow Men incorporates the entire scenario of *Up in the Hills* within a serious, even lugubrious, meditation on the political and religious strife in Ireland and, indeed, the world. This queer novel deals with an utterly naive young Irishman from Ulster, Mathew Perry, who travels the entire globe in what the narrator terms a "wild chase after the will-o'-the-wisp of universal tolerance" (HFM 40), specifically tolerance of different religious sects, rituals, and traditions. The narrator makes the odd remark that Perry's "father was dead, shot one night through the window of his house for some reason unconnected with this story, and his mother had been killed at the same time" (HFM 5); but far from being unconnected with the story, this incident leads directly to Mathew's quest, since he realizes that his parents were killed in sectarian violence and he himself wishes "to be free from the passions that had killed his father and mother" (HFM 28), in particular the vengeance the rest of his Protestant family expects him to exact for these deaths.

Mathew's peregrinations around the globe—first to Africa, where he converts to Islam; then to India, where he practices Hinduism; then to Persia, where he comes under the influence of the Bahai faith; then back to Ireland, where he resumes his Protestant leanings; then to England, where he samples both Anglican and Methodist services; then, after an interlude with fervent teetotallers, back to Ireland—are scarcely worth probing in detail: the whole point of them is to show that every faith has its drawbacks (some are exclusionary, others are held with fanatical intensity, still others have unfortunate social or political consequences), and everywhere he goes Mathew encounters intolerance from one group the moment he espouses the religion of another. Finally, under the influence of Eileen O'Shaughnessy, a Catholic woman with whom he is in love, he abandons the quest for tolerance: in a half-comic ending she tells him tartly that she will continue being a Catholic and he is "to go on being an Orangeman, and as intolerant as any of them" (HFM 224).

It is hard to know what to make of this meandering, relentlessly cheerless novel. Dunsany is hampered by a flaccid narrative tone that fails to achieve dramatic tensity at critical moments, by an inability to convey Mathew Perry's varying emotional states with any degree of precision or empathy, and by a failure of characterization generally. We are clearly meant to sympathize wholly with Mathew's quest for tolerance, but what Dunsany wishes us to regard as his sympathy with diverse religious, political, and social views occasionally seems instead a lack of principle or willpower: does not the ability to believe *everything*—every religion that human beings have created—really mean the inability to believe firmly in anything?

But whatever the novel's deficiencies, it is Dunsany's last "Irish" novel, even if, both topographically and thematically, it is not uniformly about Ireland. Its guiding principle—the conflict of Protestantism and Catholicism—returns to the theme of one of Dunsany's earliest Irish pieces, the untitled story in *Vanity Fair* of November 1919: when Mathew goes to Marseilles and sees a beautiful Catholic church there, he reflects that this is "the Church that all his life he had been taught to know as the enemy" (HFM 12). But the conclusion, whether avowedly comic or not, suggests that Dunsany felt the problem to be irresolvable, just as he knew that in Ireland "those two religions had allied themselves with politics" (HFM 28) to produce a political impasse that was equally difficult of resolution.

Dunsany, of course, remained a Unionist to the end. In the curious humorous volume *If I Were Dictator* (1934), he takes delight in referring continually to the "Disunited Kingdom"; and he makes note of the fact that he is a "convinced Unionist" in so inapposite a place as his 1947 translation of the odes of Horace (OH 134). In a letter to the London *Times* of October 22, 1948, he writes acidly: "My son was born in the United Kingdom. My grandson was born in quite another country—I am not clear what, but I believe the Irish Free State."[16] And yet, as in his fiction, whenever Dunsany could bring himself to cease thinking about the political situation—a thing that was, admittedly, difficult for someone in his position to do—he could write very movingly of Ireland and what it meant to him. Perhaps this passage from *My Ireland* is what he would like us to remember of Ireland and the Irish, and what he would like them to remember of him:

they are in a land remote from the world's affairs, a land under clouds so thick and so far away to the North that the Romans called it Winter. Their dreams have to suffice them, just as gold might have to suffice men in a land that had no copper. Green fields, castles, politics and old stones, of which I have told in these pages, are far from the real Ireland. The real Ireland is a land of dreams. . . . And if we are not looking at the stars as we walk, or looking for them at broad noon, we are looking back over our shoulders at what has gone ages since, and peering back even further through the mist and the haze of Time, to see bright and clear in the radiance, that shines from our vivid dreams, the kings and the heroes of days that never were. And that we shall part with last of all. (MI 267–68)

NOTES

1. W. B. Yeats, letter to Lady Gregory, 23 May 1909; in *The Letters of W. B. Yeats*, ed. Allan Wade (London: Rupert Hart-Davis, 1954), 530.

2. Introduction to *Selections from the Writings of Lord Dunsany* (1912); rpt. in Yeats, *Prefaces and Introductions*, ed. William H. O'Donnell (New York: Macmillan, 1989), 140.

3. See *Letters of James Stephens*, ed. Richard J. Finneran (New York: Macmillan, 1974), 16–19.

4. Ibid., 18.

5. Montrose J. Moses, "Dunsany on Art vs. Politics," *New York Times* No. 22,541 (12 October 1919): Sec. 9, p. 1.

6. *Times* (London) No. 42,637 (5 February 1921): 8.

7. *Letters of James Stephens*, 17.

8. "Lord Dunsany," *Atlantic Monthly* 195, No. 3 (March 1955): 70.

9. *Times* (London) No. 46,254 (3 October 1932): 10.

10. "Irish Academy," *Manchester Guardian* No. 26,843 (19 September 1932): 9.

11. "Irish Academy of Letters," *Times* (London) No. 46,243 (20 September 1932): 10.

12. *New York Times* No. 27,306 (28 October 1932): 17.

13. As announced in the *Times* (London) No. 46,730 (17 April 1934): 16.

14. *New York Times* No. 28,075 (6 December 1934): 10.

15. Nearly two hundred letters by Lord and Lady Dunsany to Mary Lavin are in the library of the State University of New York at Binghamton.

16. This letter was written in response to the Irish government's proposed repeal of the External Relations Act of 1936, which it was feared would compel Irish-born residents in England to be regarded as foreigners and to register as aliens. Although the act was in fact repealed, no such interpretation regarding citizenship was made.

Conclusion

I stated at the outset that it is difficult to write about an author nearly the whole of whose work is out of print and some of which has not been reprinted since its appearance in books, periodicals, and newspapers of sixty, seventy, or eighty years ago. Nevertheless, I hope I have suggested the range and general thrust of Dunsany's work, and its variegated exposition of the theme of reunification with Nature and consequent vaunting of the past over the present, the country over the city, the pagan over the Christian, and art over machinery.

And yet, one of the most obvious features of Dunsany's work—especially his early tales and plays—is its stylistic richness. It is possible to read Dunsany solely for his style; and it is also possible, I think, to maintain that his is among the most naturally musical, rhythmic, and incantatory prose in modern English literature, perhaps in all English literature. How Dunsany achieves the effects he does—effects ranging from heartrending pathos to otherworldly terror—is, however, extraordinarily difficult to analyze. It is a truism that his early style was founded primarily on the King James Bible; he himself makes no secret of it, speaking of

a Sunday [at Cheam], when we used to read a chapter of the Bible for part of the time and write out a précis of it for the rest of the time, with the book closed; and on that Sunday we had the lament of David for Jonathan. Even at that early age I saw that no précis was possible; so I learned the whole thing by heart, which I was able to do in the time, and then wrote out as much of it as I was able to do by the end of the hour. . . . [T]he reward of learning the poetry of David,

translated into the prose of our greatest period, was ... to have grand lines
dwelling deep in my memory long after they have left my recollection, for it is
from such stores as these that we draw when we write or speak. (PS 34–345)

In *The Gods of Pegāna* the influence of the King James Bible—in the
oracular tone, in systematic repetition, in faint traces of archaism—is so
obvious as to seem at times a parody: "There is also Kilooloogung, the
lord of arising smoke, who taketh the smoke from the hearth and sendeth
it to the sky, who is pleased if it reacheth Pegāna, so that the gods of
Pegāna, speaking to the gods, say: 'There is Kilooloogung doing the work
on earth of Kilooloogung'" (GP 32). I wonder if this is what Dunsany
meant when he made the otherwise cryptic admission that *The Gods of
Pegāna* was guided "by two lights that do not seem very often to shine
together, poetry and humour" (PS 111).

The primary lesson Dunsany learned from the King James Bible is the
use of paratactic construction—the lack of subordination of clauses—as
opposed to the syntactic construction derived from classical prose. *The
King of Elfland's Daughter*, that remarkable echo of Dunsany's earlier
manner, provides a canonical example:

And at that moment a wind came out of the northwest, and entered the woods
and bared the golden branches, and danced on over the downs, and led a company
of scarlet and golden leaves, that had dreaded this day but danced now it had
come; and away with a riot of dancing and glory of colour, high in the light of
the sun that had set from the sight of the fields, went wind and leaves together.
With them went Lirazel. (KED 77)

There is, of course, more to this than the old joke of beginning every
sentence with "And": the failure to subordinate clauses creates an effect
of linear simplicity reminiscent of parables, fairy tales, and other examples
of "primitive" narrative.

This King James style is maintained throughout *Time and the Gods* and
the first half of *The Sword of Welleran*. But then we come upon "The
Highwayman," which Dunsany noted as his first tale "in which all the
characters were human" (PS 133); it is also the first tale in which archaisms
are notably absent. This pattern continues with the next two tales in this
volume, "In the Twilight" and "The Ghosts"; the latter opens with a flat
and prosaic manner we would hardly have expected this early in his career:
"The argument that I had with my brother in his great lonely house will
scarcely interest my readers" (SW 170). And yet, the former story already
demonstrates that Dunsany no longer requires the owlish gravity of King

James English to create memorable effects. Consider the crispness of detail in the following description of a hallucination experienced by a drowning man:

I was lying on the warm, grassy slope of a valley in England. It was a valley that I had known well when I was young, but I had not seen it now for many years. Beside me stood the tall flower of the mint; I saw the sweet-smelling thyme flower and one or two wild strawberries. There came up to me from fields below me the beautiful smell of hay, and there was a break in the voice of the cuckoo. (SW 166)

By the time we get to *A Dreamer's Tales*, almost all the thee's and thou's are gone. I mean no criticism of Dunsany's archaistic early manner, for he was as great a master of selective archaism as Lucretius or Spenser; but I think it became gradually evident to him that that sort of thing was no longer necessary. "Idle Days on the Yann," perhaps because it is set in the dreamworld, is a fine return to that older manner: "And so Yann bore us magnificently onwards, for he was elate with molten snow that the Poltiades had brought him from the Hills of Hap, and the Marn and Migris were swollen full with floods; and he bore us in his might past Kyph and Pir, and we saw the lights of Goolunza" (DT 63). This passage is, indeed, somewhat atypical in its abundance of imagined names, just as the passage quoted above from "In the Twilight" is perhaps atypical in its unusual conglomeration of adjectives; Dunsany ordinarily requires neither the mere rattling off of jewelled names nor the assistance of labored adjectives to create his effects. In this sense his tales are very different from work that may appear superficially similar—the fairy tales of Wilde, Lovecraft's "Dunsanian" fantasies, the novels of E. R. Eddison.

The passage from "Idle Days on the Yann" brings us to the issue of Dunsany's invented names, something that gained him great renown, even notoriety, in his day. He himself addresses the matter early in *Patches of Sunlight*:

And now my head began to fill with the sounds of Greek and Latin words, and continued to do so afterwards at Eton, until my memory held the echoes of more stately syllables than I knew the meanings of; and, when geography was tumbled on top of this, my mind was very full of the material needed for the names of strange rivers and cities. And these, when I came to write, my mind put together for itself . . . (PS 31–32)

It would, however, be false to think that Dunsany's invented names derive solely from Greek or Latin roots; while there are many such (Eimes, Zanes,

Segastrion [GP 36]), there are also names that have an Oriental cast (Limpang-Tung [GP 24]), or those that are clearly Egyptian (Alhireth-Hotep [GP 57]), and others seem relatively unrelated to preexisting geography or mythology, suggesting names of primitive times (Kib, Ood [GP 12, 91]). This heterogeneous mixture of linguistic roots points to the fundamentally synthetic nature of Dunsany's imaginary realm, where not only names but many other details and conceptions are drawn heterogeneously from ancient mythology and modern philosophy.

Rather more curious, or amusing, are the rather odd names given to many of Dunsany's human characters, even those purportedly dwelling in the real world. From Thomas Shap to Smethers, the occupants of Dunsany's real world seem by their very names to belong to some other realm. Would a Thomas Shap be more susceptible of being crowned king of Larkar than a Henry Jones would be? Conversely, in *The Blessing of Pan*, does the more "normal" Anglo-Saxon name of Arthur Davidson (who may have been Pan in disguise) bespeak that entity's greater closeness to Nature than the vicar, who has the queerly artificial and Victorian name of Elderick Anwrel?

And yet, Dunsany extends this practice of anomalous nomenclature even to characters in works wholly divorced from the fantastic. Srebnitz, the protagonist of *Guerrilla*, is by no means a Greek name, and yet I can see no parodic purpose in giving him such a comic—or, at least, inapposite—name. It is as if Dunsany could not bring himself to be wholly serious or wholly realistic even in those works whose very raison d'être is realism.

The true secret of Dunsany's early style is neither archaism nor adjectives but a tremendously bold use of metaphor. I return to "The Raft-Builders" (FOT), that powerful prose-poem in which writing is likened to "sailors hastily making rafts upon doomed ships":

> See now the wreckage of Babylon floating idly, and something there that once was Nineveh; already their kings and queens are in the deeps among the weedy masses of old centuries that hide the sodden bulk of sunken Tyre and make a darkness round Persepolis.
>
> For the rest I dimly see the forms of foundered ships on the sea-floor strewn with crowns.
>
> Our ships were all unseaworthy from the first.
>
> There goes the raft that Homer made for Helen. (FOT 25)

Those spectacular metaphors—"the weedy masses of old centuries," "the raft that Homer made for Helen"—enmeshed in a "cosmic" framework that can speak with idle offhandedness of the destruction of entire civilizations give the passage a quiet but awesome grandeur that no amount of adjective-choked purple prose could have done. And Dunsany also knew, from a very early stage, the power to be derived from a judicious use of slang and colloquialism: we see it in *The Glittering Gate* (1909), and we see it in "The Workman," where the title character says derisively that " 'yer 'ole silly civilization 'ull be tidied up in a few centuries' " (FOT 27).

When Dunsany adopted his self-parodic manner in the later stories of his early period, he did so primarily by juxtaposing the real and the unreal, the archaic and the modern, in jarring contrast: "There were big diamonds in London that summer and a few considerable sapphires. In certain astounding kingdoms behind the East strange sovereigns missed from their turbans the heirlooms of ancient wars, and here and there the keepers of crown jewels who had not heard the stockinged feet of Thang, were questioned and died slowly" (LBW 54). This sort of thing may be momentarily amusing, but Dunsany wrote too many stories of this type in the later teens, and they begin to seem mechanical and repetitious. He required the few years' surcease from short-story writing in the early 1920s to develop a new style; this style was, however, already implicit in some of what had gone before, and it was the one he used for Jorkens:

When I met my friend Murcote in London he talked much of his Club. I had seldom heard of it, and the name of the street in which Murcote told me it stood was quite unknown to me, though I think I had driven through it in a taxi, and remembered the houses as being mean and small. And Murcote admitted that it was not very large, and had no billiard-table and very few rooms; and yet there seemed something about the place that entirely filled his mind and made that trivial street for him the centre of London. (TT 1)

Whereas Dunsany's early work makes us think of a sort of prose Swinburne, this later work might make us imagine that we were reading an Anglo-Irish Hemingway or Sherwood Anderson. I imagine, however, that one of the prime influences for this style—at least in its Jorkens mode—is Kipling, whom Dunsany had read as early as the turn of the century (PS 84) but whose narrative drive and plain speaking are very evident in the Jorkens tales.

There are those, even among Dunsany's supporters, who find this development in style and manner a disappointment and even a sort of betrayal of his early work. Lovecraft, gauging from the totality of his remarks, seems to have felt that this flat, deadpan, dryly ironic style had the effect of poking fun not only at itself but at the entire mode of weird writing. I do not find any such implication in Dunsany's own work or in any of his remarks about his work; indeed, it is difficult to imagine that an author would adhere to a style for thirty years simply for the purpose of parodying it. It could, however, be maintained that the tone of many of the slighter tales of Dunsany's middle and later period is so flippant as to seem both cheaply ironic and self-trivializing.

But it is by no means the case that this style is incapable of powerful emotive effects—we have found them even in the Jorkens tales, and find them again in the best of his novels, from *The Blessing of Pan* through *The Curse of the Wise Woman* and *The Story of Mona Sheehy* to *The Strange Journeys of Colonel Polders*—or that it is so uniform as to be monotonous. It may seem monotonous simply because of the sheer quantity of Dunsany's output in his last thirty years, some of which—like his countless squibs for *Punch* or the parodic detective stories in *The Little Tales of Smethers*—is indeed mechanical and uninspired, but that early work, if read too concentratedly, can be just as cloying. The one criticism that could be made of it is that it does not allow for much dramatic tensity, especially when—as in *Guerrilla* or *The Last Revolution*—a portrayal of vivid physical action is sought. And it is true that this later style is less obviously or intrinsically distinctive than that earlier manner, which has so captured the imaginations of readers then and now as to earn the adjective "Dunsanian."

Dunsany did, however, evolve an ingenious method of reinjecting quasi-archaistic prose into his later work: the use of Irish dialect. *The Curse of the Wise Woman* is a prototypical example:

"We walked down the river, Mother," said Marlin.

"Aye, the river," said she, "and one of the great rivers of the world, though it's small here. For it widens out on its way, and there's cities on it, high and ancient and stately, with wide courts shining by the river's banks, and steps of marble going down to the ships, and folk walking there by the thousand, all proud of their mighty river, but forgetting the wild bog-water." (CWW 62)

Here again prose-poetry is conjoined to paratactic construction, and passages like this are the more effective because they occur within a generally staid and sober narrative flow. They also simultaneously supply a modicum of quasi-fantasy to an otherwise realistic account and serve as a vehicle for character portrayal.

I trust I have shown that many of the standard criticisms of Dunsany's work—that it is remote from human concerns; that it fails to deal with human emotions; that it is somehow lacking in a firm and clear moral vision—all fall to the ground upon a careful reading of the entire body of his writing. Nevertheless, impediments remain toward the full appreciation of his work, in particular the facts that its self-conscious archaism creates the surface impression of being non-vital for present-day concerns and that its fantastic and supernatural orientation makes it decidedly an acquired taste for readers nurtured on the literature of social realism. H. P. Lovecraft was aware of the obstacles fantastic literature had to overcome:

The appeal of the spectrally macabre is generally narrow because it demands from the reader a certain degree of imagination and a capacity for detachment from everyday life. Relatively few are free enough from the spell of the daily routine to respond to rappings from the outside, and tales of ordinary feelings and events, or of common sentimental distortions of such feelings and events, will always take first place in the taste of the majority; rightly, perhaps, since of course these ordinary matters make up the greater part of human experience. But the sensitive are always with us, and sometimes a curious streak of fancy invades an obscure corner of the very hardest head . . .[1]

Readers and critics alike must be tutored in the rhetoric of fantasy, and shown how fantastic beings, events, and scenarios can serve as metaphors for profound human concerns.

It is, to be sure, not very likely that Dunsany will ever gain general recognition again; but if his historical importance in Irish and world literature is recognized, if the merit of his best work is acknowledged, and if he continues to have a small readership of the "sensitive," then it is perhaps all one can hope for. Other writers have had to do with less.

NOTE

1. H. P. Lovecraft, "Supernatural Horror in Literature," in *Dagon and Other Macabre Tales* (rev. ed., Sauk City, WI: Arkham House, 1986), 365–66.

Bibliography

PRIMARY

Short Story Collections

The Gods of Pegāna. London: Elkin Mathews, 1905. *Boston: John W.. Luce & Co.,
    [1916]. *Contents*: "Preface"; [Prologue]; "The Gods of Pegāna"; "Of Skarl the
    Drummer"; "Of the Making of the Worlds"; "Of the Game of the Gods"; "The
    Chaunt of the Gods"; "The Sayings of Kib"; "Concerning Sish"; "The Sayings
    of Slid"; "The Deeds of Mung"; "The Chaunt of the Priests"; "The Sayings of
    Limpang-Tung"; "Of-Yoharneth-Lahai"; "Of Roon, the God of Going"; "The
    Revolt of the Home Gods"; "Of Dorozhand"; "The Eye in the Waste"; "Of the
    Thing That Is Neither God Nor Beast"; "Yonath the Prophet"; "Yug the
    Prophet"; "Alhireth-Hotep the Prophet"; "Kabok the Prophet"; "Of the
    Calamity That Befel Yūn-Ilāra by the Sea, and of the Building of the Tower of
    the Ending of Days"; "Of How the Gods Whelmed Sidith"; "Of How Imbaun
    Became High Prophet in Aradec of All the Gods Save One"; "Of How Imbaun
    Met Zodrak"; "Pegāna"; "The Sayings of Imbaun"; "Of How Imbaun Spake
    of Death to the King"; "Of Ood"; "The River"; "The Bird of Doom and the
    End."
Time and the Gods. London: William Heinemann, 1906. Boston: John W. Luce & Co.,
    1913. *In *The Book of Wonder*. New York: Boni & Liveright (Modern Library),
    [1918]. *Contents*: "Preface"; "Time and the Gods"; "The Coming of the Sea";
    "A Legend of the Dawn"; "The Vengeance of Men"; "When the Gods Slept";
    "The King That Was Not"; "The Cave of Kai"; "The Sorrow of Search"; "The
    Men of Yarnith"; "For the Honour of the Gods"; "Night and Morning"; "Usury";
    "Mlideen"; "The Secret of the Gods"; "The South Wind"; "In the Land of Time";
    "The Relenting of Sardinac"; "The Jest of the Gods"; "The Dreams of the
    Prophet"; "The Journey of the King."

The Sword of Welleran and Other Stories. London: George Allen & Sons, 1908. Boston: John W. Luce & Co., [1916]. *In *A Dreamer's Tales and Other Stories*. New York: Boni & Liveright (Modern Library), [1917]. *Contents*: "The Sword of Welleran"; "The Fall of Babbulkund"; "The Kith of the Elf-Folk"; "The Highwayman"; "In the Twilight"; "The Ghosts"; "The Whirlpool"; "The Hurricane"; "The Fortress Unvanquishable, Save for Sacnoth"; "The Lord of Cities"; "The Doom of La Traviata"; "On the Dry Land."

A Dreamer's Tales. London: George Allen & Sons, 1910. *Boston: John W. Luce & Co., [1916]. Philadelphia: Owlswick Press, 1979. *Contents*: "Preface"; "Poltarnees, Beholder of Ocean"; "Blagdaross"; "The Madness of Andelsprutz"; "Where the Tides Ebb and Flow"; "Bethmoora"; "Idle Days on the Yann"; "The Sword and the Idol"; "The Idle City"; "The Hashish Man"; "Poor Old Bill"; "The Beggars"; "Carcassonne"; "In Zaccarath"; "The Field"; "The Day of the Poll"; "The Unhappy Body."

The Book of Wonder. London: William Heinemann, 1912. Boston: John W. Luce & Co., 1913. *In *The Book of Wonder*. New York: Boni & Liveright (Modern Library), [1918]. *Contents*: "Preface"; "The Bride of the Man-Horse"; "The Distressing Tale of Thangobrind the Jeweller, and of the Doom That Befel Him"; "The House of the Sphinx"; "The Probable Adventure of the Three Literary Men"; "The Injudicious Prayers of Pombo the Idolater"; "The Loot of Bombasharna"; "Miss Cubbidge and the Dragon of Romance"; "The Quest of the Queen's Tears"; "The Hoard of the Gibbelins"; "How Nuth Would Have Practised His Art upon the Gnoles"; "How One Came, as Was Foretold, to the City of Never"; "The Coronation of Mr. Thomas Shap"; "Chu-Bu and Sheemish"; "The Wonderful Window"; "Epilogue."

Fifty-One Tales. London: Elkin Mathews, 1915. *Boston: Little, Brown, 1917. *Contents*: "The Assignation"; "Charon"; "The Death of Pan"; "The Sphinx at Gizeh"; "The Hen"; "Wind and Fog"; "The Raft-Builders"; "The Workman"; "The Guest"; "Death and Odysseus"; "Death and the Orange"; "The Prayer of the Flowers"; "Time and the Tradesman"; "The Little City"; "The Unpasturable Fields"; "The Worm and the Angel"; "The Songless Country"; "The Latest Thing"; "The Demagogue and the Demi-Monde"; "The Giant Poppy"; "Roses"; "The Man with the Golden Ear-rings"; "The Dream of King Karna-Vootra"; "The Storm"; "A Mistaken Identity"; "The True History of the Hare and the Tortoise"; "Alone the Immortals"; "A Moral Little Tale"; "The Return of Song"; "Spring in Town"; "How the Enemy Came to Thlunrana"; "A Losing Game"; "Taking Up Piccadilly"; "After the Fire"; "The City"; "The Food of Death"; "The Lonely Idol"; "The Spinx in Thebes (Massachusetts)"; "The Reward"; "The Trouble in Leafy Green Street"; "Furrow-Maker"; "Lobster Salad"; "The Return of the Exiles"; "Nature and Time"; "The Song of the Blackbird"; "The Mist"; "The Messengers"; "The Three Tall Sons"; "Compromise"; "What We Have Come To"; "The Tomb of Pan"; "The Poet Speaks with Earth." [The American edition omits "The Poet Speaks with Earth" and adds "The Mist."]

The Last Book of Wonder. London: Elkin Mathews, 1916 (as *Tales of Wonder*). *Boston: John W. Luce & Co., 1916. *Contents*: "A Tale of London"; "Thirteen at Table"; "The City on Mallington Moor"; "Why the Milkman Shudders When He Perceives the Dawn"; "The Bad Old Woman in Black"; "The Bird of the

Difficult Eye"; "The Long Porter's Tale"; "The Loot of Loma"; "The Secret of the Sea"; "How Ali Came to the Black Country"; "The Bureau d'Echange de Maux"; "A Story of Land and Sea"; "A Tale of the Equator"; "A Narrow Escape"; "The Watch-Tower"; "How Plash-Goo Came to the Land of None's Desire"; "The Three Sailors' Gambit"; "The Exiles' Club"; "The Three Infernal Jokes."

Tales of War. Dublin: The Talbot Press; London: T. Fisher Unwin, 1918. *Boston: Little, Brown, 1918. *Contents*: "The Prayer of the Men of Daleswood"; "The Road"; "An Imperial Monument"; "A Walk to the Trenches"; "A Walk in Picardy"; "What Happened on the Night of the Twenty-seventh"; "Standing To"; "The Homing Plane"; "England"; "Shells"; "Two Degrees of Envy"; "The Master of Noman's Land"; "Weeds and Wire"; "Spring in England and Flanders"; "The Nightmare Countries"; "Spring and the Kaiser"; "Two Songs"; "The Punishment"; "The English Spirit"; "An Investigation into the Causes and Origin of the War"; "Lost"; "The Last Mirage"; "A Famous Man"; "The Oases of Death"; "Anglo-Saxon Tyranny"; "Memories"; "The Movement"; "Nature's Cad"; "The Home of Herr Schnitzelhaaser"; "A Deed of Mercy"; "Last Scene of All"; "Old England."

Tales of Three Hemispheres. *Boston: John W. Luce & Co., 1919. London: T. Fisher Unwin, 1920. Philadelphia: Owlswick Press, 1976. *Contents*: "The Last Dream of Bwona Khubla"; "How the Office of Postman Fell Vacant in Otford-under-the-Wold"; "The Prayer of Boob Aheera"; "East and West"; "A Pretty Quarrel"; "How the Gods Avenged Meoul Ki Ning"; "The Gifts of the Gods"; "The Sack of Emeralds"; "The Old Brown Coat"; "An Archive of the Older Mysteries"; "A City of Wonder"; "Beyond the Fields We Know" ("Publishers Note"; "Idle Days on the Yann"; "A Shop in Go-by Street"; "The Avenger of Perdóndaris").

The Travel Tales of Mr. Joseph Jorkens. *London: G. P. Putnam's Sons, 1931. New York: G. P. Putnam's Sons, 1931. *Contents*: "Preface"; "The Tale of the Abu Laheeb"; "The King of Sarahb"; "How Jembu Played for Cambridge"; "The Charm against Thirst"; "Our Distant Cousins"; "A Large Diamond"; "A Queer Island"; "The Electric King"; "A Drink at a Running Stream"; "A Daughter of Rameses"; "The Showman"; "Mrs. Jorkens"; "The Witch of the Willows."

Jorkens Remembers Africa. New York: Longmans, Green, 1934. *London: William Heinemann, 1934 (as *Mr. Jorkens Remembers Africa*). *Contents*: "Preface"; "The Lost Romance"; "The Curse of the Witch"; "The Pearly Beach"; "The Walk to Lingham"; "The Escape from the Valley"; "One August in the Red Sea"; "The Bare Truth"; "What Jorkens Has to Put Up With"; "Ozymandias"; "At the End of the Universe"; "The Black Mamba"; "In the Garden of Memories"; "The Slugly Beast"; "Earth's Secret"; "The Persian Spell"; "Stranger Than Fiction"; "The Golden Gods"; "The Correct Kit"; "How Ryan Got out of Russia"; "The Club Secretary"; "A Mystery of the East."

Jorkens Has a Large Whiskey. London: Putnam, 1940. *Contents*: "Preface"; "Jorkens' Revenge"; "Jorkens Retires from Business"; "Jorkens Handles a Big Property"; "The Invention of Dr. Caber"; "The Grecian Singer"; "The Jorkens Family Emeralds"; "A Fishing Story"; "Jorkens in High Finance"; "The Sign"; "The Angelic Shepherd"; "The Neapolitan Ice"; "The Development of the Rillswood Estate"; "The Fancy Man"; "The Lion and the Unicorn"; "A Doubtful Story";

"Jorkens Looks Forward"; "Jorkens among the Ghosts"; "Elephant Shooting"; "African Magic"; "Jorkens Consults a Prophet"; "A Matter of Business"; "The Invention of the Age"; "The Sultan, the Monkey and the Banana"; "Pundleton's Audience"; "The Flight in the Drawing-Room"; "The Ivory Poacher."

The Fourth Book of Jorkens. *London: Jarrolds, [1947]. Sauk City, WI: Arkham House, 1948. *Contents*: "Mgamu"; "The Haunting of Halahanstown"; "The Pale-Green Image"; "Jorkens Leaves Prison"; "The Warning"; "The Sacred City of Krakovlitz"; "Jorkens Practices Medicine and Magic"; "Jarton's Disease"; "On the Other Side of the Sun"; "The Rebuff"; "Jorkens' Ride"; "The Secret of the Sphinx"; "The Khamseen"; "The Expulsion"; "The Welcome"; "By Command of Pharaoh"; "A Cricket Problem"; "A Life's Work"; "The Ingratiating Smile"; "The Last Bull"; "The Strange Drug of Dr. Caber"; "A Deal with the Devil"; "Strategy at the Billiards Club"; "Jorkens in Witch Wood"; "Lost"; "The English Magnifico"; "The Cleverness of Dr. Caber"; "Fairy Gold"; "A Royal Dinner"; "A Fight with Knives"; "Out West"; "In a Dim Room."

The Man Who Ate the Phoenix. London: Jarrolds, [1949]. *Contents*: "The Man Who Ate the Phoenix"; "The Widow Flynn's Apple-Tree"; "Where Everyone's Business Is Known"; "The Rose By-pass"; "An Old Man's Tale"; "How the Tinker Came to Skavangur"; "The Opal Arrow-Head"; "The Sultan's Pet"; "The Descent of the Sultan of Khash"; "The Policeman's Prophecy"; "The Wind in the Wood"; "The Tiger's Skin"; "The Finding of Mr. Jupkens"; "The Awful Dream"; "Mrs. Mulger"; "The Choice"; "Rose Tibbets"; "Little Snow White up to Date"; "The Return"; "The Mad Ghost"; "The Cause"; "The Cut"; "The Sleuthing of Lily Bostum"; "The Possibility of Life on the Third Planet"; "Old Emma"; "How Abdul Din Saved Justice"; "The First Watch-Dog"; "The Chess-Player, the Financier, and Another"; "The Honorary Member"; "The Experiment"; "Down among the Kingcups"; "The Gratitude of the Devil"; "The After-Dinner Speech"; "The Je-ne-sais-quoi"; "Poseidon"; "A Near Thing"; "Ardor Canis"; "A Lapse of Memory"; "Forty Years On"; "The Iron Door"; "The Great Scoop."

The Little Tales of Smethers and Other Stories. London: Jarrolds, 1952. *Contents*: "The Two Bottles of Relish"; "The Shooting of Constable Slugger"; "An Enemy of Scotland Yard"; "The Second Front"; "The Two Assassins"; "Kriegblut's Disguise"; "The Mug in the Gambling Hall"; "The Clue"; "Once Too Often"; "An Alleged Murder"; "The Waiter's Story"; "A Trade Dispute"; "The Pirate of the Round Pond"; "A Victim of Bad Luck"; "The New Master"; "A New Murder"; "A Tale of Revenge"; "The Speech"; "The Lost Scientist"; "The Unwritten Thriller"; "In Ravancore"; "Among the Bean Rows"; "The Death-Watch Beetle"; "Murder by Lightning"; "The Murder in Netherby Gardens"; "The Shield of Athene."

Jorkens Borrows Another Whiskey. London: Michael Joseph, 1954. *Contents*: "Preface"; "The Two-Way War"; "A Nice Lot of Diamonds"; "Letting Bygones Be Bygones"; "The Lost Invention"; "On Other Paths"; "The Partner"; "Poulet à la Richelieu"; "A Walk in the Night"; "One Summer's Evening"; "A Friend of the Family"; "An Eccentricity of Genius"; "Influenza"; "The Unrecorded Test Match"; "Idle Tears"; "Among the Neutrals"; "An Idyll of the Sahara"; "The Devil among the Willows"; "A Spanish Castle"; "The New Moon"; "The Gods of Clay"; "A Rash Remark"; "The Story of Jorkens' Watch"; "The Track through the Wood"; "Snow Water"; "The Greatest Invention"; "The Verdict"; "A Conversation in Bond Street"; "The Reward"; "Which Way?"; "A Desperado in Surrey"; "Misadventure"; "A Long Memory"; "An Absentminded Professor"; "Greek Meets Greek."

Plays

Five Plays. *London: Grant Richards, 1914. Boston: Little, Brown, 1914. London: G. P. Putnam's Sons, 1925. *Contents: The Gods of the Mountain; The Golden Doom; King Argimēnēs and the Unknown Warrior; The Glittering Gate; The Lost Silk Hat.*

Plays of Gods and Men. *Dublin: The Talbot Press, 1917. London: T. Fisher Unwin, 1917. Boston: John W. Luce & Co., 1917. New York: G. P. Putnam's Sons, [1918]. *Contents: The Laughter of the Gods; The Queen's Enemies; The Tents of the Arabs; A Night at an Inn.*

If. London: G. P. Putnam's Sons, September 1921. *New York: G. P. Putnam's Sons, 1922.

Plays of Near and Far. London: G. P. Putnam's Sons, 1922. *New York: G. P. Putnam's Sons, 1923. *Contents: The Compromise of the King of the Golden Isles; The Flight of the Queen; Cheezo; A Good Bargain; If Shakespeare Lived Today; Fame and the Poet.*

Alexander and Three Small Plays. *London: G. P. Putnam's Sons, 1925. New York: G. P. Putnam's Sons, 1926. *Contents: Alexander; The Old King's Tale; The Evil Kettle; The Amusements of Khan Kharuda.*

Seven Modern Comedies. London: G. P. Putnam's Sons, 1928. *New York: G. P. Putnam's Sons, 1929. *Contents: Atalanta in Wimbledon; The Raffle; The Journey of the Soul; In Holy Russia; His Sainted Grandmother; The Hopeless Passion of Mr. Runyon; The Jest of Hāhālābā.*

The Old Folk of the Centuries. London: Elkin Mathews & Marrot, 1930.

Lord Adrian. Waltham Saint Lawrence: Golden Cockerel Press, 1933. *In *The Ghosts of the Heaviside Layer* (q.v.).

Mr. Faithful. New York: Samuel French; London: Samuel French Ltd., 1935.

Plays for Earth and Air. London: William Heinemann, 1937. *Contents:* "Preface"; *Fame Comes Late; A Matter of Honour; Mr. Sliggen's Hour; The Pumpkin; The Use of Man; The Bureau de Change; The Seventh Symphony; Golden Dragon City; Time's Joke; Atmospherics.*

Novels

The Chronicles of Rodriguez. London: G. P. Putnam's Sons, 1922. *New York: G. P. Putnam's Sons, 1922 (as *Don Rodriguez: Chronicles of Shadow Valley*). London: Pan/Ballantine, 1972.

The King of Elfland's Daughter. London: G. P. Putnam's Sons, 1924. *New York: G. P. Putnam's Sons, 1924. New York: Ballantine Books, 1969.

The Charwoman's Shadow. *London: G. P. Putnam's Sons, 1926. New York: G. P. Putnam's Sons, 1926. New York: Ballantine Books, 1973.

The Blessing of Pan. *London: G. P. Putnam's Sons, 1927. New York: G. P. Putnam's Sons, 1928.

The Curse of the Wise Woman. London: William Heinemann, 1933. New York: Longmans, Green, 1933. *London: Collins, 1972.

Up in the Hills. *London: William Heinemann, 1935. New York: G. P. Putnam's Sons, 1936.

My Talks with Dean Spanley. London: William Heinemann, 1936. New York: G. P. Putnam's Sons, 1936. *London: Collins, 1972.

Rory and Bran. *London: William Heinemann, 1936. New York: G. P. Putnam's Sons, 1937.

The Story of Mona Sheehy. *London: William Heinemann, 1939. New York: Harper & Brothers, 1940.

Guerrilla. *London: William Heinemann, 1944. Indianapolis: Bobbs-Merrill, 1944.

The Strange Journeys of Colonel Polders. London: Jarrolds, 1950.

The Last Revolution. London: Jarrolds, 1951.

His Fellow Men. London: Jarrolds, 1952.

Essays and Miscellany

Nowadays. Boston: The Four Seas Company, 1918. *In *The Ghosts of the Heaviside Layer* (q.v.). (First published in *English Review* 12, No. 3 [October 1912]: 390–97.)

Unhappy Far-Off Things. London: Elkin Mathews, 1919. *Boston: Little, Brown, 1919. *Contents*: "Preface"; "A Dirge of Victory"; "The Cathedral of Arras"; "A Good War"; "The House with Two Storeys"; "Bermondsey *versus* Wurtemburg"; "On an Old Battle-Field"; "The Real Thing"; "A Garden of Arras"; "After Hell"; "A Happy Valley"; "In Bethune"; "In an Old Drawing-Room"; "The Homes of Arras."

If I Were Dictator. London: Methuen & Co., 1934.

Building a Sentence. New York: The Marchbanks Press, [1934].

My Ireland. London: Jarrolds, 1937.

Patches of Sunlight. *London: William Heinemann, 1938. New York: Reynal & Hitchcock, 1938.

While the Sirens Slept. London: Jarrolds, [1944].

The Sirens Wake. London: Jarrolds, 1945.

The Donnellan Lectures 1943. London: William Heinemann, 1945. *Contents*: "Prose"; "Poetry"; "Drama."

A Glimpse from a Watch Tower. London: Jarrolds, 1946.

Poetry

Fifty Poems. London: G. P. Putnam's Sons, 1929.

Mirage Water. London: Putnam, October 1938. Philadelphia: Dorrance & Co., 1939.

War Poems. London: Hutchinson & Co., [1941].

Wandering Songs. London: Hutchinson & Co., [1943].

A Journey. London: Macdonald & Co., 1944.

The Year. London: Jarrolds, 1946.
The Odes of Horace. London: William Heinemann, 1947.
To Awaken Pegasus. Oxford: George Ronald, 1949.

Omnibuses and Selections

Selections from the Writings of Lord Dunsany. [Edited by W. B. Yeats.] Churchtown:
    Cuala Press, 1912.
A Dreamer's Tales and Other Stories. New York: Boni & Liveright (Modern Library),
    [1917]. *Contents: A Dreamer's Tales; The Sword of Welleran and Other Stories.*
The Book of Wonder. New York: Boni & Liveright (Modern Library), [1918]. *Contents:*
    The Book of Wonder; Time and the Gods.
The Sword of Welleran and Other Tales of Enchantment. New York: Devin-Adair, 1954.
At the Edge of the World. Edited by Lin Carter. New York: Ballantine, 1970.
Beyond the Fields We Know. Edited by Lin Carter. New York: Ballantine, 1972.
Gods, Men and Ghosts: The Best Supernatural Fiction of Lord Dunsany. Edited by E. F.
    Bleiler. New York: Dover, 1972.
Over the Hills and Far Away. Edited by Lin Carter. New York: Ballantine, 1974.
The Ghosts of the Heaviside Layer and Other Fantasms. Edited by Darrell Schweitzer.
    Philadelphia: Owlswick Press, 1980. *Contents:* "Foreword" by Darrell Schweit-
    zer; "The Ghosts of the Heaviside Layer"; "Told under Oath"; "The Fields
    Where the Satyrs Danced"; "By Night in a Forest"; "A Royal Swan"; "How the
    Lost Causes Were Removed from Valhalla"; "Correcting Nature"; "Autumn
    Cricket"; "In the Mojave"; "The Ghost of the Valley"; "The Ghost in the Old
    Corridor"; "Jorkens's Problem"; "The Revelation to Mr. Periple"; "A Fable for
    Moderns"; "The Fantastic Dreams"; "Nowadays"; "Ghosts"; "Irish Writers I
    Have Known"; "Four Poets"; "The Authorship of the Barrack Room Ballads";
    "Sime"; "Artist and Tradesman"; "Spring Reaches England"; "Triad"; "July";
    "Or But a Wandering Voice"; "After the Shadow"; "A Moment in the Life of a
    Dog"; "Seeing the World"; "A Word for Fallen Grandeur"; "Where Do You Get
    the Clay?"; "Decay in the Language"; "The Carving of the Ivory"; *The Prince*
    of Stamboul; Lord Adrian.

Uncollected Stories

"As It Seems to the Blackbird." *Empire Youth Annual,* 1951, pp. 227–34.
"The Awakening." *Poetry Review* 44, No. 5 (July–September 1953): 375–77.
"Biding His Time." *Punch* No. 5202 (27 November 1940): 629.
"A Breeze at Rest." *Time and Tide* 35, No. 35 (28 August 1954): 1136.
"The Burrahoola." *Evening News* (London) No. 21,248 (21 March 1950): 7.
"The Coming Party." *Punch* No. 5519 (2 October 1946): 413.
"A Crime Story." *Punch* No. 5693 (4 January 1950): 22–23.
"Darwin Superseded." *Spectator* No. 6484 (3 October 1952): 420–21.
"La Dernière Mobilisation." *Fabulist* No. 1 (Autumn 1915): [6–7].
"The Dwarf Holóbolos and the Sword Hogbiter." *Collins for Boys and Girls* No. 1 ([July]
    1949): 9–16.

"Fatal Mistake." *Argosy* 16, No. 4 (April 1955): 49–52.

"The Ghost in the Corner." *Punch* No. 5175 (29 May 1940): 588.

"A Goat in Trousers." *Everybody's Weekly*, 11 July 1953, 24–25.

"The Heart of Earth." *Saturday Review* (London) No. 2804 (24 July 1909): 104–5.

"Helping the Fairies." *Strand Magazine* 113, No. 2 (May–June 1947): 28–31.

"The Higher Neutrality." *Punch* No. 5311 (2 December 1942): 546.

"How Mickey Paid His Debt." *Evening News* (London) No. 21,271 (18 April 1950): 7.

"The Judgment of Mullaghagraney." *Punch* No. 5173 (15 May 1940): 544–45.

"Little Tim Brannehan." *Punch* No. 5631 (10 November 1948): 431.

"Near the Back of Beyond." *Ellery Queen's Mystery Magazine* 26, No. 5 (November 1955): 30–42.

"Neutrality over Berlin." *Punch* No. 5304 (21 October 1942): 335.

"One More Tale." *Saturday Review* (London) No. 3107 (15 May 1915): 504.

"Our Laurels." *Saturday Review* (London) No. 3083 (28 November 1914): 558.

"Our War Aims Committee." *Punch* No. 5149 (6 December 1939): 619.

"Romance." *Saturday Review* (London) No. 2796 (29 May 1909): 695–96.

"The Romance of His Life." *Harper's Bazaar* No. 2884 (March 1952): 170, 229.

"The Story of Tse Gah." *Tomorrow* 7, No. 4 (December 1947): 19–20.

"The Traveller to Thundercliff." *Colophon* (London) 1, No. 1 (March 1950): 16.

"Two Sketches." *Vanity Fair* 13, No. 3 (November 1919): 43.

"The Use of Man." *Harper's Bazaar* No. 2626 (August 1931): 85, 108.

"A Witch in the Balkans." *Everybody's Weekly*, 2 June 1951, pp. 21–22.

Uncollected Essays, Reviews, and Introductions

"Among the Ruins." *Essays by Divers Hands* (Transactions of the Royal Society of Literature), 3rd Series, 21 (1944): 15–23.

"Arming Our Ignorance with a Knife." *Time and Tide* 34, No. 38 (19 September 1953): 1209.

"The Art of Longjuju." *Saturday Review* 39, No. 51 (22 December 1956): 9.

"A Barbarous Rite." *Spectator* No. 6366 (30 June 1950): 882.

"By Ony and Teme and Clun." *Saturday Review* (London) No. 2814 (2 October 1909): 406–7.

"*Deirdre of the Sorrows.*" *Saturday Review* (London) No. 2849 (4 June 1910): 719–20.

"A Dissenting Opinion on Modern Poetry." *Tomorrow* 10, No. 3 (November 1950): 37–40.

"England Language Conditions!" *Essays and Studies* 13 (1928): 138–44.

"Faint Footsteps" [review of *The Mandrake Root: An Anthology of Fantastic Tales*, ed. Jeremy Scott]. *Sunday Times* (London) No. 6427 (16 June 1946): 3.

"The Fall of the Muses." *Poetry Review* 43, No. 4 (October–December 1952): 201–4.

"Francis Ledwidge." *Fortnightly Review* 164, No. 6 (December 1945): 407–8.

"From the Mouse's Point of View." *Open Window* No. 12 (September 1911): 327–31.

"Gondolas." *Saturday Review* (London) No. 2761 (26 September 1908): 392–93.

"Good Plays and Bad—Why?" *Theatre Magazine* No. 328 (July 1928): 7–8.

"Improving the Poets." *John O'London's Weekly* No. 1052 (9 June 1939): 337–38.

"In the House of Mammon." *Saturday Review* (London) No. 2929 (16 December 1911): 762.

"Introduction." In *The Complete Poems of Francis Ledwidge*. New York: Brentano's, 1919, 7–18. (Contains introductions to *Songs of the Fields*, *Songs of Peace*, and *Last Songs*.)

"Introduction." In *Ireland/L'Irlande/Irland: A Book of Photographs*. London: Anglo-Italian Publication, [1959], 7–23 (in English, French, and German).

"Ireland" [review of *Celtic Wonder-Tales* by Ella Young and *Irish Ecclesiastical Architecture* by Arthur C. Champneys]. *Saturday Review* (London) No. 2895 (22 April 1911): 484–86.

"Jetsam." *Saturday Review* No. 2852 (25 June 1910): 819.

"A Mountainy Singer." *Bell* 12, No. 5 (August 1946): 375–82.

"Nine Wonders." *Go . . . The Travel Magazine* 3, No. 4 (December 1950): 46–47.

"A Note on *Blanco Posnet*." *Saturday Review* (London) No. 2809 (28 August 1909): 254.

"Pens." *Saturday Review* (London) No. 2785 (13 March 1909): 332.

"The Poets Fail in Their Duty." *Saturday Review* 40, No. 42 (19 October 1957): 14–15.

"A Preface." In *Tales from Bective Bridge* by Mary Lavin. Boston: Little, Brown, 1942, vii–xii.

"Romance and the Modern Stage." *National Review* No. 341 (July 1911): 827–35.

"Tales about Dogs." *Tail-Wagger Magazine* 23, No. 2 (February 1951): 28–30.

"That Suprasensical Lear." *New York Times Book Review*, 19 July 1953, 6, 22.

"Two Hundred Times in a Blue Moon." *Saturday Review* (London) No. 2844 (30 April 1910): 555–56.

"What Have We Here?" *Time and Tide* 15, No. 15 (14 April 1934): 459.

Uncollected Letters

"Irish Academy of Letters." *Times* (London) No. 46,254 (3 October 1932): 10.

"Irish Subjects in Britain." *Times* (London) No. 51,209 (22 October 1948): 5.

Letter to W. B. Yeats (29 July 1924). In *Letters to W. B. Yeats*, ed. Richard J. Finneran et al. London: Macmillan, 1977, 2: 458.

SECONDARY

Books and Articles about Dunsany

Amory, Mark. *Biography of Lord Dunsany*. London: Collins, 1972.

Anderson, Angelee Sailor. "Lord Dunsany: The Potency of Words and the Wonder of Things." *Mythlore* No. 55 (Autumn 1988): 10–12.

Bassnett, Susan. "From Gods to Giants—Theatrical Parallels between Edward Dunsany and Luigi Pirandello." *Yearbook of the British Pirandello Society* No. 6 (1982): 40–49.

Bierstadt, Edward Hale. *Dunsany and Dramatist*. Boston: Little, Brown, 1917 (rev. ed., 1919).

Boyd, Emma Garrett. "Lord Dunsany, Dreamer." *Forum* 57, No. 4 (April 1917): 497–508.

Boyd, Ernest A. "Lord Dunsany—Fantaisiste." In *Appreciations and Depreciations*. New York: John Lane, 1918, 71–100.

Clarke, Arthur C. "Dunsany Lord of Fantasy." *Rhodomagnetic Digest* 3, No. 4 (November–December 1951): 15–18.

Colum, Padraic. "Lord Dunsany's Plays." *Irish Review* 4, No. 4 (June 1914): 217–22.

de Camp, L. Sprague. "Two Men in One: Lord Dunsany." In *Literary Swordsmen and Sorcerers: The Makers of Heroic Fantasy*. Sauk City, WI: Arkham House, 1976, 48–63.

Desmond, Shaw. "Dunsany, Yeats and Shaw: Trinity of Magic." *Bookman* (New York) 58, No. 3 (November 1923): 260–66.

Duperray, Max. "Les Mondes imaginaires de Lord Dunsany (1878–1957)." Ph.D. diss.: Université de Lyon, 1979.

Foster, John Wilson. "A Dreamer's Tales: The Stories of Lord Dunsany." In *Fictions of the Irish Literary Revival: A Changeling Art*. Syracuse: Syracuse University Press; Dublin: Gill & Macmillan, 1987, 291–98.

Gallagher, Ronald Joseph. "The Uses of the Supernatural in the Works of Lord Dunsany and James Stephens." Ph.D. diss.: University of Washington, 1990.

Gogarty, Oliver St. John. "Lord Dunsany." *Atlantic Monthly* 195, No. 3 (March 1955): 67–72.

———. "My Friends Stephens and Dunsany." *Tomorrow* 10, No. 7 (March 1951): 22–28.

Hyles, Vernon. "Lord Dunsany: The Geography of the Gods." In *More Real Than Reality: The Fantastic in Irish Literature and the Arts*, ed. Donald E. Morse and Csilla Bertha. Westport, CT: Greenwood Press, 1991, 211–18.

Joshi, S. T. "Lord Dunsany: The Career of a *Fantaisiste*." In *The Weird Tale*. Austin: University of Texas Press, 1990, 42–86.

———, and Darrell Schweitzer. *Lord Dunsany: A Bibliography*. Metuchen, NJ: Scarecrow Press, 1993.

La Croix, J. F. "Lord Dunsany." Ph.D. diss.: Trinity College, Dublin, 1956.

Littlefield, Hazel. *Lord Dunsany, King of Dreams: A Personal Portrait*. New York: Exposition Press, 1959.

Lovecraft, H. P. "Lord Dunsany and His Work" (1922). In *Marginalia*, ed. August Derleth. Sauk City, WI: Arkham House, 1944, 148–60.

———. *Selected Letters*. Edited by August Derleth, Donald Wandrei, and James Turner. 5 vols. Sauk City, WI: Arkham House, 1965–76.

———. "Supernatural Horror in Literature" (1927). In *Dagon and Other Macabre Tales*. Rev. ed. Sauk City, WI: Arkham House, 1986, 365–433.

Mahony, Patrick. "Lord Dunsany's Centennial: A Memoir." *Eire-Ireland* 4, No. 1 (Spring 1979): 126–30.

Manlove, C. N. "Anaemic Fantasy: Morris, Dunsany, Eddison, Beagle." In *The Impulse of Fantasy Literature*. Kent, OH: Kent State University Press, 1983, 133–37.

Moses, Montrose J. "Lord Dunsany's Peculiar Genius." *Bellman* No. 561 (14 April 1917): 405–9.

Pashka, Linda. "Dunsany's Other Worlds: The Prose Fantasy of Lord Dunsany." M.A. thesis: University of Calgary, 1987.

———. " 'Hunting for Allegories' in the Prose Fantasy of Lord Dunsany." *Studies in Weird Fiction* No. 12 (Spring 1993): 19–24.

Paul-Dubois, Louis. "Lord Dunsany: Le Maître du merveilleux." *Revue des Deux Mondes* 16, No. 4 (15 August 1933): 893–919.

Perrin, Noel. "Warbling His Native Wood-Notes Wild." *Washington Post Book World* 12, No. 22 (30 May 1982): 9, 11.

Rateliff, John D. " 'Beyond the Fields We Know': The Short Stories of Lord Dunsany." Ph.D. diss.: Marquette University, 1990.

[Russell, George William ("AE").] "A Maker of Mythologies." *Irish Statesman*, 17 April 1926. *Living Age* No. 4273 (29 May 1926): 465–66.

Saul, George Brandon. "Strange Gods and Far Places: The Short Fiction of Lord Dunsany." *Arizona Quarterly* 19, No. 5 (Autumn 1963): 197–210.

Sawyer, Andy. "The Horns of Elfland, Faintly Winding: Three Novels by Lord Dunsany." *Crystal Ship* No. 14 (1988): 10–20.

Schweitzer, Darrell. *Pathways to Elfland: The Writings of Lord Dunsany*. Philadelphia: Owlswick Press, 1989.

Shepard, Odell. "A Modern Myth-Maker." In *The Joys of Forgetting: A Book of Bagatelles*. Boston: Houghton Mifflin, 1929, 30–47.

Tinterri, Alessandro. "Pirandello regista e *The Gods of the Mountain* di Lord Dunsany." *Yearbook of the British Pirandello Society* No. 6 (1986): 36–39.

Weygandt, Cornelius. "The Dramas of Dunsany." In *Tuesdays at Ten*. Philadelphia: University of Pennsylvania Press, 1928, 13–42.

Yeats, W. B. "Introduction" to *Selections from the Writings of Lord Dunsany* (1912). Reprinted in *Prefaces and Introductions* (The Collected Works of W. B. Yeats). Edited by William H. O'Donnell. New York: Macmillan, 1989, 6: 138–43.

Other Works Consulted

Boyd, Ernest A. *Ireland's Literary Renaissance*. 1916. Rev. ed. New York: Knopf, 1922.

Coogan, Timothy Patrick. *Ireland Since the Rising*. New York: Praeger, 1966.

Gregory, Lady. *Collected Plays*. 4 vols. Edited by Ann Saddlemyer. New York: Oxford University Press, 1970.

Jeffares, A. Norman. *Anglo-Irish Literature*. New York: Schocken Books, 1982.

Ledwidge, Francis. *The Complete Poems of Francis Ledwidge*. Edited by Alice Curtayne. London: Martin Brian & O'Keeffe, 1974.

Stephens, James. *Letters of James Stephens*. Edited by Richard J. Finneran. London: Macmillan, 1974.

Synge, J. M. *The Plays and Poems of J. M. Synge*. Edited by T. R. Henn. London: Methuen, 1963.

Yeats, W. B. *Collected Plays*. New York: Macmillan, 1953.

———. *The Letters of W. B. Yeats*. Edited by Allan Wade. London: Rupert Hart-Davis, 1954.

Index

About the Author

S. T. JOSHI has done graduate work at Brown and Princeton and is currently senior editor of the Literary Criticism division of Chelsea House Publishers. He is the author of *The Weird Tale* (1990), has compiled bibliographies of Lord Dunsany, H. P. Lovecraft, and other authors, and is the editor of a corrected edition of Lovecraft's fiction and miscellaneous writings. He is the editor of *Lovecraft Studies* and *Studies in Weird Fiction*, and coeditor of *Necrofile: The Review of Horror Fiction*.

ISBN 0-313-29403-8

90000>

EAN

9 780313 294037

HARDCOVER BAR CODE